THE CAMBRIDGE
MOVEMENT

THE
CAMBRIDGE
MOVEMENT

THE ECCLESIOLOGISTS AND THE
GOTHIC REVIVAL

BY

JAMES F. WHITE

Assistant Professor at the
Perkins School of Theology, Dallas, Texas

CAMBRIDGE
AT THE UNIVERSITY PRESS
1962

PUBLISHED BY

THE SYNDICS OF THE CAMBRIDGE UNIVERSITY PRESS

Bentley House, 200 Euston Road, London, N.W.1
American Branch: 32 East 57th Street, New York 22, N.Y.
West African Office: P.O. Box 33, Ibadan, Nigeria

Printed in Great Britain by Latimer, Trend & Co. Ltd., Plymouth

To
RAY C. PETRY
father to many scholars

CONTENTS

PREFACE

For a century now, a single type of church building has been regarded as most appropriate for worship according to the *Book of Common Prayer*. Within this time, most of the Protestant denominations in the English-speaking world have also adopted this variety of church. Few factors have so profoundly influenced the worship of the Anglican Communion and the Protestant denominations as the type of church devised and propagated by a group of undergraduates at Cambridge University during the early years of Victoria's reign. That this particular liturgical arrangement could survive in an age when most Victorian architecture is uncritically rejected, is proof that it has so successfully altered liturgical patterns that resistance to it seems futile.

Yet resistance there now is, though still quite rare. After decades of building churches with the full neo-medieval arrangement, a few liturgical scholars have begun to question its basic suitability. There can be no mistaking the fact that the Cambridge Camden Society was actuated by distinct theological presuppositions, especially about the doctrines of the ministry and the sacraments. The reluctance of its members to engage in open theological debate never concealed from their contemporaries the fact that these men held a definite theological position.

Twentieth-century liturgical scholars of such differing backgrounds as Jungmann, Dix, and Brilioth have shown clearly that the Middle Ages were not the apex of Christian worship that an earlier generation supposed them to be. Indeed, the Cambridge Camden Society chose as its ideal a period when the common worship of the entire Body of Christ was realized much less than at many other periods in the Church's history. For the nineteenth century, as Chesterton remarked, saw the Middle Ages 'by moonlight'. The great weakness of the Cambridge Camden Society was that it neglected that most Catholic doctrine of the Church's constant guidance by the Holy Spirit. To idealize one age and to ignore the witness of subsequent centuries was a serious mistake in the members' theology. Of course, their contemporaries glorified the sixteenth century and neglected those preceding it, and we today may sometimes be tempted to do the same. Such romantic and selective views of Church History always prove defective, for the Church's witness is not confined to the expression of it by any period in time.

There can be no denying the appeal which the neo-medieval church has had to succeeding generations. Even buildings built in the contemporary styles, with few exceptions, use the liturgical arrangement developed a century ago by the Cambridge Camden Society. Here, many have felt, is a 'correct' way of building churches, and thousands of parishes all over the world have adapted their worship to fit this variety of building. But this was the real difficulty which has been ignored for so long. Worship had to be adapted to fit a pre-conceived notion of a 'correct' church building. Choirs were introduced to fill the chancels; priests were removed further and further from the congregations in which they ministered, and worship became more and more a professional art.

The twentieth century has experienced a theological reformation unparalleled in the past few centuries. Directly connected with the new frenzy of biblical and historical scholarship, a new liturgical movement has arisen which has not been confined to any denomination or country. The new architecture has finally seized the imagination of most Christian laymen except in the most conservative areas. While the liturgical movement was questioning many of the previous concepts and practices of worship, the new architecture was condemning the repetition of hackneyed forms. One may wonder how much longer the type of church pioneered by the Cambridge Camden Society will endure. Has its time run out after a century of service, or will it continue to dominate the pattern of worship for millions of Christians? One thing is certain; one cannot regard the nineteenth century or any other time as one of loss and decadence. Though many of its forms may pass, they have contributed to the development of the Church's witness. Unfortunately the Cambridge Camden Society did not realize this in its efforts to abolish the legacy of the preceding three centuries.

In writing this account of the work of the Cambridge Camden Society, I have adopted several conventions for convenience. Unless another group is specified, I have always used the term 'the Society' to refer to the Cambridge Camden Society or its successors. I have chosen to call its members 'the Ecclesiologists', realizing full well that they were not the only practitioners of this science, but that as the originators of the term they could best claim it. The term 'ecclesiology' has been used consistently in its original sense as the science of church-building and decoration. In America it has come to have quite a different meaning in recent years, but it has kept its original meaning in Great Britain. References to the chief publication of this group, the *Ecclesiologist*, appear in the text itself. The periodical is abbreviated as *E.* and reference is made to volume number and page according to the original series. A new series was introduced in 1845 but the original numbering was also retained.

The research and writing of this study were made possible through grants from the U.S. Fulbright Commission and the Danforth Foundation. I have been privileged to have the assistance of the staffs and use of the resources of many institutions, especially the Duke University Libraries, the Library of the University of North Carolina, the Harvard College Library, the Robinson Architectural Library, the Yale University Library, the Congregational Library in Boston, the Washington Cathedral Library, the Library of Congress, the Library Company of Philadelphia, the Free Library, Philadelphia, the Library of Union Theological Seminary, New York, the New York Public Library, and the Boston Public Library in the United States. In England I am similarly indebted to the staffs of the University

Preface

Library, Cambridge, the British Museum Library, the Library of Trinity College, Cambridge, and the Library of the Royal Institute of British Architects.

I began my work on the Cambridge Camden Society at the suggestion of Professor E. C. Ratcliff, Regius Professor of Divinity, Cambridge University, and his advice has continued to be most helpful. Professor Ray C. Petry of Duke University nurtured this work and contributed unsparingly of his time and knowledge as he has done so generously for many others. Mr. R. H. Harrison of the present Ecclesiological Society in London has done me the kindness of reading the manuscript and has supplied much valuable information. I am grateful to Professor Massey H. Shepherd, Jr., for reading and commenting on the manuscript. But chiefly I am indebted to my wife Marilyn for her help in typing the entire manuscript and her role as a sympathetic critic.

J. F. W.

PERKINS SCHOOL OF THEOLOGY
DALLAS, TEXAS
1 August 1961

CHAPTER I

'THE ABYSS FROM WHICH WE ARE EMERGING'

I

Queen Victoria began her long reign in 1837. Long before her death in 1901 the appearance of England's churches had been radically altered and a revolution had occurred in the way in which worship was conducted in them. Indeed, so widespread were the changes in this period, that it is now difficult to visualize the arrangement of the average Anglican parish church of the 1830's or the manner in which the services were held. In many ways the Victorian era represents the real watershed in parochial life and practice between the Reformation and the present-day Church of England.

When the Protestant Reformation began in the sixteenth century, England was already well supplied with numerous parish churches and it was over a century before the English Church was confronted with the necessity of erecting many new buildings. The chief architectural problem facing the Reformers was that of adapting medieval structures for Protestant worship. This was no simple task since the functional requirements had changed so much with the introduction of worship according to the *Book of Common Prayer*. No longer was it necessary to provide room for chantry altars or to reserve the chancel for the devotions of the clergy. A variety of experiments was performed in adapting these buildings; communion tables were set up lengthwise in the chancel or actually in the nave and an increasing part of the services was taken from the pulpit. The rubrics of the Elizabethan Prayer Book ordered: 'The Morning and Euening prayer, shalbe used in the accustomed place of the churche, chapel or Chauncell, except it shalbe other wise determined by the ordinary of the place: and the chauncels shall remain, as

I

they haue done in tymes past.' As a consequence, the chancels frequently remained empty except during the infrequent communion services, being occupied by the communicants then at the words: 'Draw nere and take this holy Sacrament to your comforte.'

Today, four centuries after the Reformation, England still retains upwards of nine thousand medieval church buildings. Not until the great fire of 1666 when eighty-six churches were destroyed in London was an extensive programme of church-building undertaken by the reformed Church of England. Sir Christopher Wren, as architect for most of the new City churches, used the ancient Roman basilica as his point of departure. More than any other person Wren determined the form which Anglican churches were to take until the Victorian era. After building more than fifty churches himself, Wren set down his principles for the benefit of a friend:

The Churches ... must be large; but still, in our reformed Religion, it should seem vain to make a *Parish-church* larger than that all who are present can both hear and see. The *Romanists*, indeed, may build larger Churches, it is enough if they hear the Murmur of the Mass, and see the Elevation of the Host, but ours are to be fitted for Auditories. I can hardly think it practicable to make a single Room so capacious, with Pews and Galleries, as to hold above 2,000 Persons, and all to hear the Service, and both to hear distinctly, and see the Preacher. ...

7. Concerning the placing of the Pulpit, I shall observe—A moderate Voice may be heard 50 Feet distant before the Preacher, 30 Feet on each Side, and 20 behind the Pulpit, and not this, unless the Pronunciation be distinct and equal, without losing the Voice at the Last Word of the Sentence.[1]

Although Wren did not object to the presence of the chancel, some of his churches had none, and the tendency to omit the

---

[1] Christopher Wren, *Parentalia: or, Memoirs of the Family of the Wrens: Viz. of Matthew Bishop of Ely, Christopher Dean of Windsor, etc. but chiefly of Sir Christopher Wren, Late Surveyor-General of the Royal Buildings, President of the Royal Society, etc. etc. Compiled by his Son Christopher, Now Published by his Grandson, Stephen Wren, Esq.* (London, 1750), p. 320.

chancel or to reduce it to a very shallow apse became wide-spread in the eighteenth century.

By the nineteenth century, the chancel was frequently considered no more than a superfluous appendage. Wren's type of church, 'fitted for Auditories' had become the prevalent model, and the dominant consideration in building new churches was the ease with which the voice of the preacher might be heard. Services were conducted almost entirely from the pulpit and reading desk, even on the rare occasions (in many parishes only three times per year) when Holy Communion was celebrated. Indeed, from the Reformation onwards, the general tendency had been towards a reduction and simplification of liturgical centres. Frequently these consisted of the three-decker (clerk's desk, reading desk, and pulpit) and a railed-in communion table on which a portable baptismal basin might be placed. These items were located as near to the congregation as possible in order to secure the greatest ease in hearing. The auditory churches exemplified a very logical approach to the problem of church-building, the dominant theme throughout a great variety of different treatments being that of the congregation's convenience in following the service.[1] (See Plate I for a typical Anglican church arrangement in the 1830's.)

Although the buildings had been arranged with a view to the maximum of comfort and convenience for the congregation, it is undoubtedly true that the maintenance of the structure itself was often neglected. By the 1830's many medieval buildings were in very poor repair. A book published in 1845 on the *Churches of Cambridgeshire and the Isle of Ely* claimed that in the village of Haslingfield: 'The church has suffered considerably from damp and neglect; the state of the floor at the west end of the north aisle is such as would certainly not be permitted in any gentleman's stable, nor, voluntarily, in the meanest cottage.'[2] It was reported that in the Cherry Hinton Church, 'the north

[1] A large number of these experiments are illustrated and described by G. W. O. Addleshaw and Frederick Etchells, *The Architectural Setting of Anglican Worship* (London, 1950).
[2] Cambridge Camden Society (Cambridge, 1845), p. 118.

Aisle is blocked off, and irreverently used as a dust-hole and rubbish depositary—an idle and unseemly custom, very common in the churches in the neighbourhood of Cambridge'.[1] Of the Histon Church, the writers commented that 'the air of dank, neglected decay which pervades the entire place, betrays the spirit of the present day'.[2]

Whatever the 'spirit of the present day' was, it certainly was not one of reverence for the church building and its contents. The Dean of Exeter, Thomas H. Lowe, told the Exeter Diocesan Architectural Society in 1842—

we may now see in most of our rural Churches a rabble of boors and boys seated on the very steps and rails of the altar, and the altar itself used to place their hats on, and perhaps, at other times, and where there is no proper vestry, employed as a table for the accommodation of the farmers in vestry assembled. This extreme irreverence, and shocking desecration of holy things is capable of no excuse.[3]

In a letter written during a tour of Somerset in 1842, John Mason Neale relates 'a thing practised in Tong Church. The Squire has built a pew in the Chancel; when the Commandments are begun, a servant regularly enters at the Chancel door with the luncheon tray!'[4] Neale soon found profanation even closer at hand. On his first Sunday as parish priest in Crawley, 'in the middle of the service . . . the Church warden, wanting to open the east window, got up on the Altar!'[5]

Reverence for the church building and its furnishings had been thoroughly leached out of Anglicanism by the 1830's. In some sophisticated circles a profane love of these items for their artistic and antiquarian associations had appeared, but even this was rare. The *Ecclesiologist*, the journal of the Cambridge Camden Society, reported that at the Church of Sts Peter and

[1] *Churches of Cambridgeshire*, p. 24.   [2] *Ibid.*, p. 70.
[3] *A Few Thoughts on the Interior Arrangement of Churches: Being the Substance of a Paper Read at a General Meeting of the Members of the Exeter Diocesan Architectural Society, March 24, 1842* (Exeter, n.d.), p. 24.
[4] *Letters of John Mason Neale, D.D., Selected and Edited by His Daughter* (London, 1910), p. 33. (Cited hereafter as *Letters*.)
[5] *Ibid.*, p. 37.

4

Paul, Moulton, Northamptonshire: 'The ancient Font was taken as a *horse-trough to the vicarage*, and has now disappeared ... its substitute is a small mortar on a stone baluster' (iii, 63). Frequently the medieval font was appropriated by the squire or clergyman as the base for a quaint sundial.

The altar received no more respect. In East Shefford Church, Berkshire, it was noted: 'On the altar itself are placed books, hats, and instruments, in utter irreverence for the holy purposes for which that altar was erected' (*E.* v, 167). Nor were the laity solely to blame: 'What must the unlearned think when they see Priests deposit their gloves and handkerchief, as is too commonly the case, on the very Table of the Lord?' (*E.* iii, 165).

The chancel itself was frequently the victim of neglect since it was rarely used except on the occasion of Holy Communion. A tract reported in 1844: 'This "deplorable waste of available space", to use the language of the cheap church-builders of the present day, ... [Chancels] are pronounced, in short, a needless expense.'[1] In 1842 the Society related that 'in nine-tenths of the new churches we shall find no attempt whatever at having a distinct Chancel, or it is at best confined to a small apsidal projection for the Altar'.[2] In many churches, especially those of medieval origin, the chancels were allowed to 'remain as they have done in times past' simply by being closed off from the church. In 1842 the Society exclaimed in horror that it was—

often the case, the Chancel has been quite shut out from the Nave by a boarded screen up to the roof, or by an overgrown pew, that most sacred part of the church is sure to be given up to dirt and decay. ... I have seen some Tables that would not be thought good enough for a kitchen, and some which serve also as cupboards for books and cushions: nay the church-chest itself is in one place used for the Eucharistick Table, and in another the same thing serves both for an Altar and a stove![3]

[1] Cambridge Camden Society, *A Few Words to Church Builders*, 3rd ed. (Cambridge, 1844), p. 14.

[2] *A Few Words to Church Builders with an Appendix Containing Lists of Windows, Fonts, and Roodscreens Intended to Serve as Models*, 2nd ed. (Cambridge, 1842), p. 6.

[3] *A Few Words to Churchwardens on Churches and Church Ornaments: Part II. Suited to Town and Manufacturing Parishes*, 5th ed. (Cambridge, 1842), p. 9.

Practical parishes occasionally put the chancel to various uses. Sometimes it was simply filled with pews and used for accommodation of prominent people of the parish, especially the squire or the clergyman's family. During the thirteenth century Bishop Grosseteste had granted the patron a stall in the choir, but in the nineteenth century several private pews often dominated the entire chancel. Pews at the entrance to the chancel were considered especially desirable, and the old roodscreens were often incorporated into pews. According to one observer, the pew belonging to the priest at Wicken Bonhurst Church, Essex, 'divides the chancel from the nave, so that access to the altar, except through it is impossible' (*E.* IV, 244).

Another very frequent function for the chancel was as a school. In Long Stanton, St Michael's Church, someone noticed:

The Chancel of this very beautiful little Early-English chapel is used for a school, a green curtain being drawn across the Chancel-arch, and a common wide *kitchen fire grate* inserted in, and projecting from, the north wall, with a huge red brick chimney behind it, for the comfort and accommodation of the teacher (who sits within the Altar rails with his chair against the Holy Table) and his flock, who thus imbibe early principles of irreverence which must be most baneful (*E.* II, 171).

It was indeed a practical time, having little interest in reverence when it interfered with utility.

The arrangement of the nave likewise emphasized the same practicality, the chief liturgical centre usually being the three-decker pulpit. 'In most modern churches it [the pulpit] is placed with the reading pew and clerk's desk, immediately before the Holy Altar, for the purpose, it would seem, of hiding the latter as much as possible from the congregation.'[1] Various experiments were tried. A letter in the *Ecclesiologist* noted: 'In a modern chapel, at a *"fashionable watering-place"*, (it is at *such* places that excesses like this are chiefly committed) the architect has fixed over the Altar twin boxes or tubs for the desk and pulpit, precisely alike in size and shape' (II, 26).

[1] *A Few Words to Church Builders*, 2nd ed., p. 24.

The nave itself was largely filled with pews, or 'pues' as their opponents preferred to call them. A pew, in the nineteenth-century sense, is almost a forgotten item, so wholesale was the destruction of them engendered by the Society. At that time a pew was a space in the church or chancel appropriated for the exclusive use and possession of a private family and enclosed with wood panelling or curtains often to a height of five feet or more. (See Plate I for an illustration of a church fitted with pews.) Some of the most elaborate ones were elevated above the pavement or even covered by canopies. A description of a pew in Exton Church, Rutlandshire, noted: 'The size of this parlour is 12 feet by 15; it is richly carpeted, and contains thirteen drawing-room chairs, and a mahogany table in the centre. On the north side is a stove with a fender and fireirons' (*E.* II, 102). Pews were undoubtedly a great abuse, reflecting the rigid class structure of the time. Many of the poor refused to attend Church services when the accommodation for them (usually benches in the centre alley or galleries) was so wretched, preferring instead the dissenting chapels, usually unpewed. A preacher of the time denounced—

the pew system—that system which has introduced so unchristian a distinction in the house of God between the sittings of the rich and of the poor, and which (there can be little doubt) is doing more to alienate the hearts of tens of thousands in every large town in England from the Church of Christ, than any one other thing that could be named.[1]

An Ecclesiologist wrote: 'We do not seldom see pews, even in the Nave, half-roofed like country villas, and sometimes even *embattled* . . . it is still worse when this great pew is fitted up like a drawing-room, with fire-place and chimney and a separate entrance.'[2] Pews occupied a great deal of space, and since the population of many towns was growing rapidly, it was frequently considered necessary to add extra aisles or galleries,

---

[1] Edward Stuart, *The Pew System, The Chief Hindrance to the Church's Work in Towns: A Sermon*, 3rd ed. (London, n.d.), p. 10.
[2] *A Few Words to Churchwardens: Part II*, 5th ed., pp. 5–6.

despite the fact that this usually disfigured a medieval church. The great majority of churches built in the seventeenth and eighteenth centuries were in one of the classical styles and many of these were constructed with galleries as a part of the original structure.

There can be little doubt but that the average English parish church at the beginning of Victoria's reign presented a rather unattractive sight, reflecting religious indifference and the worst effects of rigid social snobbery. But changes were already under way. It is difficult to chronicle a change of taste briefly, especially when the change was at least a century in developing. The first significant monument of the gothic revival is usually considered to be Horace Walpole's villa, Strawberry Hill, the reconstruction of which began in 1750. This had been preceded by the publication in 1747 of Batty Langley's *Gothic Architecture, Improved by Rules and Proportions*.[1] However, it was not until the nineteenth century that gothic architecture really achieved popularity. Some of the more than two hundred Commissioners' Churches built between 1818 and 1835 were more or less gothic, perhaps because it was considered cheaper than a classical building with a portico.

The literature of the romantic movement gave powerful impetus to the gothic revival. In an article on 'The French Académie and Gothic Architecture', the *Ecclesiologist* declared:

But, like many other signs of hope in the present day, we are disposed to trace the progress which has of late been made in a considerable degree to the writings of Sir Walter Scott: and whatever be his place among the chiefs of English Literature, he will we believe earn from posterity a higher praise than is ever the lot of any mere literary man, nor fail to draw from the truthful and attractive pictures he has given of those times which the grossness of a later age had treated with unmixed contempt (vi, 83).

Scott's novels were complemented by several series of books by

---

[1] Batty and Thomas Langley, *Gothic Architecture, Improved by Rules and Proportions, In Many Grand Designs of Columns, Doors, Windows, Chimney-Pieces, Arcades, Colonades, Porticos, Umbrellos, Temples, and Pavillions &c. with Plans, Elevations and Profiles, Geometrically Explained* (London, 1747).

'The Abyss from Which We Are Emerging'

John Britton (1771–1857) on the *Beauties of England, Architectural Antiquities of Great Britain,* and *Cathedral Antiquities.* These series ran between 1800 and 1835 and were very well illustrated.[1] In 1857 the *Ecclesiologist* noted Britton's death:

With ecclesiology in its most technical sense, John Britton had little sympathy or acquaintance. But it is undoubted that his elaborately illustrated works were among the earliest of the causes which led to that revived appreciation in England of mediaeval ecclesiastical architecture, of which ecclesiology is the complete expression. For that let John Britton be honoured in the *Ecclesiologist* (XVIII, 70).

Britton's books, surprisingly enough, were extremely popular and spread the craze for gothic architecture as well as earning their publisher a small fortune.

Books intended for the professional architect as well as for the cultured public also enjoyed a great success. Perhaps the most significant of these books was one by Thomas Rickman (1776–1841), *An Attempt to Discriminate the Styles of Architecture in England,* first published in 1819 and reaching a fifth edition in 1848. Rickman established the nomenclature for the periods of English architecture still used today: Norman, Early English, Decorated, and Perpendicular. He made over two thousand drawings of medieval buildings in every part of England and rendered a tremendous service to the scientific knowledge of gothic. Although a Quaker, Rickman designed a number of parish churches as well as the New Buildings, St John's College, Cambridge (1827).[2]

Undoubtedly the most colourful figure in the gothic revival was Augustus Welby Northmore Pugin (1812–52). Reared an Anglican, Pugin became a Roman Catholic in 1834, thus insuring lifelong resentment from all Anglicans. He did not need this extra unpopularity, however, for few people have fought for a cause with such bitter and outspoken firmness as Pugin.

---

[1] Cf. Kenneth Clark, *The Gothic Revival, an Essay in the History of Taste* (London, 1950), pp. 105–6.

[2] At his death the Society called Rickman 'the great architect to whom we are chiefly indebted for the revival of a taste for ecclesiastical architecture' (*Report of the Cambridge Camden Society for MDCCCXLI,* Cambridge, 1841, p. 4).

But even his enemies, and they were legion, had to admit his talent. The *Ecclesiologist,* perpetually annoyed by Pugin's proud Roman Catholicism and assaults on the Establishment, wrote at his death: 'Now that we have lost him—we can have no hesitation in pronouncing [him] the most eminent and original architectural genius of his time' (XIII, 352).

Pugin first acquired notoriety with his *Contrasts,* published in 1836 (two years after his conversion) at his own expense, no publisher wishing to handle such a vitriolic book. The title is indicative: *Contrasts: or, a Parallel between the Noble Edifices of the Fourteenth and Fifteenth Centuries, and Similar Buildings of the Present Day: Shewing the Present Decay of Taste: Accompanied by Appropriate Text.* It would be difficult to tell which was more explosive, the text or the eleven plates of highly satirical contrasts with which the book concluded. The theme of the book is succinctly stated on the first page: 'On comparing the Architectural Works of the present Century with those of the Middle Ages, the wonderful superiority of the latter must strike every attentive observer; and the mind is naturally led to reflect on the causes which have wrought this mighty change.'[1] It did not take him long to reveal that the cause of the change was the Protestant Reformation.[2] A few more years' experience among his fellow Roman Catholics led Pugin to modify his charges somewhat, and in the second (1841) edition of *Contrasts* he announced:

The real origin of both the revived Pagan and Protestant principles is to be traced to the decayed faith throughout Europe in the fifteenth century, which led men to dislike, and ultimately forsake, the principles and architecture which originated in the *self-denying Catholic principle and admire and adopt the luxurious styles of ancient Paganism.* Religion must have been in a most diseased state, for those two

---

[1] *Contrasts* (St. Marie's Grange, near Salisbury, 1836), p. 1.

[2] The chapter titles in the first edition (1836) of *Contrasts* are indicative: 'On the Feelings Which Produced the Great Edifices of the Middle Ages'; 'On the State of Architecture in England Immediately Preceding the Change of Religion'; 'Of the Pillage and Destruction of the Churches Under Henry the Eighth'; 'Of the Ravages and Destruction the Churches Suffered Under Edward VI, and After the Final Establishment of the New Religion'; 'On the Present Degraded State of Ecclesiastical Buildings'; 'Conclusion, On the Wretched State of Architecture at the Present Day.'

monsters, revived Paganism and Protestantism, ever to have *obtained a footing*, much less to have overrun the Christian world.[1]

In other words, the Renaissance, with its revival of classical forms of architecture, shared the blame with Protestantism.

Pugin loathed the buildings of his century and claimed 'it would be extremely difficult, if not impossible, to find one amongst the immense mass which could be handed down to succeeding ages as an honourable specimen of the architectural talent of the time'.[2] There could be no solution, he felt—'unless the same feelings which influenced the old designers in the composition of their Works, can be restored:—a result which, though I most fervently wish, I dare not at present hope for. But I feel thoroughly convinced, that it is only by similar glorious feelings that similar glorious results can be obtained.'[3] Here we have in a few words that characteristic Victorian compounding of architecture and ethics to which Geoffrey Scott gave the name 'The Ethical Fallacy'.[4] Through the efforts of Ruskin and other Protestants, the full moral vigour of Puritanism was enlisted in the cause of art, especially architecture.[5]

Pugin was eventually appointed Professor of Architecture and Ecclesiastical Antiquities at Oscott College, the Roman Catholic centre near Birmingham. In 1841 he published some of his lectures there in another significant book, *The True Principles of Pointed or Christian Architecture*. The basic thesis of the book was 'we can *never successfully deviate one tittle from the spirit and principles of pointed architecture* [gothic]. We must rest content to *follow*, not to lead.'[6] His object in the book was—

---

[1] Second edition, reprinted (Edinburgh, 1898), pp. iii–iv.

[2] *Contrasts* (1836), p. 31.

[3] *Ibid.*, p. iii.

[4] *The Architecture of Humanism, A Study in the History of Taste* (Garden City, N.Y., 1956), pp. 97ff.

[5] In 1849 Ruskin stated in comparing architecture and the other arts: 'But in architecture another and a less subtle, more contemptible, violation of truth is possible; a direct falsity of assertion respecting the nature of material, or the quantity of labour. And this is, in the full sense of the word, wrong; it is as truly deserving of reprobation as any other moral delinquency' ('The Lamp of Truth', in *The Seven Lamps of Architecture*, London, 1956, p. 33).

[6] *The True Principles of Pointed or Christian Architecture: Set forth in Two Lectures*

to set forth and explain the true principles of Pointed or Christian Architecture, by the knowledge of which you may be enabled to test architectural excellence. The two great rules for design are these: *1st there should be no features about a building which are not necessary for convenience, construction, or propriety; 2nd, that all ornament should consist of enrichment of the essential construction of the building.*[1]

These principles, so strangely prophetic of twentieth-century functionalism, formed Pugin's creed.

For Pugin, only gothic was true 'Christian Architecture'. In a tract entitled *An Apology for the Revival of Christian Architecture in England*, he attempted 'to place Christian architecture in its true position . . . as the only correct expression of the faith, wants, and climate of our country'.[2] 'To advocate Christian architecture merely on the score of its beauty,' is not enough. 'We must turn to the principles from which all styles have originated.'[3] Consequently, he found: 'The student of Christian architecture should . . . imbue his mind with the mysteries of his Faith, the history of the Church, the lives of those glorious Saints and Martyrs that it has produced in all ages.'[4]

Surprisingly enough, such ideas were accepted. In a candid moment in 1843, Pugin wrote:

The progress which the revival of pointed architecture has made within the last few years is most surprising. . . . In my own case I can truly state, that in buildings I erected but a short time since, I can perceive numerous defects and errors, which I should not now commit; and, but a few years ago, I perpetrated abominations. Indeed, till I discovered these laws of pointed design, which I set forth in my

Delivered at St. Marie's Oscott (London, 1841), p. 9n. The *Ecclesiologist* claimed Pugin's 'own idea of perfection was an absolute copy of a medieval building' (*E.* XIII, 352).

[1] *Ibid.*, p. 1.

[2] First published 1843, reprinted (Edinburgh, 1895), p. 3.

[3] *Ibid.*, p. 4. Pugin here sheds light on a leading misinterpretation of nineteenth-century architecture: the belief that it was meant to be beautiful. Elsewhere he remarked: 'Pointed or Christian Architecture has far higher claim on our admiration than mere beauty or antiquity; the former may be regarded as a matter of opinion,—the latter, in the abstract, is no proof of excellence, but in it alone we find *the faith of Christianity* embodied, and its practices illustrated' (*Contrasts*, 2nd ed., pp. 3–4).

[4] *Apology*, p. 21.

'True Principles', I had no fixed rules to work upon, and frequently fell into error and extravagance. . . . But, from the moment I understood that the beauty of architectural design depended on its being the expression of what the building required, and that for Christians that expression could only be correctly given by the medium of pointed architecture, all difficulties vanished.[1]

This strange affirmation of functionalism may have ended some of Pugin's perplexities, but there were other problems. Although Pugin found a wealthy patron and supporter in Lord Shrewsbury, his fellow Roman Catholics showed little enthusiasm for gothic.[2] His *The Present State of Ecclesiastical Architecture in England* scolds 'Catholic England' for leaving 'thy most beauteous works unnoticed and despised, to catch at foreign ideas, unsuited to their country and jarring with its national traditions'.[3] Pugin was shocked by the classical architecture of Rome, especially by St Peter's. 'He got out of Rome as soon as he possibly could "for every hour he was there he felt endangered his faith".'[4] The Roman Catholic Church brought continual discouragement in its apathy to any form of artistic or liturgical revival, and some of Pugin's gothic churches were shorn of their fastidiously correct ornaments by prelates uninterested in such matters. In *An Earnest Appeal for the Revival of the Ancient Plain Song*, Pugin conceded:

Indeed, with some few exceptions, the Churches that have been raised after the old models are become so many evidences of our degradation and our shame. The altar and the arch may belong to the ages of faith, but the singing drags us down to the concert-room of the 19th century, and is a sad and striking proof of the little sympathy which exists between the architecture and the men.[5]

Though he found few sympathetic souls in his own Church,

---

[1] *Ibid.*, pp. 15–16n.

[2] Cf. Denis Gwynn, *Lord Shrewsbury, Pugin and the Gothic Revival* (Westminster, Maryland, 1946).

[3] London, 1843, p. 15.

[4] Benjamin Ferrey, *Recollections of A. N. Welby Pugin, and His Father Augustus Pugin; With Notices of Their Works* (London, 1861), p. 151.

[5] London, 1850, p. 8. This tract was ungraciously reprinted by Anglicans as an anti-Roman tract, an act which did not make Pugin any more popular with Roman Catholics.

Pugin's ideas were soon reflected in many parts of the Established Church. His contemporary, Benjamin Ferrey wrote: 'He frequently expressed a more favourable opinion of the Anglican clergy, than of those belonging to his own Church, . . . the clergy of the Church of England as a body were entirely favourable to the revival of architecture of which Pugin was so masterly an exponent.'[1] Of course, few Anglicans were willing to admit that they had been influenced by Pugin. The safest course was to appropriate his ideas without acknowledging the source. The *Christian Remembrancer* announced: 'It is well known . . . that the writers of that journal [*Ecclesiologist*] are avowed disciples of Mr. Pugin.'[2] The *Ecclesiologist*'s version was quite different:

Shortly after the formation of the Cambridge Camden Society, the first founders of which had as yet no knowledge of his works or writings, Mr. Pugin expressed himself so warmly and even affectionately in the pages of the *Dublin Review*, with respect to our early labours and publications, that a personal acquaintance was soon formed . . . when . . . he found among Roman Catholics less sympathy and encouragement than he deserved, he seemed to value the more firm and consistent line advocated by our Society (XIII, 352-3).

Ruskin, too, denied charges of plagiarizing from Pugin.[3] Though few people cared to give Pugin full credit, it was obvious by the time of his death in 1852 that his ideas were shared by many within the Church of England.

Fortunately for the Anglican champions of gothic, there were kindred souls within the Church of England whose accomplishments could be pointed out with pride. John Henry Newman built a gothic chapel in the village of Littlemore near Oxford in 1835. A small building with neither chancel nor porch, it was nevertheless highly esteemed by those who considered Newman

[1] Ferrey, pp. 228-9.

[2] 'Styles of Church Architecture', *Christian Remembrancer*, IV (1842), 258.

[3] 'It is often said that I borrow from Pugin,' Ruskin wrote. 'I glanced at Pugin's Contrasts once, . . . [and] His "Remarks on Articles in the *Rambler*" were brought under my notice by some of the reviews. I never read a word of any other of his works, not feeling from the style of his architecture the smallest interest in his opinions' (*Modern Painters*, London, 1904, III, 428-9).

a hero.[1] In January 1845 (before Newman was received into the Roman Catholic Church) the *Ecclesiologist* reviewed this building:

Now therefore the time has come when we may, without misgiving, venture to do what we must all in some sort feel to be an act of justice, make honourable mention of Littlemore Church, first as being in itself the first unqualified step to better things that England had long witnessed: the first building for many a long year erected, showing itself to be not so much a sermon-house, as a temple of the MOST HIGH.

. . . .

In this church, so new, so strange, so startling when first built, are not to be found chancel (properly so called), sedilia, piscina, rood-screen, stalls, we believe, or font-cover; and yet Littlemore Church, with its solid walls and lofty roof, its honoured altar, its quiet half-light, and religious services, is a greater step in advance beyond what was known before it, that the most Catholically built and arranged church would be over it. Truly, without a 'graduated' scale, we can never measure the depth of the abyss from which we are emerging (IV, 32–3).

The building was subsequently considerably altered by the addition of a chancel and tower. But evidently its furnishings were startling enough to make a vivid impression on at least one contemporary. The Reverend Peter Maurice, Chaplain of New and All Souls' Colleges, recorded his visit to Littlemore Chapel: 'I felt an indescribable horror stealing over me, as I carried my eye towards the eastern wall of the building, and beheld a plain naked cross, either of stone or a good imitation of it rising up and projecting out of the wall, from the centre of the table of communion.'[2] Maurice was perturbed further by some of the stained glass and what must have been a credence table.

Another step was taken by Walter F. Hook, vicar of Leeds, in

[1] Thomas Mozley states that the Church was modelled after the chancel of his own church in Northamptonshire: 'There was to be no chancel, or vestry, or tower, or porch. The work became an object of much interest' (*Reminiscences Chiefly of Oriel College and the Oxford Movement*, Boston, 1884, I, 346). Cf. John Rothenstein, 'Newman and Littlemore', *Architectural Review*, 98 (1945), 176–7.

[2] *The Popery of Oxford Confronted, Disavowed, & Repudiated* (London, 1837), p. 53n.

rebuilding St Peter's Church, Leeds, in 1841. The *Ecclesiologist* considered it 'perhaps the first really great undertaking of the present age, which, though not in the highest architectural style, was arranged with a regard to ecclesiastical propriety previously unknown' (VII, 46). At another time, the *Ecclesiologist* called it—

the first great instance, as Littlemore chapel . . . was the first on a small scale, of the Catholic feeling of a church, . . . grasping at the altar as being rather than the pulpit the central point of worship, and yet of course not being able to compass those points of church arrangement which are the result of study and of patient research (VIII, 132).

St Peter's was a gothic structure and featured a chancel occupied by a surpliced choir of laymen.

Gothic was being favoured increasingly. Yet the spirit of these churches built in the first few years of Victoria's reign was unfettered by any dictates of correctness. Medieval buildings had been the point of departure, not the goal of the journey. The styles of the Middle Ages had been little more than playthings except for rare zealots such as Pugin. But church architecture was destined to become serious business at a time when the Church itself was caught up in a major transition.

II

No one has convincingly maintained that the early 1830's were a period of great piety in the Church of England. It was common knowledge that the Church was full of abuses such as pluralism and non-residence. John Wade took particular delight in exposing the finances of the Church. His *Extraordinary Black Book* cited with considerable relish many individual cases:

The late archbishop SUTTON is an eminent instance of the perversion of ecclesiastical patronage. The Suttons remaining in the Church are very numerous; among seven of them are shared sixteen rectories, vicarages, and chapelries, besides preacherships and dignities in the cathedrals. Of the *eleven* daughters of the Archbishop, several had the prudence to marry men in holy orders, who soon became amply endowed. Hugh Percy, son of the Earl of Beverly, married one daughter; and in the course of about as many years, was portioned off with eight different preferments, estimated to be worth £10,000 per annum.[1]

Wade goes on to point out that whereas the income of the two archbishops averaged £26,465 per year and the bishops £10,174, there were more than four thousand curates who were averaging only £75 remuneration.[2] The surge of reform evident in the rest of public life found faint response from within the sacred precincts of the Church. The suggestion of government interference aroused cries of Erastianism. Many historians, wishing to darken the night before the dawn of the Oxford Movement, doubtlessly overstate the case. But it was certainly not a time of widespread religious zeal.

This was well typified in the parochial worship of the period. It seemed in retrospect to Gladstone, that—

the actual state of things, as to worship, was bad beyond all parallel known to me in experience or reading. Taking together the expulsion of the poor and labouring classes (especially from the town churches), the mutilations and blockages of the fabrics, the baldness of the service, the elaborate horrors of the so-called music, . . . and above all the coldness and indifference of the lounging or sleeping congregation, our services were probably without a parallel in the world for their debasement.[3]

Undoubtedly the services must have been long and dull, Morning Prayer, the Litany, and Ante-Communion being frequently combined. In many parishes the Communion was only rarely celebrated. Hymn-singing was considered improper by many priests. Benjamin Webb wrote Neale in 1849: 'I expect I shall loathe your Methodistical snuffling hymnizing article. It is the oddest thing to me that you have never slipped off that Evangelical slough.'[4]

[1] London, 1831, p. 23.
[2] *Ibid.*, p. 54.
[3] W. E. Gladstone, *Gleanings of Past Years, 1843–78* (London, 1879), VI, 119.
[4] *Letters of John Mason Neale*, p. 124.

It is amazing, considering present Anglican practice, to recall that the efforts of Bishop Blomfield of London and of Bishop Phillpotts of Exeter to make their clergy wear surplices in the pulpit produced riots and had to be abandoned.[1] The churches were generally barren of anything which could be considered suggestive of Catholic ritual. Liddon noted in 1857 that during a visit to the Theological College at Cuddesdon:

The Bishops of Glasgow and London have represented to him [Samuel Wilberforce, Bishop of Oxford] in the strongest terms the necessity of making the chapel less 'gaudy.' Accordingly (1) the Cross has been removed; (2) the white and green Altar clothes are forbidden; (3) the painted figures on the wall are to be covered over; and (4) the celebrant is to stand at the end, not in front, of the Altar.[2]

In the early 1830's there were three large parties in the Church of England: Orthodox, Liberals, and Evangelicals. Of these, the Evangelicals were 'the most influential of all the parties in the Pre-Victorian Era'.[3]

But matters were soon to change. On 14 July 1833 John Keble preached his famous Assize Sermon at Oxford. Newman said: 'I have ever considered and kept the day, as the start of the religious movement of 1833.'[4] That autumn, publication of the *Tracts for the Times* began. Though advertised as 'against Popery and Dissent', they proved very unpopular within the Church of England. The last one, Tract 90, *Remarks on Certain Passages in the Thirty-nine Articles*, appeared in 1841 and produced such a violent reaction that publication was suspended. Newman was a leader of the Oxford Movement from its origin, and Edward Bouverie Pusey joined in 1834. Henceforth the Movement was frequently referred to as 'Puseyism' or as 'Tractarianism'. From the start the Movement was violently attacked, and many individuals were persecuted and harassed by the Church

---

[1] Henry Parry Liddon, *Life of Edward Bouverie Pusey* (London, 1897), IV, 213. (Cited hereafter as *Life*.)

[2] John Octavius Johnstone, *Life and Letters of Henry Parry Liddon* (London, 1904), pp. 36–7.

[3] Elliott-Binns, *Religion in the Victorian Era* (London, 1946), p. 48.

[4] John Henry Newman, *Apologia pro Vita Sua* (New York, 1947), p. 32.

and the University. But the *Tracts* and Newman's sermons at St Mary's won numerous adherents. However, some of the leaders, including Newman and Ward, eventually came to doubt the position of the Church of England, and began drifting towards the Roman Catholic Church. Newman was received into it on 8 October 1845, thus closing the first phase of the Oxford Movement.

Although initially it appeared as a reaction against Erastianism, the great principle of Tractarianism proved to be the doctrine of the Church, specifically that known as apostolic succession. Vernon F. Storr comments:

> No reader of the Tracts can fail to see that the essence of Tractarianism lies in this doctrine of the succession. Episcopacy is held up as not merely of the *bene esse* of a Church, but as something without which there can be no Church at all. The fact of an unbroken ministerial succession is not enough . . . without bishops tracing their descent through the Apostles to Christ, [there is] no duly commissioned minister.[1]

Yngve Brilioth refers to this doctrine as the 'static' concept of the Church, that is, the belief that the validity of a ministry is determined by its commissioning rather than by its fruits.[2]

Undoubtedly, the chief interest of the leaders of the Oxford Movement was that of teaching correct doctrine, especially in matters relating to the nature of the Church. Actually, they had little, if any, interest in ritualistic matters. It is a mistake, though a very common one, to think that the change in worship and architecture occurring in Victoria's reign was engineered at Oxford. Gregory Dix states: 'It was the "Cambridge Ecclesiological Society" which led the way in changes in worship expressive of the changes in theology advocated at Oxford.'[3] Indeed, some of the Tractarians, or Puseyites as they were generally called, were quite disturbed by ritualistic innovations. Pusey himself wrote in 1860:

[1] *The Development of English Theology in the Nineteenth Century 1800–1860* (London, 1913), I, 260.
[2] *The Anglican Revival: Studies in the Oxford Movement* (London, 1925), pp. 180ff.
[3] *The Shape of the Liturgy* (Westminster, 1954), p. xvi n.

I am in this strange position that my name is a byword for that with which I never had any sympathy, that which the writers of the Tracts, with whom in early days I was associated, always deprecated —any innovations in the way of conducting the service, anything of ritualism or especially any revival of disused vestments. . . . Of late years, when Ritualism has become more prominent, I have looked for a natural opportunity of dissociating myself from it, but have not found one. . . . Altogether I have looked with sorrow at the crude way in which some doctrines have been put forward, without due pains to prevent misunderstanding, and ritual has been forced upon the people, unexplained and without their consent.[1]

However, this confusion as to the instigators of ritualism is nothing new. From the earliest days of the Movement, any ritualistic changes were blamed on the Oxford men. An anonymous writer in Weale's *Quarterly Papers on Architecture* wrote in 1844: 'The matter, *architecturally* not less than *spiritually*, seems to have originated with certain "clerkes of OXENFORDE". As the tracts theological, so have the treatises church-gothical, swarmed upon us.'[2]

Despite such accusations, there is good evidence that the Tractarians were not interested in aesthetics. In 1844 John Mason Neale wrote Benjamin Webb, severely criticizing a letter of Pusey's which evidently had stated that personal purity was necessary for the building of churches:

I hope and trust that you are not going to Oxonianize. It is clear to me, that the Tract writers missed one great principle, namely the influence of Aestheticks, and it is unworthy of them to blind themselves to it. . . it is absurd to say that it does not often please GOD to raise up, as defenders of His truth, men even of immoral lifes: witness many of the Popes. If of His truth, why not of His beauty?[3]

Pusey's fear of aesthetics and ritualism seems to have been largely grounded on the apprehension lest they would lead men

---

[1] *Life*, IV, 211–12.

[2] John Weale, editor and publisher, *Quarterly Papers on Architecture* (London, 1844), II, 1.

[3] *Letters*, p. 70. Shortly thereafter, however, Neale reported that he had 'sat a long time with Dr Pusey, who is just the man I fancied, and among other things, we spoke a good deal of "Durandus". I could not wish any man to be more aesthetic than he is. How different from Newman' (*Letters*, p. 75).

from more important duties. In 1866 he addressed the English Church Union:

It is well known that I never was a ritualist. . . . In our early days we were anxious on the subject of ritual. . . . We had further a distinct fear with regard to ritual; and we privately discouraged it, lest the whole movement should become superficial. . . we felt it was much easier to change a dress than to change the heart, and that externals might be gained at the cost of the doctrines themselves. . . . We had also ground for fear lest it should be thought we were only engaged in a matter of external order.[1]

Whether or not they were motivated by a similar fear of superficiality, many of Pusey's associates remained quite indifferent to ritualism, preferring to retain the usual practices of the time. Storr tells us that: 'Keble never wore vestments, or adopted advanced ritual usages, and deprecated the fashion of non-communicating attendance at the Holy Communion on the ground that it might lead to superstition and the fostering of a belief in a "quasi-sacramental virtue" in so attending.'[2] Mozley wrote of Newman:

So little part had he in the great ecclesiological and ritual revival, which has changed not only the inside of our churches but the face of the land, that from first to last he performed the service after the fashion of the last century. At his own church of St Mary's was retained the custom, said to be from Puritan times, of handing the sacred elements to the communicants at their places down the long chancel, the desks of which, covered with white linen for the occasion, looked much like tables.[3]

Indeed, Newman placed his emphasis squarely on doctrine. 'There will be no good there or anywhere else,' he wrote Keble, 'till the doctrine of post-baptismal sin is recognized. N., N., and the Bishop of Exeter combine with the Cambridge Camden, in making a fair outside, while within are dead men's bones. We shall do nothing till we have a severer religion.'[4]

Pusey's sentiments were similar. Between 1842 and 1845 he

---

[1] *Life*, IV, 212.   [2] Storr, I, 268.   [3] T. Mozley, *Reminiscences*, I, 345–6.
[4] *Correspondence of John Henry Newman with John Keble and Others, 1839–45*, edited at the Birmingham Oratory (London, 1917), p. 195.

was engaged in building St Saviour's Church in Leeds. This large gothic structure had no stalls in the chancel, the services being performed in the crossing. Pusey corresponded with Benjamin Webb, secretary of the Cambridge Camden Society, about some details of the arrangements. Despite the objections of the Ecclesiologists, Pusey was determined to have the Decalogue erected over the altar according to the practice of the time: 'I cannot but think that, however it may have been brought about that we have the Commandments, Creed, and our Lord's Prayer near the altar, there is much good in it. . . . Needs may have arisen and have been providentially provided for even by uncatholic means . . . there is a danger in the very "beauty of holiness" without its severity.'[1]

In his own practices, Pusey was most conservative and seemed to delight in showing his ignorance of the more complicated ritualistic matters. He wrote a fellow minister in 1851:

I am grieved to hear of your trouble about your ritual. One most grievous offence seems to be turning your back to the people. I was not ritualist enough to know, until the other day, that the act of turning had any special meaning in the Consecration. And it certainly seemed against the Rubric, that the Consecration should take place so that they cannot see it. Dear Newman consecrated to the last of his Consecrations at the North end of the altar.[2]

Pusey was frequently occupied restraining young men from rushing into ritualistic practices. To J. F. Russell, one of the leading members of the Cambridge Camden Society, he wrote in 1839:

I should deprecate seeking to restore the richer style of vestments used in Edward the Sixth's reign. . . . It seems beginning at the wrong end for our ministers to deck their own person: our own plain dresses are more in keeping with the state of our Church, which is one of humiliation: it does not seem in character to revive gorgeous or even

[1] *Life*, II, 476–7. Cf. G. G. Pace, 'Pusey and Leeds', *Architectural Review*, 98 (1945), 178–80.
[2] *Life*, IV, 210. The mention of the 'North end of the altar' refers to the rubric preceding the Communion service in the 1662 Prayer Book which orders: 'And the Priest standing at the north side of the Table shall say the Lord's Prayer. . . .' This was usually interpreted as meaning the 'North end of the altar'.

in any degree handsome dresses in a day of reproach and rebuke and blasphemy: these are not holyday times.[1]

When the ritualistic practices of the younger men involved them in riots and serious troubles with their bishops, Pusey reminded them that other things were more important: 'To begin with outward things seems like gathering flowers, and putting them in the earth to grow. If we win their hearts [of the congregations], all the rest would follow.'[2] Only later in life did Pusey overcome his fears about Ritualism. In 1866 he said: 'There is no danger of superficialness now. Thirty years of suffering, thirty years of contempt, thirty years of trial, would prevent anything from being superficial.'[3]

Ritualism, then, had little appeal to the first generation of Tractarians. Nor did they appear to be much interested in medievalism. Certainly they did little to promote it within the Church. A clue to their interests may be found in their two large publishing ventures. The *Library of the Fathers* was a forty-eight volume work of extracts from the period of the early Church. This was followed by the *Library of Anglo-Catholic Theology* which is entirely post-reformation, concentrating on the Caroline Divines. According to Storr:

It was the Anglican Church of the seventeenth century and the Church of the patristic age to which the original appeal was made. The Tractarians wished to show that the Anglican Church of the nineteenth century was identical with that of the seventeenth, and was continuous in spirit and doctrine with the still earlier and undivided Church of the Fathers. They appealed to the past, but to a past different from that of Romanticism; and they appealed in a different spirit and with a different intention.[4]

Newman's choice of gothic for Littlemore Chapel appears to have been almost accidental, and in his Roman Catholic days, he showed a definite preference for Italian Renaissance architecture, much to Pugin's dismay. In a novel, *Loss and Gain*, one

[1] *Life*, ii, 142.
[2] *Life*, iii, 369.
[3] 'Address to the English Church Union, 14 June 1866', *Life*, iv, 213.
[4] Storr, i, 255-6.

of Newman's characters says: 'The basilica is beautiful in its place. There are two things which Gothic cannot show—the line or forest of round polished columns, and the graceful dome, circling above one's head like the blue heaven itself.'[1] According to Mozley, 'Newman never went into architecture. . . . Froude was most deeply interested in architecture, but it is plain that he was more penetrated and inspired by St Peter's than ever by Cologne Cathedral. . . . Keble was a latitudinarian if not a utilitarian, in architecture.'[2]

Oxford did have its own architectural society, instituted 12 March 1839 as the Oxford Society for Promoting the Study of Gothic Architecture. Among the members of the Committee were J. R. Bloxam, F. A. Faber, J. B. Mozley, and I. Williams. J. H. Newman, J. Ruskin, and W. Palmer were ordinary members. Newman was not a member long though, and Pusey did not join till May 1842, being made a vice-president the following year.[3] Unlike its Cambridge counterpart, the Oxford Society was mostly academic in its activities and did not promote gothic with the same fervour as the Cambridge Camden Society. An article in the *Eclectic Review* for January 1849 attacks the Cambridge Camden Society, but exonerates the Oxford group: 'Its sister, the Oxford Architectural, has confined itself very much to . . . the extension of our miscellaneous knowledge.'[4] Evidently gothic was an antiquarian pastime for Oxonians rather than the religious crusade which it became in Cambridge.

---

[1] *Loss and Gain, The Story of a Convert* (London, 1900), p. 306. Later in life, Newman referred to gothic as being 'endowed with a profound and commanding beauty such as no other style possesses with which we are acquainted,' but found it necessary to warn that 'as the *renaissance* three centuries ago carried away its own day, in spite of the Church, into excesses in literature and art, so that revival of an almost forgotten architecture, which is at present taking place in our own countries . . . may in some way or other run away with us into this or that error, unless we keep a watch over its course' (*The Idea of a University Defined and Illustrated*, London, 1898, p. 82).

[2] *Reminiscences*, I, 217.

[3] *Rules and Proceedings of the Oxford Society for Promoting the Study of Gothic Architecture* (Oxford, 1839 et seq.).

[4] 'The Literature of Gothic Architecture', *Eclectic Review*, xxv (1849), 33.

CHAPTER II

THE ORIGINS OF THE CAMBRIDGE CAMDEN SOCIETY

I

Oxford and Cambridge in the 1830's still remained the preserve of the Church of England. A large number of the members of the architectural societies in both Universities became clergymen upon taking their degrees. Many of these future members of the Cambridge Camden Society matriculated in the years 1833 to 1841. These were exciting years, for the *Tracts for the Times* were appearing currently and producing a tremendous excitement in the Church. Edward J. Boyce, who came up to Cambridge in 1836, recollected:

> The times when we were together at college were very stirring ones, and full of excitement caused by the most varied and opposite circumstances. It may cause a smile when I illustrate this by saying that the Oxford Tracts on the one hand, and Pickwick on the other, produced a ferment which few can understand, except those who had to mix with the religious controversies of the hour.[1]

Young men at Cambridge in the late 1830's were exposed to two intellectual currents which were to figure prominently in the activities of the Cambridge Camden Society. The first and more recent of these was the Oxford Movement. The second was the much more diffuse element of Romanticism. In some respects, the two were quite similar; yet Hoxie Neale Fairchild insists that the Oxford Movement was not a part of Romanticism which he regards as being essentially opposed to Christianity.[2] Though both Romantics and Tractarians expressed a feeling for the past, Storr asserts:

---

[1] Letter by Boyce in *Letters of John Mason Neale*, p. 13.

[2] *Religious Trends in English Poetry*, vol. IV, *1830–1880, Christianity and Romanticism in the Victorian Era* (New York, 1957), pp. 10–14. Fairchild considers Romanticism anthropocentric, though he admits that sometimes Romanticism and the Oxford Movement did overlap.

Yet between the Romantic spirit and the essential spirit of Tractarianism there is a real opposition. The Oxford Movement stood for the principle of authority. It advocated the claims of ecclesiastical system, Church order, and authoritative dogmatic pronouncement. But the essence of literary Romanticism was freedom and the assertion of the principle of individuality. . . . The Romantics felt indeed the authority of the past, its charm and glamour, and to revivify the past was one of their main objects; but each left himself at liberty to revive it in his own way.[1]

The Romantics, likewise, were primarily interested in the Middle Ages, a period which, as we have seen, the Tractarians neglected. Thus, between the two movements there were many similarities and many tensions. Throughout its career the Cambridge Camden Society was to be torn between these two forces: between ecclesiology and antiquarianism, between rigid rules of architectural correctness and the expression of artistic originality.

The Evangelical party in the Church was well represented at Cambridge, especially by the aged Charles Simeon. Some of the younger members of the Society had been influenced by adherents of the Evangelicals (as had Newman as a young man). Most of the older members of the Society showed their Evangelical colours when controversies arose. The High Church tradition had been preserved also at Cambridge, particularly by Hugh James Rose while Archdeacon Thomas Thorp and Dr W. H. Mill gave very important help to the Society.

For the most part, the younger men looked to Oxford for their inspiration, perhaps because Tractarianism appeared considerably more daring and exciting than the ideas of the Cambridge High Churchmen. The Society's first Chairman of Committees, John Mason Neale, enthusiastically subscribed to the doctrines of the *Tracts*. In 1839 he wrote Boyce: 'Confine yourself to the O. T. [Oxford *Tracts*] and—so far as I have read them, and that is very nearly all—heart and soul, entirely and completely, do I join with them; but for every loose expression of their partisans, it is too hard to be made to bear the blame.'[2]

---

[1] *The Development of English Theology in the Nineteenth Century*, I, 255.
[2] *Letters*, p. 20.

Neale could not subscribe to the violent remarks of Froude's *Remains*.[1] Neither could he agree with Newman's famous nine-tieth tract, the *Remarks on Certain Passages in the Thirty-Nine Articles*, which to Neale was an 'obnoxious book' and a 'tragedy'.[2] However, he was quite willing to identify himself with the Tractarians. In a rather humorous letter, Neale described himself as 'a great upholder and setterforth of Puseyism'.[3] During his entire life, Neale fought on the side of the Tractarians in battle after battle. Benjamin Webb, Honorary Secretary of the Society for the years 1839–68, kept up an enthusiastic hero-worship for Keble.[4] The sentiments of another stalwart of the Society, A. J. B. Hope, were similar. Years later, Hope wrote of 'my undergraduate Newman and Faber hero-worship'.[5]

Unlike the Oxford men, few Cambridge Camden Society members joined the Roman Catholic Church. The final issue of the *Ecclesiologist*, published in 1868, boasted: 'In our very early days—twenty-three years ago—two, and two only [F. A. Paley and S. N. Stokes], of those who were foremost in our cause while it was yet struggling, unfortunately accepted service in another Communion' (xxix, 316). The loyalty of the Cambridge men to the Church of England is remarkable since many of them were subjected to the same intense persecution which drove Oxford men to Rome. Shortly after Newman's reception into the Church of Rome, Neale wrote Webb: 'I cannot express to you the firmness of my conviction. It seems to grow upon me the more the others waver.'[6] Neale accepted the theory of Hope 'that the first generation of reformers may perhaps be absorbed by Rome: but that the second will remain in our Church and renovate it', and added: 'I am quite sure that if we don't desert ourselves, GOD will not desert us. If you all go, I shall stay.'[7]

Many of the older members did not realize for a long time how thoroughly the younger and more active members of the

[1] *Letters*, p. 19.   [2] *Letters*, p. 24.   [3] *Letters*, p. 60.
[4] Clement C. J. Webb, 'Benjamin Webb', *Church Quarterly Review*, LXXV (1913), 337.
[5] Irene and Henry William Law, *The Book of the Beresford Hopes* (London, 1925), p. 133.
[6] *Letters*, p. 88.   [7] *Letters*, p. 89.

Society had imbibed Tractarian doctrines. Evidently, a large number of people, especially those occupying positions of authority in the University and the Church, had joined thinking they were merely encouraging an antiquarian and artistic society with a commendable practical interest in building churches. The younger men profited greatly from the presence of many an unsuspecting bishop and University dignitary among their patrons. It was not without considerable consternation that many of these gentlemen eventually became aware that they had been sponsoring much more than a practical church-building society.

Romanticism was a much more ambiguous subject than Tractarianism, representing as it did a *Zeitgeist*. Storr analyses it in this fashion:

> In its origin it was a reaction against the over-dominance of classical standards in literature and art, and a protest against the intellectualism and rationalism of the eighteenth century. It was a plea for life, for freedom, for the claims of feeling and the spiritual nature. . . . But the movement, in its main advance, came not from religion, but from literature and philosophy. Once started on its career, it progressed with an impetus which nothing could withstand.[1]

The writings of such poets as Wordsworth and Coleridge as well as the novels of Scott and many others popularized Romanticism among the English.[2] This was recognized by Archdeacon Thomas Thorp, the President of the Society, on the occasion of Wordsworth's visit to a meeting on 7 November 1844: 'He (Mr Wordsworth), might be considered one of the founders of the Society. He had sown the seed which was branching out now among them, as in other directions, to the recall of whatever was pure and imaginative, whatever was not merely utilitarian, to the service of both Church and State' (*E.* IV, 26). The 'pure and imaginative' might very well stand for the ideal of Romanticism. Throughout the Romantic Movement there was a constant search for the 'pure' and unsullied,

[1] Storr, I, 127.
[2] Cf. Agnes Addison, *Romanticism and the Gothic Revival* (New York, 1938).

obviously lacking in the present time. Neale, who very much regretted the introduction of railroads, moaned, 'How lamentably unromantic is every thing and every body becoming!'[1] The 'imaginative' could be found by escape to another period, a vanished epoch when the problems of contemporary life were a vexation to no one. It was characteristic of Romanticism to emphasize that the natural, the intuitive, and the unaffected came closer to purity than the rational and sophisticated. A return to the past, an intense nationalism, a stress on the natural and the picturesque, the cult of the supernatural, and an emphasis on the importance of feeling, all these were characteristic features of Romanticism which were frequently evident in the activities of the Cambridge Camden Society.

And thus the Ecclesiologists, too, like so many of their generation, rode off on their own romantic quest. The presidential report in 1842 carried the words—

there may be supposed to be some period in the history of the Church, which it would be difficult and perhaps not profitable to seek very accurately to define, at which the architectural and ritual provision for Christian worship should have reached its point of perfection, to the satisfying of that external reverence man pays to his Maker, and before that reverence had yet degenerated into superstition.[2]

The search for this ideal age soon led to the Middle Ages when it was believed men were 'more spiritually-minded and less worldly-minded' than in the nineteenth century.[3] This was the sublime period whose virtues the Ecclesiologists sought to recover. Study of the period was the first requisite. In an introductory essay to the Society's publication, *Illustrations of Monumental Brasses*, Neale wrote: 'It is no wonder that our realization of the past should be so weak, when our ideas of it are so

[1] *Hierologus: or, the Church Tourists* (London, 1843), p. 90. This book, written at the age of twenty-five, is Neale's most definitely romantic work. *The Unseen World*, published four years later, is likewise very romantic.
[2] *Report of the Cambridge Camden Society for MDCCCXLII* (Cambridge, 1842), p. 16. It is interesting to note how many of the characteristically romantic elements of the Society had been anticipated by Pugin.
[3] *Ibid.*, p. 14.

inaccurate.'[1] Neale recommended the study of brasses since this method provided insight and stimulated the imagination. Elsewhere he rhapsodized about the past:

Oh the good old times of England! Ere, in her evil day,
From their Holy Faith and their ancient rites her people fell away.[2]

His poetry was to improve considerably, but the nostalgia for a golden age remained with him.

This interest in the past was nothing new. Indeed, antiquarianism almost seems a part of the English character. A reviewer in the *Ecclesiologist* wished: 'May it always be the lot of England that her young men should devote themselves to study and to antiquarian research, having special relation to holy things and holy places, rather than to political agitation, and wild seekings for new modes of constructing society' (IX, 27). At Cambridge there had been in existence for some years before the Cambridge Camden Society was founded, an Antiquarian Society, which, Eastlake tells us, was 'only incidentally engaged in those researches which were afterwards called *ecclesiological*'.[3] The earliest name of the Society, Cambridge Camden, was taken from that of the great early antiquarian, William Camden (1551–1623).[4] However, the Ecclesiologists soon came to feel themselves superior to mere antiquarians. The *Ecclesiologist*, recalling the 'antiquaries' of the immediate past, declared in patronizing fashion: 'A most useful and meritorious body of men they were, though of course in many respects behind the requirements which are now necessary to constitute an "Ecclesiologist" or even an "Archaeologist" ' (VI, 231). One reason for this superiority, evidently, was that ecclesiology had more obvious practical applications in church-building and in spreading 'Church principles'. In 1845 Ecclesiologists could boast: 'By cherishing

[1] *Illustrations of Monumental Brasses* (Cambridge, 1846), p. 2.
[2] *Hierologus*, p. 101.
[3] Charles L. Eastlake, *A History of the Gothic Revival, an Attempt to Show How the Taste for Mediæval Architecture Which Lingered in England during the Last Two Centuries Has Since Been Encouraged and Developed* (London, 1872), p. 195.
[4] Author of *Britannia* (1586), one of the earliest major works of antiquarian nature written in England.

a *Church*, not merely an *antiquarian*, spirit, the Society has helped people to *know and love the Church*' (*E.* iv, 86).

The interest in the past which was such a prominent part of Romanticism almost invariably involved a strong element of nationalism. Germans developed an interest in Teutonic legends; the British were excited by Percy's *Reliques of Ancient English Poetry* and Scott's historical novels. The Society was in the forefront of the fervid nationalism. Neale especially was adamant in his nationalism:

Do not think that for one moment I give the preference to foreign buildings over English: if in any case our own cities fall short of those in more Catholick lands, it was not so once; our ancestors' hands and hearts were not in fault—the wickedness and apathy of their descendants were the cause. Undervalue our English buildings! Oh no![1]

Indeed, Neale's persistent nationalism almost provoked a major break among the leaders of the Society. His associate, A. J. B. Hope, became in the course of time a thorough-going eclectic.[2] By 1846 the practice of including articles on foreign art in the *Ecclesiologist* had become frequent, much to Neale's dismay. Neale felt that the strength of the magazine lay in offering examples of English architecture which could safely be imitated rather than foreign examples which were taboo.

In the early years, evidently, the entire group was fiercely national in its architectural views. An important review of Petit's *Remarks on Church Architecture* condemned 'the neglect of the many beauties and peculiarities observable in the parish churches of our own country, which remain to this day but partially explored, although they contain much that is decidedly superior to the most approved German or Italian edifices'.[3] Eclecticism was explicit condemned, 'calculated as it is to ob-

---

[1] *Hierologus*, p. 97.
[2] A note in the *Ecclesiologist* characterizes an address by Hope as 'a bold vindication of the right of the architecture of the future to borrow eclectically the merits of every form of the building-art' (xx, 79).
[3] *E.* i, 92. Petit had boldly suggested ' "we are at full liberty to appropriate, by such alteration as may be necessary, any feature that pleases us" '. The reviewer reacted! 'Only conceive such a suggestion being generally acted upon!' (p. 97).

struct the progress of that improvement in our national religious architecture, which is beginning to flow from a more careful observation of the multitude of examples we happily possess in a style truly religious and truly national' (*E.* I, 132). Indeed, national style had almost a religious sanction. In condemning a new church of a foreign style, the *Ecclesiologist* complained—

that a foreign (we had almost said an unChristian) style should have been selected in preference to one which, as being the direct offspring of the Christian religion, would have been more suitable, and as connecting us in a manner with the 'holy men of old' of our own branch of the Catholick Church, has assuredly a greater claim to our regard.[1]

Nevertheless, the foreign styles were there to stay. In one of its few instances of surrender, the Society gave way and joined in eclecticism.

A love of the beauties of nature was a dominant theme in the poetry of Wordsworth and the other great Romantics. The Society likewise appropriated this feature of Romanticism, giving it an almost religious sanction:

A taste for the natural beauties of scenery and landscape is one of the many aesthetical consequences of the teachings of the Church. . . . In the Middle ages, therefore, we might naturally expect to find a love for the beauties of nature very strong; that it was so, this paper will attempt to prove. In those truly dark centuries, the latter part of the seventeenth and the whole of the eighteenth, this love was all but extinct (*E.* IV, 263).

The proof of this decadence, strangely enough, was the popularity of classical gardens in the eighteenth century. But a change was occurring. The *Ecclesiologist* noted a feeling 'in its present intensity a peculiar feature of modern times, the appreciation of what is called *romantic* scenery'. This change seemed a gift 'specially vouchsafed to the Church of our days, . . . suited to remedy the diseases of the present Church, and therefore to

---

[1] *E.* II, 21. The *Ecclesiologist* pledged itself to 'protesting against the introduction of a foreign style in church architecture, and in doing what we can to stop the evil before it extends further' (II, 20).

be thankfully received and jealously guarded' (VII, 164). Similar to the love of the natural is the love of the picturesque. Although picturesqueness alone was not enough to commend a building, it was very desirable when everything else was correct. Wooden porches were commended 'from their elegant and picturesque effect'.[1]

Few other writers in the nineteenth century used the supernatural to create emotional effects so successfully as Coleridge. This fascination attracted Neale likewise. *Hierologus* contains the statement: 'If any principle seems deeply rooted in our nature, if anything has received the confirmation of universal assent, it is that spirits do appear after death.'[2] In 1847 Neale published anonymously a volume entitled *The Unseen World: Communication with It Real or Imaginary, Including Apparitions, Warnings, Haunted Places, Prophecies, Aerial Visions, Astrology, etc.* In it he included a vast number of accounts of supernatural occurrences, prefacing it with the remark: 'With respect to stories hitherto unpublished, the writer has related none which he has not good grounds for believing; and he has endeavoured to state in each particular account, the degree of evidence by which it is supported.'[3] Neale's sincere Christian convictions on the subject are apparent in the second edition of the book which contains most of the same stories. He calls the 'intercommunion of the world of spirits with our own . . . a most consoling, belief', which 'ought to fill our hearts with gratitude, when we express our belief in the Communion of Saints'.[4] Not all members of the Society followed Neale in these interests, however. Hope, who had no great love for Neale, wrote in 1862: 'Intellectually his faith leads him greedily to swallow all modern forms of credulity, rapping, spiritualism, etc.'[5]

---

[1] Ecclesiological late Cambridge Camden Society, *Instrumenta Ecclesiastica*, First Series (London, 1847), plate XLIX.

[2] *Hierologus*, p. 137.

[3] (London, 1847), p. v.

[4] Second Edition (London, 1853), p. 201. The presence among us of departed spirits is here considered as an illustration of 'a most minutely superintending Providence'.

[5] *The Book of the Beresford Hopes*, p. 146.

A significant characteristic of Romanticism was the great stress which it placed on the importance of feeling. The Ecclesiologists had an almost naïve faith in the power of feeling: 'Ours is but an acquired, that of the ancient architects must have been an intuitive, perception of beauty. The latter is ever essentially correct; whatever be the varieties of style, situation, or proportion, it comprehends and adapts itself to all: the former generally fails in some one of these points, and therefore produces a bàd effect' (*E.* 1, 95). True feeling was much more important than knowledge, for 'we have remarkable proofs that feeling without knowledge will do more than knowledge without feeling'.[1]

True feeling for the Ecclesiologists was invariably 'Catholic feeling', a term susceptible to many puzzling uses. Of a picturesque village, Neale could say: 'It is generally the case, that with this poetry of feeling, Catholicity goes hand in hand, and the contrary.'[2] At times, 'Catholic feeling' seemed to mean simply a love of beauty: 'You will always find a love of flowers co-existent with a Catholick state of feeling in a nation.'[3] The 'delight of the bearers in the scenery', was proof that Madeira, 'with all its many faults, is still truly Catholick'.[4] The most extraordinary use of the term 'Catholick' was Neale's description of a forest as a 'grand Catholic oakwood'.[5] A 'Camdenian field-day', Trinity College Chapel, and a church monument with 'all the sweetness and composure distinctive of Catholick times' were all described in various issues of the *Ecclesiologist* as having 'Catholick feeling'.

The importance of feeling, acknowledged so frequently by both Pugin and the Ecclesiologists, went hand in hand for them

---

[1] Preface to Neale and Webb's, *The Symbolism of Churches and Church Ornaments: A Translation of the First Book of the Rationale Divinorum Officiorum, Written by William Durandus, Sometime Bishop of Mende* (Leeds, 1843), p. xxi. (Cited hereafter as *Durandus.*)

[2] *Hierologus*, p. 44.

[3] *Ibid.*, p. 174.

[4] *Letters*, p. 67. 'Protestant' was a synonym for ugliness. Neale called the Convent of Santa Clara 'horribly Protestant' and the Christmas services in Santa Luzia were 'Protestant and operatic' (*Letters*, p. 55 and p. 68).

[5] *Letters*, p. 31.

with the acceptance of a definite theological position. For Pugin, of course, this position was represented by the dogmas of the Roman Catholic Church. For the younger Ecclesiologists, it meant the doctrines proclaimed by the Tractarians, especially with regard to the ministry and the sacraments. Naturally, it was far from safe to declare publicly that the Society advocated Tractarian principles. The only theological position which the Society professed, according to its President, was 'the recognition and extension of sound principles of Church-membership'.[1] As long as one did not examine these 'sound principles' too closely this was safe ground. And this, evidently, was what the Society desired since it consistently forbade theological debates. The *Ecclesiologist* commenced its fifth volume with an 'Address' proclaiming: 'We steer clear of any thing that has the remotest appearance of doctrinal controversy' (v, 2). In the same issue appeared an article, probably by Neale, which declared: 'We have always refused to enter into religious controversy. We set out with the principle of believing what the Church believes; and that creed we are not called upon to defend. But its symbolical and material expression is our peculiar province' (v, 3).

This practice of forbidding theological debate was often a most effective smokescreen. At the tumultuous Sixth Anniversary Meeting in 1845, Professor Lee belatedly announced that 'he could not help thinking there was something more than architecture involved in the proceedings and objects of the committee'.[2] But Lee was silenced by the President on the grounds of provoking a 'theological discussion'.[3] Perhaps the most convenient use of this professed avoidance of theological matters was in the reply to Rev. Francis Close's famous sermon, *The Restoration of Churches is the Restoration of Popery*:

Now we respectfully but positively decline to argue any religious

---

[1] Cambridge Camden Society, *Report of the Cambridge Camden Society for MDCCCXL* (Cambridge, 1840), p. 4.

[2] *Account of the Sixth Anniversary Meeting of the Cambridge Camden Society, May 8, 1845* (Cambridge, [1845]), pp. 16–17.

[3] *Ibid.*, p. 17.

questions, and above all these questions with him, until he shall have cleared himself from a report which appeared in the public journals during the summer of 1844, and remains, so far as we can learn, uncontradicted: namely, that he did at a public meeting speak in laudatory terms of certain avowed Nestorian heretics. If the report be correct, we cannot but decline all religious controversy (*E.* IV, 111).

Of course, as their enemies well realized, a very important theological position was implicit in almost everything which the Society did. But in affecting not to be concerned about theology, the Ecclesiologists could inaugurate Catholic practices without too many people realizing that the Society was not interested simply in reviving quaint medieval curiosities. Even some members did not realize that their organization was in actuality a very effective machine for theological propaganda.

II

The Cambridge Camden Society began in a very informal fashion. John Mason Neale and Edward Jacob Boyce came up to Cambridge in 1836 and entered Trinity College. They spent a part of the long vacation in 1837 together visiting churches. That autumn Harvey Goodwin and several others joined them in this pursuit, and eventually about a dozen adherents justified the formation of a small group which initially took the name Ecclesiological Society.[1] Another Trinity man, Benjamin Webb, joined Neale and Boyce as leaders of the group. Boyce notes that in the group first formed for studying church architecture: 'Neale, Webb, Goodwin, Poyner, Hough, Colson, Lewthwaite, Thomas, Venables, Lingham, Young, and Boyce were its first members; and while the first members were almost all Undergraduates, such Graduates as Griffin, Paley, Codd, Eddis, Stooks, and others quickly joined it.'[2] Alexander James Beres-

[1] Edward Jacob Boyce, *A Memorial of the Cambridge Camden Society, Instituted May, 1839, and the Ecclesiological (late Cambridge Camden) Society, May, 1846* (London, 1888), p. 8. (Cited hereafter as *Memorial*.)
[2] *Ibid.,* p. 8.

ford Hope soon joined the group and in time became its most active lay member.

This small group at Cambridge eventually agreed upon a set of rules, 'framed for a small association of mutual friends resident in the University', since 'the originators never dreamt of anything beyond that'.[1] The name was soon changed to Camden Society and eventually the word Cambridge was added to distinguish it from the Camden Society in London, a literary and historical society. That it was meant to be but a small local society is indicated by the fact that one of the rules of the group levied ' "a fine on all members who did not visit some specified Church within four miles of S. Mary's Church *weekly*" '.[2]

However, the Society continued to grow, and growth brought some real problems. A blackballing incident caused much hard feeling. It was obvious 'there was a storm brewing, and the threat to start a counter Society was circulated'.[3] Never people to avoid a challenge, Neale, Webb, and Boyce decided on a thorough reorganization. The consequence was, in Boyce's words—

after ten o'clock at night, we three waited on our tutor, Archdeacon Thorp, and laid the state of the case before him. We entreated him to come to the rescue, and did not leave him until he promised to call forthwith a Public Meeting to be held in one of the Lecture Rooms of Trinity College. *At this Meeting in May 1839 the Cambridge Camden Society was instituted*, and the Ven. Thomas Thorp, M.A., Fellow and Tutor of Trinity College, Archdeacon and Chancellor of Bristol, became the President of the Society.[4]

The choice of Thorp was a wise one indeed for he was obviously in sympathy with the aims of the younger men. One of the dissidents in the Society charged that the Sixth Anniversary Meeting in 1845 'opened our eyes to the full length which the Committee were prepared to go, and to which their President

[1] *Ibid.*, p. 8.
[2] Letter by Boyce in *Letters of John Mason Neale*, p. 14.
[3] Boyce, *Memorial*, p. 9.
[4] Letter by Boyce in *Letters of John Mason Neale*, p. 15.

was willing to follow them'.[1] Another critic regretted that Thorp 'should make himself responsible for proceedings which, from the multiplicity of his avocations, he has not leisure to overlook, and thus place himself in the hands of young men, of great zeal for their own individual views, and with little consideration for *his* position and character'.[2] Thorp did intervene on occasion, but his annual presidential addresses and his yearly charges to the clergy of his archdeaconry show his essential agreement with the ideas of the younger men. In one of his presidential addresses, Thorp recalled 'having stipulated, on first accepting the office I hold among you, that I should not be expected to give any thing to it but my name'.[3] Nevertheless, he continued as a very active president for twenty years, resigning in June 1859.

This formal organization of the Society in May 1839 coincided with the formation of the Oxford Society for Promoting the Study of Gothic Architecture. In 1846 Neale looked back on the—'almost simultaneous formation of the Architectural Societies in the two Universities. Partial efforts might have been made here and there, both in one and the other Communion, but they were evidently premature. They had no connexion with each other, nor with anything else. They were the isolated efforts of minds in advance of their age' (*E.* v, 3). An Oxford University Genealogical and Heraldic Society had existed for several years prior to 1839, devoting its attention largely to the funeral inscriptions in churches. It was eventually merged with the Oxford Society for Promoting the Study of Gothic Architecture, the latter having been instituted on 12 March 1839.

Following the first meeting of the Cambridge Camden Society, a series of laws was drawn up. One declared: 'The object of the Society shall be the study of Gothic Architecture, and of

---

[1] C. A. S[wainson], *A Letter to a Non-Resident Member of the Cambridge Camden Society, on the Present Position of That Body* (Cambridge, 1845), p. 12.

[2] Letter by 'Academicus', *Cambridge Chronicle*, 31 May 1845.

[3] *Report of the Cambridge Camden Society of MDCCCXLI* (Cambridge, 1841), p. 7. Thorp's *A Charge Delivered at the Visitation of the Archdeaconry of Bristol in July, 1843* (Bristol, 1843) praises the accomplishments of the Society very highly.

Ecclesiastical Antiquities.'[1] The word 'Gothic' was eventually omitted. Another law gave the Committee of the Society the power of appointing churches for all to visit between meetings, subject to a penalty for failure. This law was soon repealed, but every effort was made to make the members study and report on old churches. (For the Laws of the Society subsequently adopted see Appendix A.) At first meetings were held fortnightly on Saturday afternoons in term, but after the first year, they were changed to evening meetings, twice a term. There were also occasional field days, i.e., excursions to visit neighbouring churches.[2]

From the first it became obvious that the Committee controlled the Society. Perhaps this was the result of experience gained in the power struggles before the May 1839 organization. The president, vice-presidents, and six ordinary members comprised the Committee (cf. Law VIII, Appendix A), and provision was made that half of the ordinary members must be from the previous year. They could also choose additional members. Thus one group was assured continuous control. Furthermore, Law XVI provided that 'No motion or communication shall be laid before the Society until it has been approved by the Committee'. Quite obviously, the Committee had complete control over the Society, a fact which they freely admitted: 'The Committee alone is responsible for the acts and publications of the Society.'[3]

The original vice-presidents were all clergymen and fellows of Cambridge colleges. They do not appear to have been particularly active in the affairs of the Society with the exception of Dr William Hodge Mill. Dr Mill, who became Regius Professor of Hebrew in 1848, had been a High Churchman long before the Oxford Movement, and provided valuable support

---

[1] Boyce, *Memorial*, p. 35.

[2] A very attractive account of 'A Camdenian Field-Day' appears in the *Ecclesiologist*, the participants rejoicing in 'so much of kindness and friendship and unanimity and catholick feeling' (I, 62).

[3] *Report of the Cambridge Camden Society, MDCCCXLIV* (Cambridge, 1844), p. 4. (Cited hereafter as *Report* according to year.)

for the organization. One Vice-President, John J. Smith, eventually became so annoyed with the Society for publishing *Church Enlargement and Church Arrangement* that he wrote a tract condemning it. Smith called upon the members of the Society to consider 'how far they are prepared to approve and support the Society's Committee in the course in which that Committee is now leading it'.[1] He went on to point out the 'extreme helplessness of the condition in which the Society, apart from the Committee, is placed by its constitution'.[2] Committee members were accused of trying 'to prove that the Committee of the Cambridge Camden Society is the Society itself; and the Society nothing but the Committee'.[3]

Without any doubt, the younger members of the Committee determined the character of the Society. Neale was chairman of committees for the first four years, a post subsequently occupied many years by Hope. Webb was constantly re-elected honorary secretary, and the turnover among the other officers was slight. The Committee also formed the editorial board of the *Ecclesiologist*. So actually, even when the membership was numbered in the hundreds, a small nucleus of officers was the real governing body. In almost every instance, they were men faithful to Tractarian ideas, men of quite 'advanced' views on theological and ritualistic matters. Even President Thorp said he occasionally found it necessary 'to moderate . . . between the forward zeal of the Society's executive, and the fears, suspicions —I will not say the antipathies—of those who may have wanted sympathy with its views, or have been startled by its progress'.[4]

The declared purposes of the Society hardly seemed controversial. The first law simply stated: 'The object of the Society shall be, to promote the study of Ecclesiastical Architecture and Antiquities, and the restoration of mutilated Architectural remains.' The *Ecclesiologist*'s first issue contained the smooth

---

[1] *A Few Words on the Last Publication of the Cambridge Camden Society* (Cambridge, 1843), p. 16. Smith took this occasion to resign as vice-president.
[2] *Ibid.*, p. 17.
[3] Letter by 'A Camdenist', *Cambridge Chronicle*, 3 May 1845.
[4] *Report* (1844), p. 9.

words: 'This we must look to as a main instrument of our usefulness—the spirit of love and admiration for our venerable
churches, founded on a careful study and just appreciation of
their excellencies, full as every part of them is both of meaning
and beauty' (i, 18).

Such seemingly innocuous purposes attracted many. Neale
wrote in the *Ecclesiologist*:

Those who were engaged in the work can never forget their astonishment at the spread of their principles:—how, for example, at Cambridge, before the law of the Camden Society was abrogated, which
imposed a fine on all members who did not visit some specified
church within four miles of S. Mary's weekly, it already numbered
associates in every county of the kingdom. A new science was springing up; and a new science demanded a new name; that name,
Ecclesiology, was first heard in the English church (v, 4).

The first members of the Society, those joining at the institution
of the Society in 1839, numbered a mere thirty-eight. But these
members were vigorous recruiters wherever they went. After
speaking to the churchwardens in Milverton, Somerset, Neale
noted that he 'also got three members for the C.C.S'.[1] Such
work was very successful. In a *Report* of the Society, we read:
'The year is not completed since it came into being: but in that
period it has enrolled above one hundred members,' to which
a footnote adds: 'Its number now (May 1841) amounts to about
three hundred.'[2] The third annual *Report* (1842) claimed that
250 members had been admitted since the last meeting.[3] By
1843, Boyce tells us, the membership included: '2 Archbishops,
16 Bishops, 31 Peers and M.P.s, 7 Deans and Chancellors of
Dioceses, 21 Archdeacons and Rural Deans, 16 Architects, and
over 700 ordinary members.'[4] In May 1844 the Society could
claim the addition of 148 new members since the previous anniversary meeting.[5] It is doubtful whether the membership ever

[1] *Letters*, p. 34.
[2] 'Address Delivered at the First Evening Meeting of the Cambridge Camden
Society, March 28, 1840 by the President,' *Report* (1841), p. 7.
[3] *Report* (1842), p. 19.
[4] *Memorial*, p. 10.
[5] *Report* (1844), p. 25.

reached the one thousand mark owing to the major upheaval in the Society in 1845.

There were several types of membership included within the group. Ordinary members were 'Members of the University of Cambridge; who are proposed by any Member of the Society in a fixed form, and who, after the suspension of their names for at least a week in the Society's rooms, are balloted for at an ordinary Meeting' (*E.* I, 15). Nominations for membership could be rejected by twenty per cent of those voting. People who were not university men, as well as honorary members, were admitted in the same fashion, provided their names were approved of by the Committee. Law V provided that: 'The Chancellor of the University, the High Steward, and such of their Lordships the Bishops, and of the Heads of Houses, as shall signify their pleasure to become Members of the Society, shall be admitted as Patrons without ballot.' Through this provision, the Society could boast by its second anniversary of such patrons as the Archbishops of Canterbury and Armagh, the Bishops of London, Winchester, Bath and Wells, Lincoln, Chester, Gloucester and Bristol, Ely, Hereford, Worcester, Nova Scotia, and Edinburgh, as well as a number of high University officials.[1] Before the third year was ended, however, the Bishop of London asked that his name be withdrawn, and other patrons who initially had no idea of the real spirit of the Society were soon to make similar requests. Their prestige undoubtedly had been a big asset to the Society in its early years.

Other architectural societies were springing up, though none maintained so successfully the 'dogmatic spirit' which Neale considered 'to be the life and soul of the *Ecclesiologist* and of the C.C.S'.[2] The group in Oxford, subsequently renamed the Oxford Architectural Society, was perhaps the best known of these other groups. Its *Rules* declared 'the objects of this Society be to collect Books, Prints, and Drawings; Models of the Forms of Arches, Vaults, &c.; Casts of Mouldings, and Details; and such other Architectural Specimens as the Funds of the Society will

---

[1] *Report* (1841), p. 43.   [2] *Letters*, p. 93.

The Origins of the Cambridge Camden Society

admit'.[1] In 1840 the establishment of a friendly relationship between the Oxford and Cambridge societies (for mutual attendance at meetings and purchase of publications) was heralded by the Cambridge Camden Society:

Our junction with the Oxford Architectural Society is a matter of congratulation. Engaged in the same objects, actuated by the same motives, and using in a great measure the same means, it had long been a wish on our part that pledges of good will should be interchanged between us. Yet it became us to remember, that if the more numerous, we were also the younger Society, and to wait for the first formal overtures from the sister University. The union is now accomplished; and it is pleasing to know that there is thus a bond of fellowship established between five hundred labourers in the same cause.[2]

There were, as it developed, some major differences. For one thing, the *Ecclesiologist* noted that the Oxford group refused to call Gothic 'the one Christian style, to the exclusion of all others' (I, 111), and that 'they have never yet committed themselves, as we have done, to any decided principles of church-building or restoration. . . . We are by no means prepared to assert that our sister Society holds in every thing the same views as ourselves' (II, 154). The Oxford Architectural Society did not confine itself to churches, but interested itself in old bridges, manor houses, and such secular buildings. Eastlake noted that the Oxonians were less ardent in reviving gothic and more temperate in restoring buildings.[3] Certainly they were more innocuous in the public eye. The old antagonist of the Cambridge Camden Society, Weale's *Quarterly Papers on Architecture*, praised the Oxford Society: 'We are half disarmed, and half defrauded of our quarry, first, by the modest tone which pervades their work, and secondly by the well-intentioned direction they have followed.'[4]

---

[1] *Rules and Proceedings of the Oxford Society for Promoting the Study of Gothic Architecture* (Oxford, 1840), p. 4.
[2] *Report* (1841), p. 35.
[3] *Gothic Revival*, p. 203.
[4] *Quarterly Papers on Architecture*, IV (1845), 2.

Relations between the two societies, despite the Oxonians' lack of 'dogmatic spirit' were friendly, although the Oxford Society published a report about the time of the Cantabrigians' crisis in 1845, blaming them of a lack of discretion. To this the *Ecclesiologist* tartly replied: 'We more than doubt the good taste of such references to the late secession from the Cambridge Camden Society.' It then proceeded to rap the Oxford group for its delay in effecting 'an actual restoration. . . . we want something practical,—something really effected,—something that may give ocular proof of the knowledge which the Society undoubtedly possesses' (IV, 219).

The *Ecclesiologist* carried frequent reports of the activities and meetings of the Oxford Architectural Society and many other similar groups. Most of these thrived, though on a much smaller scale than the Cambridge Camden Society, which often was their model. Many were organized on diocesan or county lines, and frequently were more antiquarian than ecclesiological. A branch of the Society was formed in the Diocese of Down, Connor, and Dromore in Ireland but was an early casualty due to the demands of various members that all connexions with Cambridge be dropped or they would withdraw from other charitable organizations of the Diocese.[1]

The Cambridge Camden Society provided a useful service in unifying all these efforts through its journal, the *Ecclesiologist*. The immediate reason for establishing the magazine, however, was the dispersion of the members after leaving the University, many of them receiving livings in the southern counties, Lon-

---

[1] A clergyman writing under the pseudonym of Clericus Connorensis, produced a tract entitled *Ecclesiologism Exposed: Being the Letters of 'Clericus Connorensis' as Originally Published in the Belfast Commercial Chronicle* (Belfast, 1843). More successful societies included: Exeter Diocesan Society, Lichfield Society for the Encouragement of Ecclesiastical Architecture, Salisbury Diocesan Church Building Association, Bristol Architectural Society, Yorkshire Architectural Society, Lincolnshire Society for the Encouragement of Ecclesiastical Architecture, Wykeham Brotherhood (Roman Catholic), Cambridge Architectural Society, Middlesex Archaeological Society, Architectural and Archaeological Society for the County of Buckingham, Somerset Archaeological and Natural History Society, Irish Ecclesiological Society (Roman Catholic), and Worcester Diocesan Architectural Society.

don, and elsewhere.[1] Neale visited Boyce in October 1841, and Boyce suggested that the Society should have a periodical. Neale, nothing loath, 'wrote off at once to the President and the Secretaries (Webb, Young, and Paley), mentioning the suggestion, giving a sketch of the design for a monthly publication and proposing that the name should be The Ecclesiologist'.[2] The first issue, appearing in November 1841, contained the following 'Address':

The principal design of the present periodical, is to furnish such members of the Cambridge Camden Society as may reside at a distance from the University, with the information which they have a right to expect, but at present cannot easily obtain, unless at long intervals and from uncertain sources, respecting its proceedings, researches, publications, meetings, grants of money, and election of members. . . . The *Ecclesiologist* is therefore, strictly speaking, a periodical report of the Society, primarily addressed to, and intended for the use of, the members of that body. But it is contemplated at the same time to conduct the publication in such a manner that its pages may convey both interesting and useful information to all connected with or in any way engaged in church-building, or the study of ecclesiastical architecture and antiquities. It is intended to give with each number, among other matters pertaining to Ecclesiology in general, critical notices of churches recently completed, or in the process of building: to give publicity to projects of church-building or church enlargement, . . . to suggest, where it can be done without unwarrantable interference or presumption, alterations or improvements in the arrangements and decorations of new designs: to describe accurately and impartially the restorations of ancient churches: to point out those which, . . . are peculiarly deserving of repair, and to suggest means of effecting it: and to supply notices and reviews of any antiquarian researches, books, or essays, connected with the subject of Ecclesiology (I, 1–2).

These were the main principles on which the *Ecclesiologist* was conducted throughout its twenty-nine volumes, although at

[1] Upon leaving the University, Neale accepted a living at Crawley in Sussex, Boyce became a Curate of Holyrood, Southampton, and Webb went to Godalming, Surrey.
[2] Letter by Boyce in *Letters of John Mason Neale*, p. 16.

times the limits of 'unwarrantable interference or presumption' seemed rather elastic. Many of the articles were merely of anti-quarian interest, but a sufficient number dealt with contem-porary issues so that the editors could boast of 'the proudest distinction of THE ECCLESIOLOGIST—its character, namely as a work strictly *practical*' (IV, 260).

The Committee of the Society retained tight control over the *Ecclesiologist*. Not only did they edit it, but evidently they wrote a large number of the articles. Few of the articles, with the exception of short communications (often signed with a pseudo-nym), bear the name of the author. Boyce states:

If any contributors to the *Ecclesiologist* deserve pre-eminent credit for its success from first to last, few will dispute that John Mason Neale and Benjamin Webb are two of these.

I find from a copy of vol. I, belonging to Neale, which has initials in ink to each article, that out of 158 contributions to that volume Neale made 47, Webb 46, and Paley 36. Under Neale's name in vol. III, I find written, *et quorum pars magna fui*.[1]

The anonymity which the magazine provided permitted much frank speaking. Evidently articles were discussed jointly before publication, for the 'Address' of the second volume de-clares: 'While another journal decides with the consistent in-fallibility of a monarchal editor, we can only pronounce the resultant judgment of the deliberations of a committee' (II, 2). As mentioned above, the Committee consisted of some of the more radical members of the Society. Boyce admitted that:

In connexion with the *Ecclesiologist*, while it was edited by Members of the Committee of the Cambridge Camden Society, it is not too much to say that the oftentimes unguarded severity of some of its criticisms . . . raised from the first month of its publication, and from time to time, a certain amount of prejudice: and even as early as the second month of its issue . . . [it was suspected] of 'a desire to convert the Society into an engine of polemical theology; instead of an instrument for promoting the study and practice of Ecclesiastical Architecture'.[2]

[1] *Memorial*, p. 17.   [2] *Ibid.*, p. 12.

The *Ecclesiologist* was never cautious about new ideas, and it came in for its share of criticism. But it is safe to say that the publication of this periodical determined the character of the Society and was the most useful method for promoting its ideas.

CHAPTER III

DEVELOPING THE SCIENCE OF ECCLESIOLOGY

I

The word 'ecclesiology' not only provided a name for the Cambridge Camden Society's periodical, but also indicated the chief interest of the group. The origin of the term in English is obscure. Eastlake declares: 'It is to be observed that the words "Ecclesiology" and "Ecclesiologist", though now commonly adopted, were originally invented and first used by the Cambridge Camden Society.'[1] The *Ecclesiologist* at one time claimed credit for the invention of the term ecclesiology, 'that peculiar branch of science to which it seems scarcely too much to say, that this very magazine gave first its being and its name' (IV, 2).

Other evidence indicates that the word first appeared in the *British Critic*, a high-church periodical which Newman edited for a short period beginning in 1838. A correspondent, writing under the pseudonym of 'Etymologist', suggested to the *Ecclesiologist* in 1842 that the proper spelling was 'Ecclesialogist', the spelling used in the *British Critic*. He was informed 'that the word *Ecclesiologist* or *Ecclesiology* was not invented, but adopted by us; we believe it was first used by a writer in the *British Critic*, to whom therefore any blame on the grounds of its supposed inaccuracy should attach rather than to ourselves' (I, 78).[2] In this instance, the *Ecclesiologist* correctly traced the origin of the term, though differed in spelling it. The January 1837 issue of the *British Critic* had contained an anonymous article calling for a new science of '*Ecclesialogy*' and claiming the invention of the term. It was explained:

[1] *History of the Gothic Revival*, p. 198.
[2] Boyce shows the same uncertainty about the term. In the *Memorial* he traces it to the *British Critic* (p. 8), but in a letter in *The Letters of John Mason Neale*, he repeats the phrase from the 1845 *Ecclesiologist* that the periodical gave 'first its *being* and its name' to ecclesiology (p. 16).

Developing the Science of Ecclesiology

We mean then by *Ecclesialogy*, a science which may treat of the proper construction and operations of the Church, or Communion, or Society of Christians; and which may regard men as they are members of that Society, whether members of the Christian Church in the widest acceptance of that term, or members of some branch or communion of that Church, located in some separate kingdom and governed according to its internal form of constitution and discipline.[1]

The article is chiefly concerned about the position of the Church of England in regard to the state and the current proposals for reform of the Church by Parliament. Despite the use of the word 'construction', the author was not speaking of church buildings.

The Society gave the term 'Ecclesiology' a quite different meaning from that which the *British Critic* had intended. In the opinion of the Society, ecclesiology was the science of church architecture. The word is still used in this sense in Great Britain. At times ecclesiology was given a wider meaning; once it was defined as 'the science of Christian Aesthetics' (*E.* vii, 2). By 1848 the *Ecclesiologist* could recall its early days when 'we had then to force upon the public the conviction that there is a science of Ecclesiology. This we have long done; and our present task is to develope that science when occasion requires' (viii, 326). The Ecclesiologists were fond of calling their specialty an 'inductive science'. J. S. Howson, a member of the Committee, testified: 'It must be remembered, that Ecclesiology, like Astronomy and Geology, is an Inductive Science. No sound and truthful generalizations can be hoped for without a careful examination of particulars; and for this work our Society is peculiarly adapted' (*E.* i, 60).

A definite methodology applied to ecclesiology when it was treated as an inductive science. In 1846 the *Ecclesiologist* explained its purpose in inaugurating the new feature, 'Ecclesiological Notes':

And it is by treasuring up such facts as these, that we form, and amplify, and check our ecclesiological creed. The same takes place,

---

[1] 'Ecclesialogy', *British Critic*, xxi (1837), 220.

49

of course, in other sciences; but Ecclesiology has so lately come to be treated as a science, that people are apt to forget that it is subject to the like laws with them; and thus forego one great assistance towards the study of it (v, 75).

It was believed that the larger the number of particular examples examined was, the more accurate the knowledge resulting would be. Of course, only buildings in their original unrestored condition could be considered reliable sources: 'It is plain, that the only safe way to arrive at any general principles of Ecclesiology, is to observe and describe the details and arrangements of unmutilated churches, or parts of churches; and from a large collection of such observations, if carefully recorded, much advantage may accrue to the science.'[1]

Although they admitted their own ignorance at many points, the Ecclesiologists had a firm conviction that medieval architecture and its glories were not accidental. Ecclesiological research was always directed to discovering the principles which, it was supposed, guided medieval builders. For some strange reason, trial and error was not considered a method worthy of the gothic architects. And so, tremendous time and energy were devoted to investigating the principles of church-building through the inductive method. A writer in the *Ecclesiologist*, commenting on a paper which Hope had read to the Oxford Architectural Society, asserted: 'Given that there exists a certain general idea of church-building and church-arrangement in which we have a right to share; Ecclesiology is the science of rightly using this privilege, of investigating, expanding, and practically exhibiting this idea' (vii, 88). In addition to this general idea, the Ecclesiologists had faith that every detail of a medieval building had a specific meaning. Little or nothing was attributed to the builder's idiosyncrasies. According to Hope, by careful investigation: ' "Every stone, every window was found to tell its own appropriate tale, to bear its own peculiar meaning" ' (*E.* vii, 88). Some meaning had to be found

---

[1] Cambridge Camden Society, *A Few Hints on the Practical Study of Ecclesiastical Antiquities for the Use of the Cambridge Camden Society*, 3rd ed. (Cambridge, 1842), p. 16. (Cited hereafter as *Few Hints.*)

even for the grotesque carvings which adorn many churches. True Ecclesiologists took their work too seriously to think that the obvious humour did not hide some esoteric meaning. The *Hand-Book of English Ecclesiology* conjectured that 'the grotesque was felt to be, in its due mixture and proportion, an ingredient of the sublime'.[1] It is no wonder that diligent research was necessary to advance the science of ecclesiology. No medieval item was considered too insignificant since it might provide a clue to some forgotten and mysterious principle.

But ecclesiology was something more than a science in the usual sense of the term. Intellectual curiosity was by no means the sole motivation for enthusiastic Ecclesiologists. Neale marvelled that 'when we add the sanctity of feeling that attaches itself to our pursuit, and the practical influence which it possesses on the worship of God in this land, one wonders that any can look on it as uninteresting, or refuse to give up themselves to it with all their ardour'.[2] Nothing offended the Ecclesiologists more than doubt as to their high seriousness. An indignant writer in the *Ecclesiologist* complained:

The whole science of Ecclesiology is by many persons regarded as a hobby. They look on it as a kind of child's play: as only a game for grown up children. That we have principles as real as those of the Church itself which they symbolize, is an idea which is utter scorn to many well meaning people (VI, 176).

Ecclesiology, to its adherents, represented not a mere amateur interest in science, but a significant ally of the Church.

Because of this affiliation with the Church, the Ecclesiologists devoted their energies to a wide sphere of concerns. 'Ecclesiology, however', according to Neale, 'is a different thing from mere Church architecture, as embracing both it and all its collateral branches of information as to Church history and antiquities.'[3] The *Ecclesiologist* affirmed: 'Liturgical science indeed ranks far higher than architectural skill and knowledge as

---

[1] Ecclesiological late Cambridge Camden Society, *A Hand-Book of English Ecclesiology* (London, 1847), p. 68. (Cited hereafter as *Hand-Book*.)

[2] *Hierologus*, p. 4.

[3] *Ibid.*, p. 189.

a qualification of the ecclesiologist' (*E.* vii, 86). Neale found it convenient to distinguish between 'ritual Ecclesiology' and 'aesthetic' ecclesiology.[1] In the Society's latter years, many fields of interest became prominent, though architecture always remained the paramount concern. The hundredth issue of the *Ecclesiologist,* published in 1854, observed: 'Church architecture is no longer tentative. It approaches to something of the completeness of an exact science. It is admitted to be a subject not so much of taste as of facts. It has its rules, principles, laws. . . . Not forgetting that architecture is our first work, we have associated Church Music as a parallel branch of ecclesiology' (xv, 3).

Whether interested in architecture, music, or ritual, the members of the Cambridge Camden Society were not the only medieval enthusiasts of their time. Indeed, in every field the Society was indebted to the researches and publications of others. Mention has already been made of Britton, Rickman, and Pugin. Though they were among the most famous architectural writers of the time, they were by no means the only ones. Writers on architectural subjects abounded, ranging in sophistication from the author of *Aunt Elinor's Lectures on Architecture* to John Henry Parker's volumes on architectural history. Much of the literature was of a high quality, although some writers filled in the gaps of their information with an undue amount of speculation.

A large portion of the credit for the rapid increase in knowledge about gothic architecture belongs to the country parsons who wrote guides to the churches of their vicinity or the local antiquaries who contributed articles to historical magazines. A writer, antagonistic to the Cambridge Camden Society, admitted that the Ecclesiologists had 'actually done something for the increase of our knowledge in this direction', but rapped them soundly for claiming—

to have done much more,—to have been, in fact, originative of that tone of thought and feeling of which it has been only an accidental embodiment. For as we have already estimated, this general trans-

---

[1] *Letters,* p. 312.

ition of taste is altogether a much larger matter; belongs to the spirit of the age, not to that of the Universities, or of the Tractarian portion of the Establishment.[1]

Perhaps the writer was too harsh. Undoubtedly the Cambridge men profited greatly from the researches and work of others. But they themselves made a contribution second to none.

No other group had such resources at its command. At one time the Society's membership was over eight hundred and fifty. Rickman spent much of his lifetime making over two thousand drawings of medieval churches and is reputed to have visited three thousand churches. The Society's members could have equalled this in a short time. In addition, the Ecclesi- ologists had at times considerable funds which could be used for hiring engravers, having measured drawings done, or paying travel expenses to remote areas. The Society had its own library and for many years kept a constantly expanding collection of drawings, casts, and models. It also had the *Ecclesiologist* as an organ for the publication of its researches.

With such resources at its command, it is no wonder that the Society made great advances in developing the science of ecclesiology. There were two methods by which this new science was advanced. One was the actual examination of buildings, ruins, or their furnishings. The other was by research in par- ochial, monastic, diocesan records (especially visitation articles), and many other documentary sources. Both methods of research went on together, but they can best be analysed separately.

II

In the middle decades of the nineteenth century, church architecture was something of a fad for many people. The dilettanti, who in the preceding century would have been en- thusiastic about archaeological discoveries in Greece, now found a pastime closer at hand in which they could actively partici- pate. They were guaranteed a sufficient means for displaying

[1] 'The Literature of Gothic Architecture', *Eclectic Review*, xxv (1849), 37.

both artistic taste and religious piety, indeed a good investment for their time. The translators of Durandus found church architecture a very popular activity: 'The study of Church Architecture has within the last few years become so general, and a love for it so widely diffused, that whereas, in a former generation it was a task to excite either, in the present it is rather an object to direct both.'[1] The Cambridge Camden Society considered itself especially well adapted for this task of direction. The *Ecclesiologist* observed: 'The question is very often asked, . . . I am inclined to take an interest in Ecclesiology, but how am I to attain it as a science?' (I, 87). To such a query, a reply could be made without hesitation. The first step, of course, was to join the Cambridge Camden Society. Then one might acquire a scientific knowledge of ecclesiology by using the various publications of the Society while visiting churches. An impressive array of materials was assembled in order to enable both the fledgling Ecclesiologist and the expert to participate in research.

Probably the most useful and popular of these methods was the Church Scheme, or as it was sometimes called, 'A Blank Form for the Description of a Church'. This very ingenious device was a checklist of the various items and arrangements which might occur in any parish church. It was used in 'taking' a church, as the Ecclesiologists called the process of making a written description of buildings. Successive editions added new items as more features were discovered. According to Boyce, 'the number of particulars mentioned in the first edition as requisite to be noted in a Church, was 58; in the second, 84; in the third, 113; in the fourth, 236; and the seventh edition has 260'.[2] (See Appendix C for a copy of the seventh edition.) Subsequent editions added a few more items, the sixteenth containing about fifteen more than the seventh. Obviously no single church would have all the items specified in the Schemes, but there could be few medieval features not noticed in the late editions. Most of the common seventeenth-century additions,

---

[1] 'Introductory Essay', *Durandus*, p. xviii.

[2] *Memorial*, p. 28. The first edition appeared in May 1839 and three more followed the same year. The seventh edition was published in 1841.

such as the Commandments, reading-pew, and hour-glass stand were also included. The Schemes provide a remarkably thorough guide for exploring gothic buildings, but porticoes and other items appearing only on classical buildings are not mentioned.

A very convenient method of using the Schemes was developed: 'There are two impressions of the Church Schemes; the one on a long strip of folio paper, on which the visitor will take an account with his pencil in the church, . . . the other a quarto sheet, into which the account will afterwards be transcribed before it is presented to the Society.'[1] The *Hand-Book of English Ecclesiology* provided full instructions for those using the Schemes:

The visitor who uses them is supposed to describe the inside of a church first, beginning with the chancel: to enter the windows and piers, as 1, 2, &c., from east to west, or from north to south, as the case may be: in giving an account of a tower, to number its stages from the top:—and is requested, in case (which will in every way be easiest) he uses contractions, to employ those only which we have given in Appendix A, [actually they appear in Appendix B] and have tested by application to many hundreds of churches.[2]

Measurements were likewise considered of great importance, forming the first question on the Scheme after the identification of the building. The *Hand-Book* recommended 'that a plan with measurements should be drawn and sent in together with the Scheme. Where, from want of time, this cannot be done, it will be sufficient to measure the length of chancel and nave; a measurement which should never be omitted.'[3]

The Schemes were an item of great importance to the Society. Not only did they provide hundreds of people with an effective means of learning ecclesiology, but since it was expected that a completed copy of each Church Scheme would be forwarded to the Society in Cambridge, a great amount of data on medieval buildings was assembled. It is no wonder that Boyce said that 'in these Schemes the great and original strength of the C.C.S.

---

[1] *Few Hints*, 3rd ed., p. 16.   [2] *Hand-Book*, p. 2.   [3] *Ibid.*, p. 37.

was considered to lie'.[1] Many amateurs obtained copies of the Schemes, then found it necessary to read *A Few Hints on the Practical Study of Ecclesiastical Antiquities* or the *Hand-Book of English Ecclesiology* in order to understand the terminology. This launched them upon their first tour, and before long the Society had both a new adherent and a source of information.[2] Members in remote parts of the British Isles were valued for their information on seldom-visited churches. The *Few Hints* declared: 'It is the Society's wish to procure a complete and accurate description in detail of as many churches as possible; but especially of such as either, from their antiquity or any other causes, may contain objects peculiarly worthy of record, or, from their remote situation, may have hitherto escaped the researches of Ecclesiologists.'[3] The use of a Scheme was recommended to all those visiting churches, 'because experience has proved it to be the best practical method of ensuring that no essential feature of a church has been overlooked'.[4]

The amount of information secured from the Schemes must have been enormous. With hundreds of Ecclesiologists visiting churches on their travels, the reports accumulated rapidly. The *Report* for 1841 devotes twelve pages in small type to a 'list of Reports of Churches sent in from May 1839 to May 1841', and this was while the Society was in its infancy. Reports came in from every county of England as well as Wales and Scotland. Neale himself frequently mentions walking six or seven miles to 'take' a church not previously visited.[5] It would be impossible to tell whether every medieval church in England was reached

[1] *Memorial*, p. 28.

[2] A fanciful 'Sketch' in the *Ecclesiologist* narrated the experiences of a country parson, Mr Herbert, his wife, and a Miss Newmarsh upon their first adventure with a Scheme. Not only is Miss Newmarsh (who proves to be a valiant antagonist to such a suspicious system) won over, but some painted wood panels are discovered. All ends happily as the Herberts realize the benefits of ecclesiology and the Society receives another completed Scheme for its files (1, 76).

[3] *Few Hints*, 3rd ed., p. 16.

[4] *Hand-Book*, p. 2.

[5] In the Library of the Royal Institute of British Architects there are five volumes of Schemes filled out by Neale, Webb, and a few of their friends. The dates run from May 1839 through 1841 and cover many churches in Sussex, Somerset, Cambridge, Yorkshire, and Wales. A number of sketches are included.

by this method or not. Such wholesale exploration was entirely new and produced a vast amount of information about medieval architecture, a subject which had been, at best, but little understood. The effect locally on the churchwardens (who usually had to be located to find the keys and often stayed to watch the proceedings), on the incumbent, and on the local population must have been great. In the investigations many concealed brasses, painted panels, and bricked-up piscinae were recovered and admired for the first time in centuries. The consequences were far reaching.

The first tract published by the Society, *A Few Hints on the Practical Study of Ecclesiastical Antiquities for the Use of the Cambridge Camden Society*, has already been mentioned.[1] The *Few Hints* is keyed directly to the Schemes and was calculated to promote actual research in the field. The first paragraph indicates:

It is hoped that the following Hints will prove not altogether useless to those, who, having acquired from books some little knowledge of Ecclesiastical Antiquities, are at a loss how to apply that knowledge to the examination and description of real buildings. . . . [this tract will] suffice at least as a directory to the learner, until he shall have made some advancement in the study, and familiarized his eye to those more minute details, which should be seen to be thoroughly understood.[2]

The *Few Hints* begins with a brief history of architectural development from the Anglo-Saxon period to the 'Debased Perpendicular' of the Elizabethan and Jacobean era. A list of books for further reading on architectural history is included. Bloxam, Rickman, Pugin, Britton, Lyson, Weever, Willis, Whewell and Grose were among the favoured authors. 'Remarks on the Church Schemes' follow with an item by item commentary on the Schemes. A Scheme for the Church of Sts Mary and

---

[1] The first edition appeared in 1839. It was rewritten and greatly expanded for the second edition in 1840. Two other editions appeared, the third in 1842 and a fourth in 1843. The revisions, we are told, were made possible through 'much curious and valuable information collected from the Church Schemes and drawings' (*Report*, 1842, p. 20).

[2] *Few Hints*, 3rd ed., p. 3.

Michael, Trumpington, is filled in to illustrate the proper method.

The *Few Hints* was eventually superseded by the much larger volume, *A Hand-Book of English Ecclesiology*.[1] The *Hand-Book* gives a very good indication of the progress of ecclesiological knowledge in the years since the Society's organization. As the Preface claims, it constituted 'the labour of years, on the part of at least fifty, more or less active, fellow-labourers'.[2] Neale, Hope, F. H. Dickinson, and Webb seem to have been the chief editors. The *Hand-Book* was published after the Society's crisis of 1845. Neale wrote Webb concerning it: 'But money in this case is not the great object—reputation is. We must do something to show that we are still working.'[3] The 266 pages of text and 118 pages of Appendixes were doubtlessly sufficient indication of the Society's continued activity.

The book was intended, as the opening pages declare—

to serve as a pocket companion to church visitors, more especially to those who are in the habit of using the Church Schemes published by the ECCLESIOLOGICAL LATE CAMBRIDGE CAMDEN SOCIETY. It is wished to point out what is most worthy of observation, and how to observe it best; to enable the Ecclesiologist, on a tour, and thus precluded from consulting larger works, to decide on the value of a discovery, or the rarity of an arrangement; to lay before him, in a condensed manner, the latest researches that have been made in the science; to assist him in familiarizing his eye with the more important features of churches, and to enable him to 'take' them well and thoroughly, and at the same time expeditiously.[4]

The *Hand-Book* is basically a greatly expanded version of the *Few Hints*, but one can gauge the progress in research since the last edition of the *Few Hints* (1843) by noting the expansions. The *Hand-Book* devotes thirty-six pages to a brief historical sum-

[1] Only one edition (London, 1847) of this book appeared.
[2] *Hand-Book*, p. iv.
[3] *Letters*, p. 97.
[4] *Hand-Book*, pp. 1-2. The Preface indicated: 'It is intended for active and *travelling* Ecclesiologists: it is meant to be the companion of their church tours, along with their portfolios, schemes, lead tape [for determining the profile of moldings], heel-ball [for rubbing brasses], &c' (p. iii).

mary of English architectural history from the Anglo-Saxon period to the seventeenth century. Two hundred and thirty pages are needed to explain and to illustrate the various items of the Church Schemes. The amount of information contained in this outline is remarkable. Perhaps even more extraordinary is Appendix A with its 118 pages of information on the ecclesiology of each county in England. This data, gathered from thousands of Church Schemes, gives the general character of churches in the county, describes the usual building materials, lists prevailing features, and mentions outstanding buildings and ornaments. It is indeed an impressive display of ecclesiological information.

Perhaps the most unusual research problem undertaken by the group was one connected with the orientation of churches. The *Hand-Book* instructs readers:

It is important to notice the deviation of the direction of a church from the True East, because an idea has prevailed, it would seem without any very good reason, that the chancel points to that part of the horizon where the sun rises on the Feast of the Patron Saint. It would be interesting to prove or to disprove this idea. The point requires very careful examination before any decision can be formed.[1]

In order to reach a definite conclusion on this point, a gadget called the 'Orientator' was invented. It consisted of a rectangular card with a disc attached. On the disc was a place for a compass and lines indicating magnetic north and the direction in which the sun was supposed to rise on various saints' days. According to the booklet which accompanied this device, 'the design of this instrument is, in general, to determine the point of the compass to which a church is directed; and more particularly to ascertain whether that point be the sun's place of rising on the festival of the Saint in whose honour the church is dedicated'.[2] The booklet gives instructions on placing the card parallel to the wall of the church, locating north with a compass

[1] *Hand-Book*, pp. 39-40.
[2] *The Orientator, A Simple Contrivance for Ascertaining the Orientation of Churches* (Cambridge, 1844), p. 1.

on it, and then observing the spot where the sun appeared at daybreak. A table of saints' days was provided in order to discover 'whether the supposed rule of Orientation was strictly adhered to'.[1] It is not known how many hardy souls arose at sunrise to check this theory, but the Society seems to have lost interest in it without establishing any conclusive results.

In 1843 Neale published *Hierologus: or, the Church Tourists* with the intention of arousing interest in ecclesiology. According to the review in the *Ecclesiologist*, *Hierologus* 'is written after the agreeable manner of good Walton's Complete Angler; and appears well calculated to stimulate many an errant-knight to essay his first church tour' (III, 52). In *Hierologus* Neale relates his travels in England and Wales, visiting churches and making frequent comments on the joys and principles of ecclesiology.

All these efforts to encourage an interest in ecclesiology soon began to bear fruit in the form of scholarly publications. From its start the *Ecclesiologist* printed many papers which were the result of careful research, in addition to shorter pieces dealing with strictly practical or polemical matters. Learned discussions appeared on such varied subjects as church-yard crosses, poppy-heads, communion plate, and the inscriptions on bells. After the crisis of 1845, the magazine became predominantly a scholarly periodical specializing in studies of medieval architecture, art, and worship. Papers read at meetings of the Society, the Oxford Architectural Society, and a few of the other societies frequently appeared in full or condensed versions in the *Ecclesiologist*. Reviews of all the important books published on ecclesiology and its related fields are a prominent feature in each issue. Although the reviewers were ruthless and dogmatic in their criticisms, the reviews form a valuable catalogue to the literature of the period.[2]

From a scholarly standpoint, one of the most valuable of the Society's publications was the *Transactions of the Cambridge Cam-*

---

[1] *The Orientator*, p. 8.

[2] Not untypical is the treatment received by a book entitled *The Book of Symbols for Church Needlework* by 'T. T.' The review declares: 'We repeat our hope that no one who values our opinion will think of buying this expensive and worthless book' (v, 260).

den Society, published in three parts.[1] They contain a number of the more important papers read at the regular meetings of the Society during the six years of its existence in Cambridge. Twenty-five papers are included altogether, a number being by such stalwarts as Neale, Webb, John S. Howson, and Philip Freeman. Representative papers are: 'On the Crypts of London', 'On the Ecclesiology of Argyllshire', 'On Foliated Wooden Roofs', and 'On the Adaptation of Pointed Architecture to Tropical Climates'.

One of the most profusely illustrated of the Society's publications was a volume entitled *Churches of Cambridgeshire and the Isle of Ely*.[2] Five churches, all within a few miles of Cambridge, are depicted in the excellent lithographs. The letterpress contains a brief history of each parish, including a list of rectors or vicars. This is followed by a minute description of every item of interest in the building as well as its general style and age. The description of St Andrew, Histon, follows the plan of a Church Scheme. The plates, which include details of mouldings, floor plans, and elevations, are probably the most valuable feature of the book.

The *Illustrations of Monumental Brasses*, published in 1846, was another scholarly work. This book, the work of seventeen contributors identified by their initials, contains lithographs of twenty-five monumental brasses with a brief history of the person represented. Neale, who wrote the 'Introduction', considered the brasses to be accurate facial representations, and spoke of the book as a 'portrait gallery'.[3] The illustrations of the brasses are excellent and of great interest. Brasses were still being destroyed or stolen from parish churches, and undoubtedly this work helped arouse interest in their preservation.

In the course of time, the Ecclesiologists turned their attention to churches on the Continent, though at first this subject was

---

[1] Cambridge, 1841–45.

[2] Cambridge, 1845. This volume and the *Illustrations of Monumental Brasses* were originally published serially.

[3] Cambridge, 1846, p. 5. Other contributors, who can be identified from their initials, include Webb, F. A. Paley, Thomas Thorp, and Hope.

strictly taboo. As late as 1846 Neale wrote: 'I have grieved, as you know, in almost every number of the *Ecclesiologist* at the enormous space devoted to foreign art. It is this which is cutting down our influence. . . . Do you really suppose that nine-tenths of our subscribers care one straw for our foreign matter?'[1] But Neale was ignored on this. The opening 'Address' in the 1846 volume of the *Ecclesiologist* declared that henceforth the magazine should 'be considered as offering a repository of *general* Ecclesiological intelligence'. A new feature was to be added to the magazine, news of 'the progress of the Ecclesiological movement on the Continent'. To that end, the Society had undertaken to be 'regularly supplied with the *Annales Archéologiques*, and *Kölner Domblatt*' (v, 2). Selections from these appeared frequently, and a large number of treatises on foreign ecclesiology found their way into the *Ecclesiologist*. Important books from the Continent were also reviewed.

Two important members of the Society published books on foreign ecclesiology. Benjamin Webb's *Sketches of Continental Ecclesiology or Church Notes in Belgium, Germany, and Italy* was published independently of the Society.[2] It is, as Webb indicates, 'a string of church-notes gathered by the way'.[3] A paragraph or more is devoted to each church which he considered noteworthy, and frequent comparisons of Anglican and Roman Catholic practices appear. Neale turned his attention in his latter years to studying the Orthodox Churches of the East. Many of his most important works deal with the history of Eastern Orthodoxy and its worship. In 1861 he published a book of *Notes, Ecclesiological and Picturesque, on Dalmatia, Croatia, Istria, Styria, with a Visit to Montenegro*, recounting noteworthy features which he had observed in these areas during a tour taken in 1860.

Despite the best efforts of the Ecclesiologists, both at home and overseas, some vexing problems remained to plague them. Had they been less certain that each feature of a medieval building represented some purpose once widely known, had

---

[1] *Letters*, p. 100.   [2] London, 1848.   [3] P. x.

they given credit to the place of personal idiosyncrasies in buildings, they could have remained untroubled by these problems.
The usual practice was to gather all the information possible on
any mysterious feature through examination of a large number
of churches. The Church Schemes were especially useful for this
purpose. Then, with the usual location and characteristics of
the item in question determined from the comparison of a large
number of particular instances, theories could be advanced,
especially if documentary research had given any information.

The most difficult problem of all was that proposed by an
item which the Ecclesiologists named a 'lychnoscope'. The
Hand-Book observed: 'This had been a *vexata quaestio* with ecclesiologists for several years. It is well known that by lychnoscopes
are meant those low side windows which frequently occur in the
north-west or south-west parts of chancels, more especially in
First-Pointed work.'[1] Actually, to this day no one really knows
the purpose of these small unglazed apertures which occur in a
considerable number of parish churches. An unromantic current
suggestion is that they may have been intended for ventilation,
a function necessitated by the burning of large numbers of
candles during services.[2]

The Ecclesiologists, however, made valiant efforts to solve
this mystery, and the process reveals their technique of investigation. The intense interest which the Society took in symbolism
after the publication in 1843 of the translation of Durandus led
an anonymous writer to conjecture that 'lychnoscopes are nothing else than the symbolical representation of the Wound in the
SAVIOUR's Side'. The same writer mentions that Ecclesiologists
had noticed ' "something very odd" about the western windows
of aisles', and suggested that 'the position of the western windows of the aisles would represent that of His Feet'[3] (*E.* v, 165).
A paper in the following issue of the *Ecclesiologist* called them
'Vulne-Windows', but pointed out that the theory of the win-

[1] *Hand-Book*, p. 201.
[2] G. H. Cook, *The English Mediæval Parish Church* (London, 1954), p. 177.
[3] It was assumed that the ground plan of the medieval church was a representation of Christ's body as it hung upon the cross.

dows representing wounds was endangered by the fact that the place where lychnoscopes occurred, the chancel (the head), is above the transepts (the arms), and this made the theory difficult, to say the least (v, 188). The *Few Hints*, revealing documentary research on medieval worship, suggested:

The following hint is thrown out to its [the lychnoscope's] real use. During the three last nights of Passion Week lights were kept burning in the Holy Sepulchre, and at all times in Chantries and upon High Altars. This window probably served for those whose business it was to keep them in, to satisfy themselves that all was right; the other windows being too high for the purpose.[1]

Various other theories were suggested: the lychnoscopes were to allow lepers to participate in the mass without contaminating others, they were to permit parishioners to observe the elevation during the daily Mass, or to facilitate the ringing of the sacring bell. The *Hand-Book* brushed these theories aside and suggested: 'We have now to state why we believe, though without wishing to state it positively, that lychnoscopes were contrivances for hearing at certain times what has been called "the confession of all comers".'[2] The evidence adduced for this theory is interesting. The examination of 'a large number of examples' had produced a list of nine characteristics, none of which disqualified this explanation. Research had produced a letter to Thomas Cromwell which stated: ' "We think it best that the place where these Friars have been wont to hear outward confession of all comers at certain times of the year be walled up, and that use to be foredone for ever".'[3] This seemed to be the perfect solution of the problem, but even this conclusion had its difficulties. The last volume of the *Ecclesiologist* admitted: 'It seems curious that though many theories have been brought forward, the question still baffles our learned ecclesiologists' (xxix, 81).

But such was not usually the case. After visiting a large number of churches and applying the inductive method, the Ecclesiologists usually found an explanation. Not all of these have stood up under modern examination, and many were pushed to

[1] *Few Hints*, 3rd ed., p. 26.   [2] *Hand-Book*, p. 202.   [3] *Ibid.*, p. 205.

absurd extremes when the Society turned to codifying its information. On the other hand, research conducted in the actual buildings produced a vast amount of new and valuable information about medieval churches and worship. Assembling this new knowledge was one of the most valuable accomplishments of the Society.

III

At the same time that research was being done among the actual buildings, a great deal of work had been begun on medieval documents. So much medieval research was accomplished during the nineteenth century, that it is difficult to imagine how elementary men's knowledge of the period was at the beginning of the century. The Middle Ages were considered by many people as only a dark era of superstition and ignorance. The poets took the lead in discovering the fascination of medieval sources. Scott's *The Lay of the Last Minstrel* was written in 1805 and based on an old border tale. The popularity of such literature continued. Tennyson's *Idylls of the King* (1859–85) was inspired by the Arthurian legend. Carlyle based his romantic account of Jocelin of Brakelond on documentary research. The Middle Ages provided a rich source of raw material for many writers.

One of the greatest hindrances to research, however, was the inaccessibility of sources. Much material had remained unexplored for centuries in cathedral libraries, at private estates, and in government archives. Numerous societies sprang up to publish these sources. Scott himself founded the Bannatyne Club for the publication of old Scottish documents. The Aelfric Society, Caxton Society, English Historical Society, Hakluyt Society, Wycliffe Society, and the Camden Society (of London) began publishing documents in the 1830's and 1840's. The Germans had been at work for some time on their *Monumenta Germaniae Historica.*

This period saw a tremendous increase in knowledge on medieval matters of ecclesiastical interest. The Cambridge Camden Society soon found it was impossible to understand the functions of medieval churches without diligent research into service books, visitation articles, parochial records, and the devotional and dogmatic writings of the Middle Ages. 'Such knowledge', Hope wrote, 'is not to be acquired by us like holiday tourists through studying prints alone, and visiting buildings; books, crabbed, learned books, and half-obliterated manuscripts must be perused and digested. Holy Fathers must be conned, and mediaeval chroniclers with no less care' (*E.* vii, 90). Sources from the seventeenth century were considered especially valuable when they showed the continuation of medieval practices after the Reformation. In addition to written materials, funeral monuments and illuminated manuscripts provided important sources for tracing vestments and the ornaments of churches. The *Ecclesiologist* was always at hand to publish the results of such research and some short documents were first published in its pages.

Several smaller publications of the Society represented the result of documentary research. In 1841 the Society published a small tract entitled *An Argument for the Greek Origin of the Monogram IHS*.[1] The author evidently was Benjamin Webb and the tract attempted to prove that the commonly accepted Latin phrase, *In hoc signo*, was antedated by the Greek abbreviation for Jesus. Another paper printed by the Society, *On the History of Christian Altars*,[2] was probably by F. W. Collison. It was one round of a long tract battle over the use of the terms 'altar' or 'Lord's Table' in which the actual issue was the doctrine of eucharistic sacrifice. On this occasion, Collison insisted that his intention was historical rather than doctrinal and showed that ancient documents revealed the use of both wood and stone altars. Yet, he shows a preference for the use of stone altars, a favourite theme among Ecclesiologists. A famous tract in its

[1] *An Argument for the Greek Origin of the Monogram IHS: A Paper Read before the Cambridge Camden Society on Tuesday, May 25, 1841* (Cambridge, 1841).
[2] *On the History of Christian Altars: A Paper Read before the Cambridge Camden Society, November 28, 1844* (Cambridge, 1845).

time was *The History of Pews*,[1] undoubtedly written by Neale. For this work, Neale examined many documentary sources 'to prove that pues were not in use before the Reformation', and 'to trace historically the gradual intrusion of pue, reading-pue, gallery, and the other encumbrances of modern churches'.[2]

Perhaps the most important scholarly work published under the auspices of the Society was *Hierugia Anglicana or Documents and Extracts Illustrative of the Ritual of the Church in England after the Reformation*.[3] Like several of the Society's other publications, this appeared initially in serial form between the years 1843–8. *Hierugia* is important as one of the first and most careful attempts to use sources since the Reformation to advocate a change in ritual. It contains a very impressive array of extracts compiled from such varied sources as Strype's *Annals*, seventeenth-century funeral sermons, cathedral inventories, visitation articles, and a host of Puritan pamphlets.

There can be no mistaking the purpose of the book. The Preface pronounced:

The design of the present work is to produce in a collected form, the historical facts concerning the retention of certain rites and usages since the Reformation, which shall speak as it were for themselves, and set forth in the words of eye-witnesses the actual practice of the Church in points which are now viewed by many with suspicion and jealousy. . . . They [the editors] hope from the most authoritative sources to collect so great a number of illustrations of Anglican Ritual as shall enable their readers to gain a much clearer idea of what the Anglican Church has allowed, and shall convince those who have distrusted the late improved feeling on these points that such ceremonial is entirely compatible with the most dutiful allegiance to our own Communion.[4]

---

[1] *The History of Pews: A Paper Read Before the Cambridge Camden Society on Monday, November 22, 1841, with an Appendix Containing a Report Presented to the Society on the Statistics of Pews on Monday, December 7, 1841* (Cambridge, 1841). A second edition and a *Supplement* appeared in 1842 and a third edition followed in 1843.

[2] *Ibid.*, 3rd ed., pp. 5 and 15.

[3] Edited by Members of the Ecclesiological late Cambridge Camden Society (London, 1848). A three-volume new edition, revised and considerably enlarged by Vernon Staley, was published (London, 1902–4). Staley claims that John F. Russell had edited the original edition.

[4] *Hierugia*, pp. i–ii.

To no other charge was the Society so sensitive as to the accusation that it was interested in 'romanizing'. The *Hierugia*, despite its scholarly façade, was a very powerful polemic weapon. It sought to show that many ritualistic practices were encouraged by such men as Laud, Andrewes, Matthew Wren, and Cosin and even tolerated by men as Protestant as Grindal. The fact that many of these usages and ceremonies had disappeared long before the nineteenth century was attributed to the period of Puritan supremacy or to 'the laxity and coldness which characterized the last century'.[1]

The *Hierugia* represents the assembling of a vast array of extracts from many varied documents. The editors neglect to point out, though, that many of the examples certainly represent exceptional cases, accounting for the practices being considered noteworthy by contemporaries. Many of the extracts from Puritan writers attack rare instances of the survival of disliked forms. Nevertheless, *Hierugia* represented a landmark in the development of Ritualism since it cited so many seventeenth-century authorities for practices which had subsequently disappeared from Anglicanism. This publication set the precedent for a great deal of similar research in the next half century.

The most important book by the Ecclesiologists, unlike those above, was published under the names of the translators instead of the Society. In 1843 Neale and Webb published *The Symbolism of Churches and Church Ornaments: A Translation of the First Book of the Rationale Divinorum Officiorum, Written by William Durandus, Sometime Bishop of Mende*. It is difficult to overestimate the importance of this work for it materially changed the course of ecclesiology. Symbolism had not been unknown previously; indeed the *Ecclesiologist* in 1842 recommended Poole's *The Appropriate Character of Church Architecture* 'as containing the best exposition of symbolism that has hitherto appeared' (I, 125). But the publication of *Durandus* in the following year marked the real adoption of symbolism as a significant feature of ecclesi-

---

[1] *Hierugia*, p. iv.

ology. The consequences for church building and restoration were tremendous.

William Durandus was a thirteenth-century cleric who spent most of his life in the papal service at Rome. He was made Bishop of Mende in 1286 though he continued to reside in Rome, not visiting his diocese until 1291, five years before his death. He wrote several learned treatises, but the *Rationale Divinorum Officiorum*, written between 1286 and 1295, is the most famous. The full work consisted of eight books with explications of the church building, the members of the Church, vestments, the Mass, the other Divine Offices, the dominical feast days, saints' days, and the calendar. Neale and Webb translated only the first book, although brief excerpts from the others are included in the Appendixes together with the first two chapters of Hugh of Saint Victor's *Mystical Mirrour of the Church*.

The translators considered *Durandus* 'the most valuable work on Symbolism which the middle ages can furnish',[1] but it was by no means the only such work. Amalarius of Metz, Alcuin, Agobard, Amalarius of Treves and many others engaged in the same type of writing. A modern Roman Catholic scholar, Louis Bouyer, feels that 'in the late Middle Ages . . . this kind of fanciful explanation of the liturgy attained what we might call a luxurious as well as a very unhealthy growth'.[2] Recent research has done much to show the significance of symbolism in the life of the medieval Church.

Evidently the work of translation was not accomplished without difficulty, since Neale and Webb had left Cambridge and were working in different places. But the really important portion of the book was not the translation but their 121-page 'Introductory Essay, Sacramentality: a Principle of Ecclesiastical Design'. As the Preface indicates, they—'considered it necessary to prefix an Essay on the subject [Christian Architecture]; in which we have endeavoured to prove that Catholick Architecture must necessarily be symbolical; to answer the more common objections to the system; and to elucidate it by refer-

---

[1] *Durandus*, p. vii.   [2] *Liturgical Piety* (Notre Dame, 1955), p. 278.

ence to actual examples, and notices of the figurative arrangements of our own churches'.[1] This 'Introductory Essay' is of
great importance for it is the first statement of many ideas which
came to be the dogmas of ecclesiology. It also represents the
first attempt at a philosophical approach to ecclesiology. In
this endeavour it was far from successful and the limitations of
the authors in this type of writing are obvious. Perhaps this was
apparent to them, for the introduction to *Durandus* was their
only major effort of this variety.

The 'Introductory Essay' has but one real purpose, to establish the necessity of symbolism in church architecture, or
'sacramentality', as the authors preferred to call it. Neale and
Webb had noticed the great difference between old churches
and new buildings. It was never very difficult to tell a real
medieval edifice from a reproduction. Somehow the former was
'church-like', but the modern building lacked this quality. This
was not due to lack of association, to incorrect details, the failure
to make a picturesque appearance, or to the absence of mechanical ingenuity. The authors had discovered—'that *Sacramentality* is that characteristick which so strikingly distinguishes
ancient ecclesiastical architecture from our own. By this word
we mean to convey the idea that, by the outward and visible
form, is signified something inward and spiritual: that the
material fabrick symbolizes, embodies, figures, represents, ex-
presses, answers to, some abstract meaning.'[2] Sacramentality,
then, was the clue to genuine Christian architecture.

It is far from clear exactly how sacramentality applies to
church architecture in the thought of Neale and Webb. At one
place they pledge themselves to—'shew how essentially Church
architecture . . . is a part of the Ritual system. And if Catholick
worship is expressed and represented by Catholick ritual, and if
Church architecture is a part of this ritual, then is Church
architecture itself an expression and exponent of Catholick wor-

---

[1] *Durandus*, pp. vii–viii.
[2] *Ibid.*, p. xxvi. Sacramentality was superior to Pugin's principle of 'reality' which
was 'true so far as it goes, but . . . it does not go far enough' (p. xxvii).

ship.'[1] The application of this, evidently, was the belief 'that at first certain given wants induced and compelled certain adaptations to those wants; which then *did* symbolize the wants themselves; and which afterwards became intentionally symbolical'.[2] This seems like saying that a bed symbolizes sleeping. Indeed it does, but one would hardly consider it worth noting. After 121 pages, one wonders whether Neale and Webb have anything more profound to say than that the purpose of an object determined its shape. Of course, now we are conditioned to accept as axiomatic that 'form follows function' in architecture. Yet mere functionalism was never a satisfactory explanation for any item to Neale and Webb. They endeavoured to show that a cruciform floor plan had no utilitarian advantage 'in the case of churches *as anciently arranged*; in which the transepts were utterly useless for the accommodation of worshippers; and in which there is a mechanical evil . . . from the lateral pressure on the lantern piers'. 'Yet', they continue, 'it is undeniable that the cross form was chosen for its symbolical meaning; and this in spite of mechanical disadvantages.'[3] Thus, church architecture, in their eyes, became 'essentially a "petrifaction of our religion": a fact which, once admitted and realized, becomes to succeeding Church-builders, whether they will or not, a rule and precedent for intentional symbolical design'.[4]

This dictum cast a very heavy burden on the church-builders of the nineteenth century. But more than just mere knowledge of symbolical detail was expected of them:

A Catholick architect must be a Catholick in heart. Simple knowledge will no more enable a man to build GOD's material, than his spiritual, temples. In ancient times, the finest buildings were designed by the holiest Bishops. Wykeham and Poore will occur to

---

[1] *Durandus*, p. iv.

[2] *Ibid.*, p. xxviii.

[3] P. cxvii. A more utilitarian (and less imaginative) age would disagree. Cook says of transepts: 'Their sole purpose was to furnish space for much-needed altars which were set up against the eastern walls' (*The English Mediaeval Parish Church*, p. 103). There are easier methods of accommodating worshippers, but altars traditionally abut against an eastern wall. Even so, only a small percentage of English churches are cruciform.

[4] *Durandus*, p. lix.

every Churchman. And we have every reason to believe, from GOD's Word, from Catholick consent, and even from philosophical principles, that such must always be the case.[1]

This is one of the prime sources of the 'ethical fallacy'. Neale himself wrote: 'We know that Catholick ethics gave rise to Catholick architecture; may we not hope that, by a kind of reversed process, association with Catholick architecture will give rise to Catholick ethics?'[2] Much of the responsibility lay with the architects:

At all events, in an investigation into the differences between ancient and modern Church architecture, the contrast between the ancient and modern builders could not be overlooked: and it is not too much to hope that some, at least, may be struck by the fact, that the deeply religious habits of the builders of old, the Hours, the cloister, the discipline, the obedience, resulted in their matchless works; while the worldliness, vanity, dissipation, and patronage of our own architects issue in unvarying and hopeless failure.[3]

Clearly a new type of architect was called for: 'We are not prepared to say that none but monks ought to design churches. . . . But we do protest against the merely business-like spirit of the modern profession, and demand from them a more elevated and directly religious habit of mind.'[4] Among the restrictions to the architect's practice was the injunction that he 'must design in one style, and one style only', that style being the favoured Decorated architecture of the fourteenth century.[5] Furthermore, architects must 'take a *religious* view of their profession', for 'a religious *ethos*, we repeat, is *essential* to a Church architect'.[6] No wonder the Ecclesiologists were regarded as their mortal enemies by many architects! Yet, in R. C. Carpenter and William Butterfield the Society discovered architects who fitted its ideal.

[1] *Durandus*, p. xx.
[2] *The Place Where Prayer Was Wont to Be Made. The Reintroduction of the System of Private Devotion in Churches Considered in a Letter to the Venerable The President of the Cambridge Camden Society* (Rugeley, 1844), p. 20.
[3] *Durandus*, p. xxv.
[4] *Ibid.*, pp. xxi–xxii.
[5] *Ibid.*, p. xxiv.
[6] *Ibid.*, p. xxv. Ruskin and Pugin were also vigorous promoters of the idea that only good men created good architecture.

The main portion of the 'Introductory Essay' consists of five 'arguments' for symbolism. Frequently the reasoning in these arguments seems opaque and the repetition is constant. The first of the five arguments for symbolism is entitled 'The Argument À Priori'. This begins with the statement: 'It will first be proper to consider whether, regarding the subject *à priori*, that is, looking at the habits and manners of those among whom the symbolical system originated, if it originated anywhere, we have reason to think them at all likely to induce that system.'[1] In the early Church, we are informed, symbolism was omnipresent. The chief purpose of this argument appears to be to show the antiquity of Christian symbolism.

The second argument, 'The Argument from Analogy', is more complicated. Basically the intention is to 'shew that, from analogy, it is highly probable that the teaching of the Church, as in other things, so in Her material buildings, would be symbolical'.[2] The proof of this point begins with a discussion of the Jews whom God chose 'to teach . . . the sacramentality, not only of things, but of events', by making 'their most famous ancestors, chiefs, and leaders, . . . most remarkable types of the MESSIAH'.[3] The Old Testament provided the Church with many obvious types for Christian doctrines. Neale and Webb explain that if they themselves press symbolism too far, they are only following the hallowed example of the Fathers. The New Testament, especially Revelation, is full of symbolism. The conclusion of this argument is: 'This quality, then of symbolism cannot be denied to one, and a most important expression of the teaching of the Church, namely its architecture.'[4]

The third argument bears the title 'Philosophical Reasons for Believing in Symbolism'. The topic is introduced with the statement: 'We now propose to offer a few remarks on the philosophical reasons there seem to be for concluding that Ecclesiastical architecture has some esoterick meaning, some figurative adaptation, more than can be appreciated, or even discerned, by the casual observer, to the uses which produced it, and which

[1] *Ibid.*, p. xxxv.　　[2] *Ibid.*, p. xli.　　[3] *Ibid.*, p. xli.　　[4] *Ibid.*, p. xlix.

73

have always regulated it.'[1] The 'philosophical' approach seems to consist of the conviction that physical matters are a reflection of the 'subjective and unseen'. Familiar platonic language is avoided, but the sentiment is similar: 'In other words, we would allege that everything material is symbolical of some mental process, of which it is indeed only the development: that we may see in everything outward and visible some inward and spiritual meaning.'[2] This theory could be used in two ways. The material church might be used as a source for deriving the abstract doctrines of Christianity, or else one might show how the doctrines prefigure the design of the church building. Either way the conclusion is the same—there is a real connexion between the doctrine and its physical embodiment and both are immutable.

'The Analytical Argument' comes next, and is perhaps the weakest of the five. If a hypothetical person, having no knowledge of Christianity, were to visit a Catholic country, we are told, he would soon notice the prevalence of large churches built on a cross plan. This would suggest some special reason for the adoption of such an 'inconvenient' form. Likewise the three altar steps and the declination of the chancel from the axis of the nave would indicate some particular symbolism. The conclusion is obvious—

if these acknowledged peculiarities in Christian architecture be utterly unintelligible on any other supposition than this of a symbolical meaning, surely it is not unreasonable to receive so ready a solution of the difficulty: and, the principle admitted, why may not reasons of the same figurative nature be assigned for other arrangements, in themselves on any other interpretation not only meaningless but obviously useless or absurd?[3]

---

[1] *Durandus*, p. 1.   [2] *Ibid.*, p. li.

[3] *Ibid.*, p. lxii. A contemporary analysis would seek utilitarian explanations for unusual arrangements and symbolical interpretations would be largely ignored. Actually Neale and Webb overstate their case, for transepts were utilitarian, altars were frequently raised to give space to a crypt below, and chancels out of line were probably a consequence of poor surveying. In addition, the majority of churches do not have transepts and the elevation of the altar may vary, even being lower than that of the nave in places. Nevertheless, symbolism certainly was a factor in the design of medieval churches, particularly numerical symbolism.

The final proof, by 'The Inductive Argument', is more convincing. It was intended to establish—'that without any actual acquaintance with the plan, details or arrangement of existing churches, we might gather from other sources, not only the probability, but the fact, that there was some reason (not merely mechanical or accidental) for the selection and universal observation of particular forms and ornaments, and peculiar roles of distribution'.[1] Ancient writers are cited to indicate the existence of a definite set of rules for church-building commonly acknowledged: 'Durandus, S. Isidore, Beleth, and the rest, seem to quote from some Canons of church symbolism, now unknown to us. Their words are often, even where they are not very connected nor intelligible, the same.'[2] Neale and Webb seem to ignore the fact that 'the type or pattern of a church . . . universally recognized',[3] which they postulate, may have been the consequence of certain uniform functional requirements in the conduct of public worship rather than any symbolical intention. At any rate, here they rest their case, convinced that they have argued successfully for the presence of symbolism in church architecture.

The reader's attention is next directed to a massive array of examples of symbolism. Many of these are English examples, supplementing the vast assortment of symbolical items and practices which Durandus had catalogued. Some reason is found for every item appearing in churches, and we are even told the symbolical reason for crosses being made ornate and another symbolical purpose in their being left plain. Indeed, there is nothing in the medieval church which is without some esoteric meaning. This type of symbolical explanation was soon adopted by other Ecclesiologists. The *Hand-Book* is full of such explanations.[4]

In a chapter intended to anticipate possible objections, Neale

---

[1] *Ibid.*, p. lxiii.   [2] *Ibid.*, p. lxxv.   [3] *Ibid.*, p. lxxiii.
[4] Concerning chancel arches, the *Hand-Book* remarks: 'True symbolism, it need hardly be said, requires them to be of small dimensions, because "strait is the gate, and narrow is the way that leadeth to Life": and, as we shall presently observe, the Kingdom of Heaven is typified by the chancel' (p. 71).

and Webb appear to retreat somewhat from the position of previous chapters: 'Now we never asserted that it was necessary that all, or indeed any, given things should be intentionally symbolized. We have pointed out that some things are essentially symbolical; others accidentally and occasionally.'[1] Symbolism, then, is more optional than we have been previously led to believe. 'It has never been asserted', they explain, 'that every church shall have Nave and Aisles: but if a church has Nave and Aisles it will be symbolical of a great doctrine; and for this reason it is better for a church to have Nave and Aisles.'[2] Symbolism is a variable factor, after all, and some churches may be much more symbolical than others.

The writers turn next to a highly interesting treatment of the development of symbolism. Here we encounter an interesting illustration of that nineteenth-century phenomenon which Geoffrey Scott called the 'Biological Fallacy', the belief in the early vigour, maturity, and decline of an art form.[3] The tenth chapter was intended as 'a brief sketch of the history of symbolism, . . . its rise, progress, and decline, in England'.[4] It seemed obvious to Neale and Webb that the facts of Christianity are received by a newly converted nation before its doctrines are. In Norman architecture, they maintained, 'we shall find an almost exclusive reference to history, in arrangements and details'.[5] The shift to a more doctrinal interest in symbolism occurred in Early English, as illustrated by fonts which instead of representing the Fall took an octagonal form 'implying our need of regeneration, . . . [and] setting forth the doctrine itself'.[6] The peak was reached in Decorated, but Erastianism somehow blighted it. Perpendicular was a period of decline for the Church: 'Above all, do not the reintroduction of horizontality, the Tudor Arch, the depressed Pier, speak of Her want of Spirituality?'[7] This view of

---

[1] *Durandus*, p. cxvi.

[2] *Ibid.*, p. cxvii. The nave and north and south aisles represented triplicity, the symbol of the Trinity. In the Middle Ages one or more aisles were often added to accommodate an increasing population.

[3] *The Architecture of Humanism*, pp. 127 ff. The theory of evolution gave increased impetus to this mode of thought.

[4] *Durandus*, p. cxix.   [5] *Ibid.*, p. cxx.   [6] *Ibid.*, p. cxxii.   [7] *Ibid.*, p. cxxiv.

history was a prominent theme throughout the writings of the Ecclesiologists, though it probably originated in the first edition of Pugin's *Contrasts* (1836).

The influence of Pugin is likewise very apparent in a verbal contrast which forms the last chapter of the 'Introductory Essay':

Let us look at a Protestant place of worship . . . On entering, the pulpit occupies the central position, . . . galleries run all around the building . . . the Altar stands under the organ gallery. . . .

We need not point out how strongly all this symbolizes the spiritual pride, the luxury, the self-sufficiency, the bigotry of the congregations of too many A PUE-RENTED EPISCOPAL CHAPEL.

In contrast to this, let us close with a general view of the symbolism of a Catholick church.

Far away, and long ere we catch our first view of the city itself, the three spires of its Cathedral, rising high above its din and turmoil, preach to us of the Most Holy and Undivided Trinity.[1]

Enough has been quoted, no doubt, to show that the translation of Durandus and the 'Introductory Essay' were bound to be controversial. A vice-president of the Society, J. J. Smith, was perturbed since this interest in symbolism was reflected in various tracts published by the Society. He called it 'a system which opens to the imagination a wild range, and familiarizes the thoughts with violations of truth, both in articles of faith and in points of practice'.[2] The Regius Professor of Hebrew, Samuel Lee, was more to the point. He found it 'scarcely possible to conceive of a production so puerile in its conceptions' as the publication of *Durandus*.[3] The work was both 'absurd' and instinct with 'Roman Catholic feeling', in short, '*a damnable heresy*'.[4] The contrast of the Protestant chapel and the Roman cathedral produced a 'fair *Chamber of popish imagery*. . . . speaking in language not to be misunderstood, "MYSTERY, BABYLON THE GREAT, THE MOTHER OF HARLOTS, AND ABOMINATIONS OF THE

---

[1] *Ibid.*, pp. cxxviii–cxxx.
[2] *A Few Words on the Last Publication of the Cambridge Camden Society*, p. 8.
[3] *A Second Letter to the Venerable Archdeacon Thorp, President of the Cambridge Camden Society, on Symbolism* (London, 1845), p. 5.
[4] *Ibid.*, p. 13.

EARTH!" '.[1] No doubt the *Ecclesiologist* was justified in feeling that 'such attacks must do it [the Society] good' (IV, 216).

A more sophisticated objection came from a respected authority on gothic architecture, E. A. Freeman of Oxford. Freeman objected to the 'symbolism of Durandus' on the grounds that 'the system appears . . . to be one of merely arbitrary association; there is no natural or philosophical connexion between the type and the anti-type' (*E.* V, 179). The *Ecclesiologist* countered that—

the Durandic symbolism had a substantive and an authoritative existence; that in short, it was a law of mediaeval church-architecture and church arrangement, . . . recommended by so general a consensus of wise and holy men, as to be hardly less binding upon the conscience of a meek and reverential architect of those days, than if it had come armed with the strongest denunciations of Decretals against its violators (V, 219).

But the *Ecclesiologist* was destined to change its mind. In 1849 a review of Poole's *A History of Ecclesiastical Architecture in England* admitted:

Of course some symbols may be far-fetched, and little applicable, and ought therefore to be allowed to perish with their conception. Such we are willing to own in the instances adduced by our author, from Messrs. Neale and Webb's Durandus. . . . But when we reflect how many years (comparatively) have elapsed since that work was published, and how young and ardent its translator-authors were, and when we weigh the fascinating interest of the new field of thought that it opened out to them, we can only be astonished that they were not more often led to seek for resemblances, where their more matured judgments would tell them none could wisely be found (X, 128–9).

Eventually a more moderate view of symbolism prevailed. This did not, however, alter the abiding effects of the work of Neale and Webb. The translation of Durandus and the 'Introductory Essay' enhanced ecclesiology, for it showed that this new science had an unmistakable religious significance. Symbolism was not to be sought in secular buildings (although

[1] *A Second Letter from the Venerable Archdeacon Thorp*, p. 44.

doubtlessly it could be found there by any determined seeker). The sanctity of ecclesiology was demonstrated by *Durandus*, for this book lent evidence to the claim of the Ecclesiologists that only a good churchman could really understand their pursuit. No longer was the Ecclesiologist to be confused with the 'mere antiquarian'. It could be maintained that the study of ecclesiology provided support for the doctrinal and ethical principles of the Church. Ecclesiology was a highly useful as well as a most interesting science.

CHAPTER IV

PROCLAIMING THE LAWS OF ECCLESIOLOGY

I

A most unfortunate consequence of the science of ecclesiology was the propensity which its adherents showed for turning the conclusions of their research into laws for church-building. The process began early in the history of the Society as sympathetic clergy and churchwardens appealed to the group for instruction on building new churches and restoring old ones. The *Ecclesiologist* and each annual *Report* list numerous applications of this nature. Whenever possible, advice was sent.

Early in its career the Society began drawing up a code of architectural laws with which to promulgate its standards for church-building. The last issue of the *Ecclesiologist* declared in retrospect: 'Our ecclesiastical position has been that of sons of the Church of England, working out from the teachings alike of our own Communion and of the Church Catholic laws of Church arrangement and Church service' (XXIX, 315). There can be no doubt that publicizing these 'laws of Church arrangement and Church service' occupied as much of the Society's attention as did pure research. As indicated previously, *Hierugia Anglicana* and *Durandus* were definitely intended to popularize certain conceptions about buildings and worship.

This tendency to dogmatism was perhaps the Society's tragic flaw. The Ecclesiologists could be dogmatic about the smallest detail and their intolerance towards disagreement was extreme. Their outspoken criticism of buildings alienated many who otherwise would have considered themselves allies. The Society's positions on many subjects have been shown to be unreliable by subsequent research. This seems especially unfortunate when it is considered how obstinately these positions were maintained. It is even more ironic in view of the fact that the medieval architects had been so extremely flexible in their own work and eager to adopt innovations in their trade. New ideas in architecture swept across England with amazing speed in the Middle Ages, and novelty never seemed to trouble medieval builders.

The conclusions derived from research provided the raw material for the Society's architectural code. An insight into the methodology of the Ecclesiologists is obtained from an article in the *Ecclesiologist* on 'Altar-Screens'—

in the attempt to revive ancient architecture, we have no safe course but to find out by induction some (at least) general rules, and to lay down some general principles: by which we must try our own attempts at imitation; by which, should they be confirmed by use and experience, we may test the truthfulness and excellence even of the ancient remains themselves. It will therefore be of small use to bring forward a solitary example of a detail or arrangement as authority for its imitation (III, 34).

It is implied that disputed points could be settled by producing the greatest number of medieval examples. No better system for collecting such evidence could have been devised than the Church Schemes. Through the Schemes statistical information could be gathered when necessary, and this provided a guide for the legislators. To a bit of correspondence on the prevalence of the priest's door in medieval churches, the *Ecclesiologist* appended a note: 'He [the correspondent] rightly remarks that it is *invariably* found in ancient churches; and ought therefore to be introduced in every modern design' (III, 61). This is an important 'therefore' for it shows clearly the thought-pattern of the Ecclesiologists.

Behind this attempt to reach rules for church-building was a clear conviction that the ancient church-builders had possessed such laws. Reference has already been made to the fact that Neale and Webb believed the ancient builders possessed 'some Canons of church symbolism, now unknown to us', but which

had been 'a rule and precedent' to architects of the past.[1] Neale
asserted: 'That there is a proportion observed between every
part of an ancient church is an unquestionable fact; we feel and
know it to be so, though we cannot at present explain its rules,
nor analyse its principles.'[2] The Ecclesiologists turned their attention to the recovery of these mysterious laws, using the inductive method to find their evidence. So dogmatic did they
become, once they had found an overwhelming amount of evidence on a topic, that they occasionally criticized medieval
buildings for incorrectness. The *Hand-Book* noted: 'Sometimes,
especially in Staffordshire, there is a clerestory to the aisles, a
thing entirely at variance with all true principles.'[3] This over-
confidence is most regrettable for it led to the many 'restorations' which, in seeking to 'correct' real medieval buildings,
destroyed numerous ancient features.

Correctness came to be a dominant theme in all the Society's
judgements of new buildings. A constant barrage of criticism was
poured upon any architect unfortunate enough to introduce an
original and (consequently) incorrect feature in a building.
Originality, except on the part of a few favoured architects, was
considered a deadly sin. The *Ecclesiologist* spoke with contempt
'of the extreme presumption of wilful departure in a case of such
importance [Westminster Abbey] from those acknowledged
laws of Cathedral arrangement, which may be almost said to
carry with them the authority of a "golden rule" ' (III, 99).
According to Boyce, in the year 1842 the Society submitted a
petition asking the Incorporated Society for Promoting the Enlargement, Building and Repairing of Churches and Chapels to
revise its *Suggestions and Instructions*. This publication carried
such obnoxious advice as the suggestion that 'the most approved
forms are a parallelogram and an octagon; but a polygon or a
semi-polygon, or a figure of three straight sides and one poly-

[1] *Durandus*, pp. lxxiv–lxxv.
[2] *Church Enlargement and Church Arrangement* (Cambridge, 1843), p. 8. Recent
research, especially von Simson's *The Gothic Cathedral* and Lesser's *Gothic Cathedrals
and Sacred Geometry*, has made this seem more reasonable than Neale's contemporaries believed.
[3] *Hand-Book*, p. 84.

gonal would bring a large congregation nearer to the preacher than any other'. Boyce continues:

The Incorporated Society received the Memorial with that respect which was due to its weight, and consented to re-consider and alter those *Instructions* to which strong objection was made.

The consequence was that on May 2, 1842, amended *Suggestions and Instructions* were issued, which the Committee of the Cambridge Camden Society characterized 'as containing an almost unexceptionable guide to Church builders who may desire to erect new Churches in conformity with ancient usage, as to materials, construction and arrangement'.[1]

The final authority, in every case, was to be 'conformity with ancient usage', or, more precisely, the Society's concept of an 'ancient usage'. A vigorous condemnation was heaped upon a new church in Cambridge on the grounds that its 'style of architecture and plan of internal arrangement should have been after some approved ancient model' (*E.* I, 27). Moreover, style and plan were not the only items involved: 'Details, however plain, should be scrupulously *correct.*'[2] Such correctness could be tested against actual medieval architecture as the authority. Reviews of new churches included such remarks as: 'We believe that there is sufficient authority for the unusual arrangement of *diagonal* buttresses at the corners' (*E.* I, 21), or 'there is direct authority for facing a large area with brass . . . in the south transept of the Cathedral Church of Amiens' (*E.* I, 43). The lack of authority could be a most damaging criticism; a tower was condemned because the 'style of the pinnacles have, we fear, no authority whatever' (*E.* I, 19). Actually the concept of architectural authority was nothing new since many eighteenth-century architects had treated Andrea Palladio (1518–80) as a lawmaker or used archaeological books on Rome and Greece as their lawbooks. But the Ecclesiologists went even further and demanded authority for every item in the church, from the tower to the altar ware.

The rules, once enacted, were not likely to be changed. In

---

[1] *Memorial*, pp. 20–1.
[2] *Few Words to Church Builders* (Cambridge, 1844), 3rd ed., p. 3.

1854 the *Ecclesiologist* commented: 'What we are we shall most likely continue to be. We are neither bigots nor waverers. It has happened to us to reconsider details: our principles, as we have not foregone, we are not likely to alter' (xv, 6). Comparatively few details were changed after the Society had ruled upon them. An article in the *Ecclesiologist* established the rule for towers: 'And we would lay down as a canon of church-building:—*Every church, not being cross, should have its tower or bell-cot at the west end,* unless there be some stringent reason to the contrary' (iv, 205). In the volume on Cambridge churches, the Society took 'the present opportunity for recording our deliberate opinion, that an early Tower without a spire is a solecism'.[1] Any architect guilty of such a mistake could expect to be severely reprimanded.

One of the most interesting (and strangest) of the Society's enactments was that regarding western triplets of lancets. The highly respected John Jebb wrote the *Ecclesiologist* in 1842:

Sir,—Although it must appear presumptuous in an individual to express a doubt upon an architectural point already ruled by the Cambridge Camden Society, still it may be well to state it, in order to secure the advantage of a solution from some member of that Society in one of your future numbers. . . . The point upon which I feel a doubt is, the rule more than once laid down in your publication, that triple windows are inadmissible in the western ends of small churches (i, 170).

Obviously the Ecclesiologists had noted the rarity of such a feature and decided there must be a reason, leading them to formulate a law for it: 'We believe that the Canons we have been endeavouring to establish may be more generally expressed, so as to include every class of church: thus—*In Early-English churches, the number of lights at the east end must exceed that at the west*' (*E.* i, 173). Even the discovery of a few ancient examples of western triplets could not dissuade them:

Yet these are so few as not in the least to impugn our opinion that, as an *architectural law,* (subject, like most laws to occasional excep-

---

[1] *Churches of Cambridgeshire,* p. 48.

tions,) *western Triplets were not adopted by the ancient architects.* . . . we consider it important to do more than *recommend—to insist upon it as a law,* which ought not rashly to be broken, and cannot be so without great risk of a gross architectural impropriety (*E.* II, 37).

But the controversy continued; issue after issue of the *Ecclesiologist* contains essays on the subject. The magazine itself admitted:

Probably no opinion expressed by the Cambridge Camden Society has met with more opposition even from those who generally think with it, than that which condemns the use of a Triplet of lancets at the West end of a church . . . we have been accused of a wish to fetter down the originality of modern design, and to make a rule only for the sake of making it (II, 65).

Nevertheless, the Society stuck to its rule and defended it on the grounds of its beauty, its symbolism, and its propriety. The Ecclesiologists argued that the western end of the church symbolized a door which represents Christ. Some representation of the Saviour was necessary and a couplet did this, rather than a symbol of the Trinity. Therefore western triplets were inadmissible. It was eventually decided 'to restate our Canon in different words, protesting at the same time against Western Doors in small churches: *Western Triplets ought not to be employed, except there be a Western Door: or except there be more than a triplet at the East end*' (*E.* II, 67–8). On most of the Society's enactments there was less discussion. Once the law was made, any architect guilty of violating it could expect severe criticism.

II

No factor was more important in the formation of the ecclesiological code than the Society's concept of the relation of architectural development and church history. According to the Ecclesiologists' understanding of architectural history, the artistic and structural advances of any period depended on the vitality of the Church. The translators of Durandus asserted:

But, hardly had Early English finished its course of splendour, when while traces of rare glory were developing daily, the Statute of Mortmain began to tell upon the Church: and though the impulse already given yet continued for some time to act, the end was near. No magnificent Cathedral was built after the full effects,—not so much of that act, as of the Erastianism which contrived and allowed it,—were felt.[1]

The debilitating forces of Erastianism were blamed for the decline of gothic rather than the financial consequences of the Statute of Mortmain. The Ecclesiologists considered piety the necessary prerequisite for good architecture. A discourse in the *Ecclesiologist* on 'Ecclesiastical Architects' stated of medieval builders: 'To their entirely religious calling and lives must be attributed the solemn and beautiful effect of every building to which they turned their hands' (IV, 279). Consequently, those times which the Ecclesiologists considered the most pious also produced the architecture which they deemed most inspired.

The basic rule of the Ecclesiologists was that gothic, or 'pointed architecture' as they called it, was the only permissible style of church architecture. They admitted: 'This assertion is *the* point upon which our system may in some sort be said to depend, the assumption . . . that in pointed architecture Christian symbolism has found its most adequate exponent' (IV, 49–50). Their consistent display of 'dogmatic spirit' on this point was impressive. In 1844 it was announced:

We are not now called on to prove that GOTHICK IS THE ONLY CHRISTIAN ARCHITECTURE. We believe that, after a well-fought battle, this point has been conceded: and that, though second-rate architects may, for a few years yet, employ Romanesque or revived Pagan, those who are at the head of their profession will be guilty of such serious errours no longer.[2]

Clients as well as architects were advised that only gothic would do. The *Ecclesiologist* frankly told people who owned houses built in a classical style and who wished to build chapels: 'Boldly acknowledge the former mistake, and let your chapel at least be in correct style, and the first fruits of your amended

[1] *Durandus*, pp. cxxiii–cxxiv.
[2] *Few Words to Church Builders*, 3rd ed., p. 5.

taste' (IV, 145). Gothic came to be so closely identified with Christianity that the *Ecclesiologist* remarked: 'Pointed Architecture seems to be so true a correlative to Christian doctrine, that we cannot suppose, . . . that any future style will be discovered, in which the Pointed spirit shall not predominate' (V, 52). Even such a sympathetic periodical as the *Christian Remembrancer* could not help but protest against the Society's 'idolatry' of gothic: 'It is utterly preposterous to assert, as Mr. Pugin has done, and as the Camden Society have re-echoed, that a style of architecture is exclusively christian and catholic which was not introduced till twelve long ages of Christianity had lapsed, and with which not more than half of Christendom was ever acquainted.'[1] Criticism never shook the Society's loyalty to gothic as the true Christian architecture.

But the Society was even more specific:

We wish however to restrict the choice of style still further than this. No one can, sensibly, employ Norman, and perhaps not judiciously even Perpendicular, when free to choose another style. Early English, though it must perhaps be allowed occasionally, should be used very sparingly. The Decorated or Edwardian style, that employed, we mean, between the years 1260 and 1360, is that to which only, except from some very peculiar circumstances, we ought to return. The reason of this is plain. During the so-called Norman era, the Catholick Church was forming her architectural language: in the Tudor period, she was unlearning it.[2]

The Decorated style was without any doubt the Society's real favourite. The 'Anglican architect' was told that 'for his own style, he should choose the glorious architecture of the fourteenth century'.[3] Frequently, in the *Ecclesiologist*'s criticisms of buildings, a new edifice was simply dismissed as being of an unapproved style. An opponent of the Society felt it necessary to call to the attention of the Ecclesiologists that beauty appears in all styles: 'It belongs to all, when all are alike treated with reference to their fitness to the character and purpose of the

---

[1] 'Church Architecture', *Christian Remembrancer*, III (1842), 356–7.
[2] *Few Words to Church Builders*, 3rd ed., pp. 5–6.
[3] *Durandus*, p. xxiv.

building erected. The question is not the relative beauty of this style or that, but the appropriateness which will allow of its beauty being developed.'[1] Such criticism was unheeded. The Society stuck to its dogma of the absolute superiority of Decorated.

A curious battle was waged on the proper nomenclature for the various styles. Rickman's terms ('Early English', 'Decorated', and 'Perpendicular') were criticized for 'the irremediable defect of a want of Catholicity', since they applied only to English architecture (*E.* IV, 51). The terms 'ascetic' and 'spiritual' were discussed but dropped. Hope preferred the terms 'early', 'middle', and 'late Plantagenet' (*E.* I, 193). The *Ecclesiologist* suggested 'naming the three styles First, Middle, and Third-Pointed' (IV, 52), and these became the favoured terms, though those of Rickman were frequently employed.

Norman architecture was brushed aside as a style for contemporary building, possibly because Evangelicals seemed to have a predilection for it, but ostensibly because as a variety of Romanesque, its 'prototype is undeniably Pagan, though its development, so far as it went, was essentially Christian' (*E.* II, 112). Strangely enough, Norman was recommended for new churches to be built in New Zealand—'because, as the work will be chiefly done by native artists, it seems natural to teach them first that style which first prevailed in our own country; while its rudeness and massiveness, and the grotesque character of its sculpture, will probably render it easier to be understood and appreciated by them' (*E.* I, 4–5). What was fit for New Zealand, however, was not suitable for the more refined mother country.

The invention of the pointed arch, the transition between Norman and Early English, freed medieval churchmen 'from those traces of paganism which cling to Romanesque architecture'.[2] The *Hand-Book* claimed that the pointed arch 'was the necessary result of the teaching of the Church, as being the only

[1] 'On the Present Condition and Prospects of Architecture in England', *Quarterly Papers on Architecture*, II (1844), 7.
[2] *Churches of Cambridgeshire*, p. 69.

legitimate expression of uprisingness and verticality'.[1] Early English was considered the style next best to Decorated: 'Indeed, for consummate taste, infinite variety of device, ingenuity of construction, perfect knowledge of effect, lightness combined with strength, and the instinctive knowledge of true principles, —the thirteenth century has never been surpassed.'[2] But even this was not enough for modern buildings. A discussion of 'The Architectural Room of the Royal Academy, 1846', strongly deprecated 'the employment of severe First-Pointed in modern times', as being 'after all only Romanesque improved' (*E.* v, 254).

The Decorated architecture of the first half of the fourteenth century was the Ecclesiologists' ideal. Neale and Webb declared: 'No other period can be chosen at which all conditions of beauty, of detail, of general effect, of truthfulness, of reality are so fully answered as in this.'[3] The Society's first preference was early Decorated: 'In truth, in the early or transitional period of this style, the workmanship was so exquisitely fine, and the ornaments so profuse and yet so delicate, that this may justly be regarded as the age in which Christian architecture attained the most consummate beauty.'[4] It was this style which the Society demanded that architects imitate. A very prominent architect of the time, Sir George Gilbert Scott, in latter years recalled—

the tendency of the 'Ecclesiologist' towards late decorated. Their dictum had been in favour of the earlier state of the flowing decorated, or, as my friend, Mr. E. A. Freeman, used to say, they would call it in their own nomenclature, 'the early late middle pointed'. . . . So imperious was their law, that any one who had dared to deviate from or to build in other than the sacred 'Middle Pointed', well knew what he must suffer. . . . They held it as a religious duty, though they now seem to have forgotten this phase of the history of their faith, and are very irrate when it is referred to.[5]

The choice of Decorated was especially unfortunate since it was

---

[1] *Hand-Book*, p. 16. [2] *Ibid.*, p. 23. [3] *Durandus*, p. xxx.
[4] *Few Hints*, 3rd ed., p. 7.
[5] *Personal and Professional Recollections* (London, 1879), p. 203.

perhaps the most difficult style to imitate, especially on a limited budget. From a modern perspective, it would seem highly dangerous to idealize any particular style since each period had distinct attractions. But the Ecclesiologists wanted Decorated, and Decorated they managed to get in many instances.

The abandonment of Decorated by medieval architects had to be explained. This was done by noting the progress of Erastianism:

In England, from the time that Edward IV. directed the execution of Archbishop Scrope, when the State interfered, it was with a strong arm, cramping and confining, obliging the Church to confine herself to ritual observances, and forbidding Her to expatiate in the grand objects for which She was ordained. Now could there be a more fitting expression of this than the Perpendicular style?[1]

The defects of Perpendicular architecture had a moral origin: 'Perpendicular employed meretricious enrichments, and *made* ornament for its own sake; . . . because the Tudor architects forgot their high vocation of setting forth truth by beauty, and symbolized worldly pomp instead of the Catholick Faith; instead of the teaching of the Church, the promptings of Erastianism.'[2] There were several objections to Perpendicular: 'We approve of its short chancels and enormous lateral chapels, as little as we do the horizontalism of its tendency, and the tautology of its ornaments' (*E.* IV, 270). Even such a splendid edifice as King's College Chapel was accused of 'violating that great principle of gothic architecture, vertical ascendancy', by its use of the flat Tudor arch.[3] Perpendicular did have one redeeming asset, its wooden roofs, 'the only feature in which this style surpasses its predecessors'.[4] However, the objections to the style overwhelmed this sole virtue as far as the Ecclesiologists were concerned. Other champions of the gothic revival were not so prone to reject Perpendicular. The *Ecclesiologist* noted that an active member of the Oxford Architectural Society, Mr E. A. Freeman, 'stands distinguished from his fellow-students in that

[1] *Durandus*, p. cxxiv.   [2] *Few Words to Church Builders*, 3rd ed., p. 6.
[3] *Few Hints*, 3rd ed., p. 8.   [4] *Hand-Book*, p. 32.

science [ecclesiology] by his championship of Third Pointed as the most perfect style', but it was hoped 'that further study may lead him to abandon these peculiar notions' (v, 53–5).

The styles which followed Perpendicular were hardly worth the Society's attention. They were given the contemptuous name 'Debased', which applied to the period between Edward VI and the Puritan Revolution, although the term was occasionally used to describe Tudor gothic. Sometimes the word 'Pagan' was used to show the derivation of the classical styles from Roman and Greek sources. The *Hand-Book* spoke in no uncertain terms of this period:

Of a style which we trust will never be revived, and which it is much to be wished had never been invented, we shall give no examples; since there is no rarity in them to make such a list necessary.

About the time of the Reformation, the practical recurrence to classical forms, induced by the vitiated and unhappy taste for Italian architecture, completely corrupted the pure Pointed style by giving birth to various anomalous compositions, generally termed Debased. It is unnecessary to particularize all the barbarisms which but too frequently occur in churches of the subsequent period.[1]

The only period which could be worse was the architecture of the eighteenth century, 'that *ne plus ultra* of wretchedness, the Georgian style'.[2] Whatever signs of hope there had been during the time of Laud were cut short by the Puritan ascendancy. The *Ecclesiologist* carried a treatise on 'Church-Building Since the Reformation', which claimed that 'from the beginning of the reign of George I. to the year 1820, not one satisfactory church was built. The age was one of indifference to the interests of religion' (VII, 43). The architecture of the Renaissance was often referred to as 'Italian', a term which was meant to be derogatory. Gothic was the true English national style, and the pagan Italianate forms of the previous two centuries were forbidden to anyone who desired the favour of the Ecclesiologists.

The style of the building was only one part of the Society's regulations, and perhaps not the most important one at that.

---

[1] *Hand-Book*, p. 35. [2] *Durandus*, p. cxxvii.

The Ecclesiologists had in mind an ideal form for a church, and though they preferred to see it executed in Decorated gothic, they would give their grudging consent to buildings in other gothic styles which exhibited this perfect design. Neale and Webb related: 'As it is we have framed a sort of *beau ideal* of a church, fully formed and developed, which we should propose as a perfect model. We are not qualified as yet to blame the ancient churches which do not come up to this ideal, but we cannot be wrong in praising such as do.'[1] During the 1840's the Ecclesiologists filled out the details of this '*beau ideal*'.

The Society constantly maintained: 'The most important requisite in erecting a church is that it be built in such a way that the Rubricks and Canons of the Church of England may be consistently observed, and the Sacraments rubrically and decently administered' (*E.* I, 10). There can be little doubt that this was the dominant factor in forming the concept of the ideal church. But this was not as simple as it might sound. The means of observing the 'Rubricks and Canons of the Church of England' varied considerably. The Society had definite ideas on this, for the Ecclesiologists considered it to be 'a sound rule, that a doubtful Rubric of our Church should be interpreted in the way most accordant with Catholick practice' (*E.* II, 27). Ritualistic propriety, as the Society conceived it, was the highest criterion for a church, surpassing even that of beauty. The Ecclesiologists did not hesitate to condemn those who put 'aesthetical beauty' ahead of the demands of the rubrics.

Perhaps the most questionable step in the logic of the Ecclesiologists was the assertion that ritualistic propriety led to medieval forms: 'We boldly assert the old arrangement to be very well suited to Common Prayer' (*E.* IV, 211). Hope told the Oxford Architectural Society: ' "that the same shell which contained the apparatus of medieval worship was, speaking generally, suited to contain that of modern worship. . . . In one word, it was manifest that in all general matters the post-reformational idea of Catholic church-arrangement was identical with the

---

[1] *Durandus*, p. cxvii.

ante-reformational one, and totally opposed to Calvinian bareness" ' (*E.* vii, 87).

The consequence of this assumption is obvious—medieval churches were to be reproduced exactly. An article on 'Ancient Models' asserts: 'It would be difficult to assign any reason why ancient churches should not be exactly copied as models for new ones. . . . The old churches are everywhere decaying and falling away from time. . . . They are, in fact, *worn out.* . . . Yet how well worthy of imitation are the least and humblest of these' (*E.* iii, 134). Architects were advised to copy medieval churches exactly. Although most architects had copied ancient details from a number of churches, few had copied an entire building. If this were done, 'we should thus replace by new and perfect buildings the worn-out and mutilated edifices of our pious ancestors' (*E.* i, 134). Obviously the Ecclesiologists were far from being pure antiquarians. The copying which they advocated would hardly be considered worthy of the name of architecture today, but architects then were told: 'It is no sign of weakness to be content to copy acknowledged perfection: it is rather a sign of presumption to expect to rival it in any other way' (*E.* i, 134). The *Ecclesiologist* explained that such 'mechanical imitation' was necessary at present in order to obtain a knowledge of 'true principles'. 'For while we copy with exactness, we are more likely to investigate and recover the lost principles which we compel ourselves to adopt, though we do not understand them, than when we blindly follow the dictates of our own unrestricted judgment and tastes' (iii, 11). Imitation of ancient buildings came to be held up as the ideal for architects, though caution had to be exercised in choosing the right model. A review of a new church mentioned: 'We give it the highest praise when we say that many have mistaken it for an old church' (*E.* iii, 88).

The most important ecclesiological legislation concerned the chancel, an item which was frequently ignored or misused at the time. The translators of Durandus boasted that the Ecclesiologists 'Were the first who dwelt on the absolute necessity of a distinct and spacious Chancel.'[1] It did not take the Society long to formulate laws for chancels. The third issue of the *Ecclesiologist* replied to an architect who had sought a definition of a chancel: 'Every church of whatever kind, size, or shape, should have a distinct Chancel *at least* one-third of the length of the Nave, and separated from the latter, internally at least, if not externally, by a well-defined mark, a chancel-arch if possible, or at least by a screen and raised floor' (i, 45). The arguments for chancels were varied. Their beauty was mentioned but more important was their almost universal use in medieval times. They had a very important place in the symbolism of churches. Furthermore, the great Anglican bishops of the seventeenth century approved of chancels, and the rubrics did not condemn them (*E.* ii, 12).

Undoubtedly the greatest problem in reintroducing chancels was the rather basic one of finding a use for them. Medieval chancels had been intended primarily for the worship of collegiate clergy or groups of religious. At this time, however, few churches except cathedrals had many resident clergy, and the orders had not yet been revived. Anglicans had managed quite well for two centuries without using chancels, or using them only on the rare occasion of Holy Communion. The Society intended the chancel to be the exclusive property of the clergy. 'The stalls north and south of the Chancel are the seats set apart for ecclesiasticks who are not immediately engaged in the service', said the *Ecclesiologist* in 1843 (ii, 90). But few parishes cared to build a large and expensive chancel for the use of the clergy only. A hostile writer criticized the Society's condemnation of so many new churches for lacking 'well developed chancels'. He added: 'But we perceive numberless instances in the small chapels recently erected, where the chancel is of a depth, not only most unnecessary as respects its purpose, but most disportionate in reference to the main structure.'[2] Pugin also objected: 'A deep chancel, under the present system is an ab-

---

[1] *Durandus*, p. xxxii.
[2] George Wightwick, 'Modern English Gothic Architecture', *Quarterly Papers on Architecture*, iii (1845), 6.

surdity; the very principles on which the Book of Common Prayer was framed are against it.'[1] Maybe Pugin was jealous; he was fighting a losing battle to convince his fellow Catholics of the need for deep chancels. Roman Catholics had found shallow apses quite sufficient during the past two centuries and saw no reason to add expensive chancels now.

In commenting on *A Few Words to Church-Builders*, the *Christian Remembrancer* disagreed with the Society's demand for chancels with rows of stalls for the clergy:

> *cui bono?* . . . our ancestors had monks to fill these seats . . . but we have no monks. Except in cathedral and collegiate churches, we have no supernumerary clergy; our *hare therefore must first be caught before we can cook him.* First provide your choristers in parish churches, and then we may listen to your injunctions about the miserere seats for the antiphonal chanting of psalms.[2]

Why build chancels when there was no one to occupy them in parish churches? The solution to this dilemma was close at hand and produced a major change in Anglican and Protestant worship.

In 1841 Walter Farquhar Hook, Rector of Leeds, rebuilt his parish church. Hook took the advice of his friend John Jebb, Canon of Hereford, and introduced the cathedral form of choral service into the new church, placing a choir of laymen in the chancel. Jebb published an important volume in 1843 on *The Choral Service of the United Church of England and Ireland: Being an Enquiry into the Liturgical System of the Cathedral and Collegiate Foundations of the Anglican Communion.* Jebb was convinced that 'the highest, most perfect, and most ancient mode [of worship] is that which is properly called CHORAL or CATHEDRAL service'.[3] He went on to say:

> Of late several parish Churches and Chapels have adopted the Choral service either partially or wholly. At Leeds, every part of the Liturgy, on the evenings of all week days, and at all the services on Sundays and Holidays, is performed according to the strictest and

[1] *Present State of Ecclesiastical Architecture in England* (London, 1843), p. 133.
[2] 'Church Architecture', *Christian Remembrancer*, III (1842), 358–9.
[3] (London, 1843), p. 20.

The Cambridge Movement

best Choral precedent, those parts even being sung which are usually omitted in Cathedrals.[1]

Jebb also had definite ideas about where the choir should be placed: 'The proper place was, and still is, the Chancel. . . . here the Choir, or those assistant in divine service, ought always to be placed. . . . No Church, however small, ought to be without a regular Chancel.'[2] So familiar has this practice of placing a lay choir in the chancel become, that it is rarely realized that 'the practice, however common, is not old. The first church of any note in which it was adopted, is the present parish church of Leeds'.[3] Hook and Jebb made a very profound impact on contemporary Anglican and Protestant worship. Jebb would have objected to one modern practice; he considered female choristers as 'inconsistent with that retiring, dependent, and domestic character so proper to all Christian women'.[4]

Hook and Jebb had found a practical use for chancels, but the Ecclesiologists were reluctant to adopt it at first since they did not like the idea of having laymen in the chancel. Rather than this, they hoped that each large church might eventually have a 'college of Priests-Vicars' who could occupy the chancel. For laymen, the Society recommended the east end of the nave and frequently condemned the current practice of placing the village choir and band in a west gallery. But the Ecclesiologists soon decided that lay choirs could be admitted to the chancel and by 1843 they were speaking of the chancel, and 'they who ought to be there, namely the singers'.[5] The surpliced choir in the chancel caught on and won the battle for deep chancels by giving them a practical purpose. By 1850 the *Ecclesiologist* could quote with great satisfaction a newspaper report that the Archbishop of Canterbury ' "has become convinced of the propriety

[1] *The Choral Service*, p. 152. Hook considered the novel experiment a success, though expensive. Cf. W. R. W. Stephens, *The Life and Letters of Walter Farquhar Hook*, 7th ed. (London, 1885), p. 332.
[2] *The Choral Service*, pp. 187–8.
[3] Addleshaw and Etchells, *The Architectural Setting of Anglican Worship*, p. 213.
[4] *Three Lectures on the Cathedral Service in the Church of England*, 2nd ed. (Leeds, 1845), p. 113.
[5] *Church Enlargement and Church Arrangement* (Cambridge, 1843), p. 16.

of the priests and choir being confined as of old, to the chancel, from seeing the good effects of it in some of the new churches he has lately consecrated in his diocese" ' (XI, 215). And fourteen years later, it was noted of a new church that 'to the right and left of the chancel the *choir is accommodated, as is becoming the system in many towns*' (*E.* xxv, 51). The battle for the chancel had been won.

The practice of admitting laymen, albeit choir members, into the holy precincts of the chancel, led to a further refinement. In 1846 a paper 'On the Distinction of Chancel and Sacrarium' belatedly admitted: 'Our end in the present paper is . . . to call attention to a point which has perhaps been somewhat over-looked in the revived feeling about chancels, we mean the right of the sacrarium to be considered as an integral part of a rightly ordered church' (*E.* v, 134). The 'sacrarium' was to be distinguished from the chancel by its elevation or by the altar railing. An 1867 issue of the *Ecclesiologist* prophesied:

So long as the altar rises conspicuous at the end of the wide and deep and well-elevated sanctuary, and between sanctuary and congregation is interposed the chancel or chorus cantorum, with its stalls for clerks, lay or in holy orders, so long will the living witness exist in the Church of England to the especial dignity of the Eucharist, to the antiphonal form of worship, and to the special attributes of the clerkly function (xxviii, 231).

The requirements for the other parts of the building were less stringent than for the chancel. Pews, of course, were forbidden, but benches and chairs might be arranged in a variety of ways, as long as adequate alleys were left. Galleries, however, were strictly prohibited. They were condemned for various reasons, the most telling being that galleries 'were never admitted into ancient churches, and are therefore an innovation: which alone is enough to condemn them'.[1] Other reasons included the isolation from the rest of the congregation and their 'theatrical appearance'. It was claimed that galleries spoilt the beauty of the building by concealing medieval features and frequently

---

[1] *Ibid.*, p. 6.

weakened the structure. They also reflected an unwillingness to build a 'sufficient number of churches', resulting in crowding more people into the old building.[1]

Organs were also opposed, partly because of their novelty (in small parish churches) and partly because they were suspected of bringing in 'a showy but hollow secularity without a particle of solemnity or devotion' (*E.* III, 3). The Ecclesiologists were convinced 'that church musick is almost exclusively *vocal*', and testified that they 'earnestly deplore and deprecate the introduction of organs into old churches not yet provided with them, or new churches to be built' (*E.* III, 4). The preferred position for the organ was at the west end on the ground level, though if it were desired to have it near the choir, the best place was under a chancel aisle arch (*E.* III, 164). This latter position, of course, is familiar in most churches today.

No matter what the plan or arrangement of the building might be, a basic rule was the prohibition of any imitation materials: 'The first great canon to observed in Church-building is this: LET EVERY MATERIAL EMPLOYED BE REAL.'[2] Nothing provoked the wrath of Ecclesiologists faster than the discovery of deceitful materials. The *Ecclesiologist* announced that the Society had, from the start, been engaged in 'an internecine war against the use of any sort of cement or other sham material' (II, 36). Brick, purporting to be stone, was forbidden. Any architect guilty of such deception could expect to be exposed ruthlessly.

These, then, were the general principles of the Ecclesiologists' code for church architecture. As one of their publications stated: 'Our three leading principles have been, REALITY, THE ABSOLUTE NECESSITY OF A DISTINCT AND SPACIOUS CHANCEL, and THE ABSOLUTE INADMISSIBILITY of PUES and GALLERIES in ANY SHAPE WHATEVER.'[3]

In the building, thus constructed, it was enacted that certain furnishings and arrangements were alone proper. Some of these

---

[1] *Church Enlargement*, p. 6.
[2] *Few Words to Church Builders*, 3rd ed., p. 5.
[3] *Ibid.*, 3rd ed., p. 29.

had great theological significance, others had none. (The Society's 'favourite Catholick arrangement' appears in Plate II.) First and foremost, of course, was the chancel, and it is worth while describing its arrangement in detail:

We suppose then a Chancel raised a single step of six inches' depth at the Chancel-arch, and considerably Eastward of this, on two other steps at least; that it has a plain Altar of substantial material placed lengthwise under the East window, and well furnished with changes of hangings and with Sacred Vessels of proper shape; that the south wall is furnished with a single Piscina to carry off the water in which the Priest has washed his hands before Celebration, and westward of this with three Sedilia, or seats for the Celebrant, Epistler, and Gospeller, constructed, if possible, in the masonry of the wall, if not, consisting of oaken tabernacle-work of appropriate pattern; that the north wall is provided with a Credence, resembling either a table, or a niche or bracket; and that in all other respects our Chancel is entirely free, open, and unoccupied: what more does it require? (*E.* III, 161).

The clergy were to occupy their stalls in the chancel except during Holy Communion when three of them sat in the sedilia. The westernmost stall on the south side formed a reading pew, and the Society instructed that the prayers 'of both matins and evensong ought to be offered by the officiating clergyman from his stall'.[1] Needless to say, three-decker pulpits or any reading desks in the nave were forbidden. Evidently, the people sometimes communicated in the stalls rather than at the rails, for as late as 1844 it was conceded that 'the Communicants may receive in the chancel stalls, coming up for that purpose'.[2]

The altar, of course, formed the focal point of the chancel. The Society definitely preferred 'a fixed Altar of stone', but if a stone altar were impossible, churchmen were instructed 'not to attempt one of wood, but let your Altar be a moveable table' (*E.* III, 6). In its early days, at least, the Society seemed to prefer an altar which was not solid, but open in front, and this is the type they placed in the restored Round Church. Neale stated that 'the proper English method . . . [is] a slab, with octagonal

[1] *Few Words to Church Builders*, 3rd ed., p. 15.   [2] *Ibid.*, p. 27.

shafts as supports'.[1] The Ecclesiologists did not advocate more than one altar in a church. That was a late development of Ritualism. In its early days, the Society was reluctant to sanction a reredos:

> The reredos, dossel, or altar-screen IS AN ORNAMENT, it cannot be too often repeated, FIT ONLY FOR A LARGE CHURCH. It should seldom be erected in a modern building, and then should be of stone: and wherever it is adopted, there must be no niches, unless there are figures. Reredoses for the Commandments are intolerable. Perhaps more money has been wasted on dossels than on any other ornaments of churches.[2]

As to whether the altar was to be enclosed with rails (a very rare feature before the sixteenth century), opinion was divided, although there was no doubt that 'if there be no Roodscreen, Altar-rails are indispensably necessary' (*E.* III, 88). It could be said in favour of altar rails that a few medieval examples existed, that some of the Caroline bishops used them, and that giving the laity communion at the roodscreen was most inconvenient (*E.* I, 59). However, altar rails were considered unnecessary when a roodscreen was present.

The roodscreen was one of the most important items for the Ecclesiologists and their publications constantly advocated it. They seem to have been among the first to promote it. In 1844 it was claimed: 'Till lately, the Cambridge Camden Society stood alone in its insisting on the roodscreen, to separate the Church from the Nave.'[3] The *Hand-Book* applied a 'mystical meaning' to the roodscreen: 'It, as dividing the chancel, which is the Church Triumphant, from the nave, which is the Church Militant, signifies death; and therefore carries the Image [the Rood] of Him Who by His Death hath overcome death . . . the doors always open inwards.'[4] However, the chief reason for advocating the roodscreen was quite functional: 'Its practical use now is the separation of the Clergy from the Laity. . . . And it is to be preserved now on the grand rule, "The chancels shall

---

[1] *Hierologus*, p. 128. [2] *Few Words to Church Builders*, 3rd ed., p. 14.
[3] *Ibid.*, 3rd ed., p. 22. [4] *Hand-Book*, p. 81.

remain as they have done in times past".'[1] Mention has already been made of the fact that the governing theological motif of the Oxford Movement was its high doctrine of the ministry. This conception was very forcefully expressed by the Society in its constant advocacy of the roodscreen:

The worshippers who are to assemble in our church are not all on equality. There are some who are endowed with high privileges as being those consecrated to the immediate service of the sanctuary. In early times so real a thing was the distinction between Clergy and the Laity, that the Church being divided into these two classes, the material edifice displayed a like division: and the Nave and Chancel preach to posterity the sacredness of Holy Orders, and the mutual duties arising from the relation in which the flock stand to their shepherds. . . . After the Reformation the great distinction between Clergy and Laity became lost or undervalued: accordingly the chancel-screens in many places disappeared, as symbolical in their absence as in their existence.[2]

There can be no mistaking the clericalism of this position. It was reiterated constantly that the clergy should sit in the chancel, divided from the laity by the screen, and 'so exhibiting, what is so wholesome for both to remember, the distinction which must exist between the Clergy and their flocks' (*E.* II, 91).

The campaign for roodscreens, however, was quite unsuccessful. As the *Christian Remembrancer* pointed out, roodscreens 'were undoubtedly monastic and conventual appendages to a church, —partitions, in fact, by which the choir, occupied solely by the monks, was shut off from the rest of the church'.[3] Evidently nineteenth-century congregations thought that if their priest were to be removed from his convenient spot in the nave, at least he still ought to be visible. In 1842 the Society spoke of 'the Chancel screen, that most beautiful and Catholick appendage to a church', and inquired: 'Why is it that *not one* modern church has it?'[4] Even churches built by the Society's favourite architects rarely had roodscreens. Anglican Congregations were

---

[1] *Ibid.*, p. 73.   [2] *Durandus*, pp. lvi–lvii.
[3] 'Church Architecture', *Christian Remembrancer*, III (1842), 358.
[4] *Few Words to Church-Builders*, 2nd ed., p. 20.

determined to see and hear their services, but medieval churches had never been designed for this purpose and the roodscreens would have effectively prevented it. The Society's crusade for roodscreens was a failure, and in some instances parishes removed ancient screens when they began using chancels again. With exasperation, the *Ecclesiologist* exclaimed in 1848: 'It is almost useless for us to repeat for the thousandth time, that we consider the screen the proper separation between the clerks and the laity' (IX, 148).

But if they lost the battle for roodscreens, the Ecclesiologists seem to have won almost every other campaign in popularizing the arrangement and furnishings they desired, both of which now appear in almost every Anglican church whatever the style may be. The despised reading pew was replaced by a lectern, and builders were told 'that the lettern [*sic*] for the Holy Bible, whence lessons are read, should be either an eagle or pelican of brass or wood, or made in the simpler form of a double sloping desk' (*E.* III, 164). A litany desk was also necessary: 'The accustomed place then of singing the Litany is ... the Eastern part of the Nave, where the Priest and the quire are to kneel. It follows that in this place a Litany-desk or faldstool is required' (*E.* III, 165). The pulpit is supposed to be at 'the north-west corner of the Chancel-arch ... its most appropriate place'.[1] The traditional spot at the western entrance was frequently advocated for the font. It was to be provided with a proper cover and a padlock. Almost any modern church furnishings catalogue contains examples of the accessories reintroduced or promoted by the Society.

Besides these liturgical objects, the Society devoted its attention to many details of no theological significance whatsoever. They were extremely concerned about roofs, constantly advocating the removal of the plaster ceilings which had been erected in many churches during the eighteenth century, and demanding that the exterior should have a steep pitch. It was felt that 'A high pitched roof is far more essential to the Christian

---

[1] *Churches of Cambridgeshire*, p. 22.

effect of a church than is a tower or spire.'[1] Churches with concealed rafters were subjected to a constant barrage of criticism. Towers, likewise, were subject to review and criticism as to placement, height, openings, and termination. Though no theological motivation can be detected, many items were often censured. In St Paul's Church, Cambridge, 'The huge clock; the disproportionate octagonal Turrets; the great four-centred Belfry windows without cusping or mouldings: . . . the square clerestory windows; the enormous windows in the Aisles; . . . the graduated parapet of the Nave' are among the numerous items called 'quite indefensible', though no theological reason can be found for such criticism (*E.* I, 9). Many such statements, evidently, were based on taste rather than on theological principles, though nothing offended the Ecclesiologists more than to be told that they were ruling on grounds of taste. In one of their many struggles, the Ecclesiologists protested 'most decidedly against the assumption that theirs is simply the province of "taste" ' (*E.* I, 26). Yet, frequently, no other motive can be seen in their arbitrary decisions.

Partly because of their uncritical admiration of things medieval, and partly because of a pronounced theological concept of the distinction of clergy and laity, the Ecclesiologists invented the neo-medieval church plan. The altar at the east end was to be seen throughout the church (despite the roodscreen), but it was to be withdrawn from the congregation by the length of a deep chancel. It was a strange compromise between a conspicuous altar (now become the dominant liturgical centre) and a secluded altar (the sole preserve of the clergy). Clericalism and the common prayer were strangely united in a new invention, the ecclesiological church.

This neo-medieval arrangement was defended in a remarkable paper, entitled 'Moral Effect of Catholick Arrangement, in Promoting Community of Worship' which appeared in the *Ecclesiologist* in 1845. This claimed that the separation of the 'clerks' from the laity encouraged all 'to take their own appro-

---

[1] *Few Words to Church Builders*, 3rd ed., p. 21.

priate share' in worship. 'The not *seeing* the clerks', it asserted, 'need not prevent the congregation taking part in the service which they hear.' The article continued: 'In general we only see one priest in the stalls, . . . but we know that when there are more, they too will sit in clerkly guise. We perceive the reality of the arrangement, and our moral perceptions are satisfied' (IV, 212–13). Exactly what this means is rather mysterious, but evidently it was intended to suggest that the unseen presence of the clergy, in their proper places, helps promote community of worship.

Whatever they thought, the church arrangement championed by the Ecclesiologists belonged neither to the Middle Ages nor to the Reformation. It was a serious misunderstanding of medieval worship to believe that the laity were meant to join in the worship of the clergy in the chancel, especially in the choir offices. According to E. C. Ratcliff, by the thirteenth century it was considered that 'the Offices were pre-eminently the concern of the clergy . . . the Offices ceased to be in practice, if not in theory, the common prayer of the Christian people'.[1] Thus, almost at the inception of the period of gothic building, a clear distinction was made in the facilities for the worship of the laity and that of the clerics—'the interior arrangements of an English medieval parish church were such that the worshipper could see or hear relatively little of the service; the worship, however resplendent and mysterious, lacked that corporateness which all sections in the Church of England believe to be an essential part of liturgy'.[2] The remarks of the *Christian Remembrancer* were succinct and to the point: 'Let then our architectural antiquarians, who would have us build after the manner of the thirteenth and fourteenth centuries, prove to us that we ought to worship after the manner of those centuries.'[3] The Ecclesiologists did not consider this necessary, for they felt the medieval buildings eminently suited for Anglican worship as they desired it. And so the

[1] 'The Choir Offices', in *Liturgy and Worship*, edited by W. K. Lowther Clarke and Charles Harris (London, 1940), pp. 265–6.
[2] Addleshaw and Etchells, p. 15.
[3] 'Styles of Church Architecture', *Christian Remembrancer*, IV (1842), 265.

type of building which the Church of England had developed during the previous two centuries in order that clergy and laity could participate together in worship was to be discarded. It was to be replaced by the double rectangle of chancel and nave, designed to keep clergy and laity apart. Today this neo-medieval arrangement has been adopted throughout the Anglican communion and in many Protestant denominations.

III

The widespread acceptance of the neo-medieval church is due to the remarkable zeal with which the Society proclaimed its new architectural laws. It is safe to say that no university society before or since has campaigned so long and so steadfastly for the adoption of a specific architectural code. That 'dogmatic spirit' which Neale considered 'the life and soul of the *Ecclesiologist* and of the Cambridge Camden Society',[1] was quite apparent in the Society's persistent efforts to establish the principles of correct church-building. Without doubt, this constancy of purpose was the clue to many of the really substantial accomplishments of the Society.

It was not long before the efforts of the Ecclesiologists became worldwide in scope. Boyce reported: 'In fact, it may be said without exaggeration that not only from every part of the British Isles, but from almost every Colony of the British Empire, applications for designs and advice were received by the Committee almost every month without intermission.'[2] As a consequence, the Committee decided 'to select such ancient churches as will, with the least alteration or modification, best suit the requirements of colonial church-building, and to provide tracings from full working-drawings of the same' (*E.* III, 116–7). This proved quite easily done, and North America, Australia, and New Zealand are full of nineteenth-century churches copied from the type advocated by the Ecclesiologists.

Although they did not hesitate in recommending 'the purest

---

[1] *Letters*, p. 93.   [2] *Memorial*, p. 23.

style of Pointed Architecture as the most fitting' in temperate climates, the Committee felt 'the question of the propriety of adapting English Architectural styles to tropical climates one of extreme difficulty'.[1] This provided a continuing theme of discussion in the *Ecclesiologist* and was the subject of a paper by Webb, 'On the Adaptation of Pointed Architecture to Tropical Climates'. The problem, as Webb stated it, was 'the adaptation of Pointed Architecture (assumed to be the Christian style) to every climate'. He went on to say that the Society had received appeals for 'assistance from the Canadas, Bombay, Ceylon, Sierra Leone, the Mauritius, the Himalaya, Tasmania, Guiana, Australia, and New Zealand, and Newfoundland, from Egypt, and from Hong Kong'.[2] Some concessions were to be made in tropical climates. Webb proposed to adopt some of the characteristics of the gothic of southern Europe (thick walls, low roof, vestibules, loggia) in creating a modified gothic.[3] At the Thirteenth Anniversary Meeting (9 June 1852), the cave-like or 'speluncar' style was proposed for tropical areas (*E.* XIII, 276).

Perhaps the most intensive campaign which the Society ever waged was the long battle against pews, a crusade of which it evidently was the originator. The real beginning of the movement to abolish pews appears to have been an address on the 'History of Pews' which Neale delivered at a meeting of the Society on 22 November 1841. This address was supplemented by a report of a sub-committee on the 'Statistics of Pews' on 7 December 1841. The report was bound with the *History of Pews* and both were widely circulated. Neale's work was obviously the result of much documentary study of ecclesiology. It begins with an inquiry: 'For what is the HISTORY OF PUES, but the history of the intrusion of human pride, and selfishness, and indolence, into the worship of God?'[4] The blame for pews is

---

[1] *Report* (1844), p. 29.

[2] *Transactions*, Part III, 218. Graphic evidence as to how seriously the Society's advice was taken in such places can be seen in Basil Clarke's *Anglican Cathedrals Outside the British Isles* (London, 1958). Clarke shows how the neo-medieval church followed the British flag in the nineteenth century.

[3] *Transactions*, Part III, 218.

[4] *History of Pews*, 3rd ed., p. 3.

laid upon the Puritans whom the Society hated passionately. Neale accuses the Puritans of having invented pews so that they could not be presented for such offences as refusing to bow at the name of Jesus, not standing for the *Gloria Patri*, and not kneeling for the communion when distributed in pews. The fact that most pews dated from after the Restoration is explained by saying 'England's character had been puritanized'.[1] The committee investigating the statistics of pews came to the obvious conclusion that pews occupied too much space: 'We repeat it in order that the fact may not be forgotten—20 per cent., or one-fifth of the "available space" in the floor of a church, is lost by the most economical puing.'[2]

This publication was followed by a four-page leaflet, *Twenty-three Reasons for Getting Rid of Church Pews or Pues*, probably by Neale.[3] The reasons are varied:

I.—BECAUSE, in the good old times, when churches were first built, and for many years after, there were no Pues at all.

. . . .

VI.—Because the system of Pues is a selfish and unchristian system.

. . . .

IX.—Because, from the room they take up, the poor, who have no Pues, have often been tempted to leave off going to church, and to go to meeting instead: thus becoming guilty of the fearful sin of schism.

X.—Because they cause more quarrels in a parish than any thing else.

. . . .

XII.—Because Pues, unless they have a faculty, (which very few have) are ILLEGAL.

. . . .

XXIII.—Because they prevent the congregation from seeing or

[1] *Ibid.*, p. 44.   [2] *Ibid.*, p. 59.   [3] Cambridge, n.d.

being seen from the altar; towards which every worshipper ought to be turned.[1]

Eventually the leaflet was renamed *Twenty-Four Reasons*, 'the nuisance of Pue-Openers' being the additional reason. The arguments presented by this propaganda were certainly forceful and convincing. Hope shows the real religious conviction behind the crusade against the Pew system: 'Its being right or wrong is a question of religious character. The solution depends upon the degree in which the Christian Church is realized as "the *communion* of saints".'[2] This, he explains, accounts for the fact that High Churchmen 'have been the foremost in the fight for free and open worship'.

The crusade against pews soon won many adherents. A General Committee on the Pew System and the National Association for Freedom of Worship joined the Ecclesiologists in the cause. Tracts appeared in large numbers, such as one by John W. H. Molyneux entitled *Preaching the Gospel to the Working Classes Impossible under the Pew System*.[3] The *British Critic* commended the Ecclesiologists, calling pews 'the rotten boroughs of our churches'.[4] Francis E. Paget, a member of the Oxford Architectural Society, made pews the subject of a novel, *Milford Malvoisin; or Pews and Pewholders*. He traced the disgraceful origin and shameful history of a particular pew.[5]

With such support, the battle against pews was largely victorious although some parishes withstood the onslaught. A poster was put up in the church at Tuxford, 'calling upon the "Protestants of Tuxford" to arise and defend their sacred rights: . . . your seats to which yourselves and ancestors have liberally contributed, are now to be wrested from you by Jesuitical intolerance' (*E.* II, 101). In less suspicious parishes, the Ecclesiologists proved quite successful as iconoclasts: 'We have known occasions on which our own joy in destroying some of these abominations [pews] has been exceeded by that of the carpenter's

---

[1] *Twenty-three Reasons*, pp. 1–4.
[2] A. J. B. Hope, writing under the pseudonym of 'D. C. L.', *Letters on Church Matters: Reprinted from the 'Morning Chronicle'* (London, 1851–2), 3 vols., III, 60.
[3] London, 1858.   [4] 'Pews', XXXII (1842), 457.   [5] London, 1842.

workman called in to help us in the task' (*E.* II, 3). As a result of such activities, great quantities of fine seventeenth and eighteenth-century woodwork and carving were destroyed. The Ecclesiologists certainly had no more appreciation of Georgian work than the Puritans had had of medieval art. Eighteenth-century funeral monuments (now widely admired) were regarded by the Ecclesiologists as 'eyesores'. It is perhaps only just that some moderns refer to the architecture of the nineteenth century as 'Victorian monstrosities'.

The question of replacing the pews and pens (as large square pews were called) was settled at first by the use of benches. In 1845 the Society began to advocate the use of chairs on the grounds that they were more ancient, cheaper, and less formal (*E.* IV, 270).

After less than a decade of crusading against pews, the Society, pleased with its successes, turned its attention to other related causes. A valiant, but quite unsuccessful, effort was made to teach 'the propriety and necessity of dividing the sexes during the publick offices of the Church' (*E.* V, 41). A campaign was also launched against sepulchral vaults in churchyards as occupying too much room which should be common property. The vaults were likened to pews: 'Vaults, therefore, are pues for dead men, as pues are vaults for living sleepers' (*E.* IV, 258).

The Society also decided, as the next step, to 'ask that our churches, those of them at least which are situated in crowded and poor neighbourhoods, . . . may be daily kept open at stated and convenient hours . . . for the purposes of private devotion' (*E.* XI, 2). The concern that the poor might have some place for private prayer is apparent, as was the fear that pews tended to exclude them from public worship. A very commendable concern for the underprivileged appeared, though political reforms were generally very unpopular among the Ecclesiologists.

The Society adopted many methods in proclaiming its architectural rules. A large collection of drawings and models of buildings worthy of imitation was assembled and made available to interested parties. Some of the drawings were lithographed and sold, with the expectation that they could be copied by architects.[1] An ideal specimen for imitation was offered in a very large folio by the architect George Gordon Place, *Plans, Sections, and Elevations of the Chancel of All Saints' Church, Hawton, Nottinghamshire With Descriptive Account.*[2]

A number of sheets were printed in order to promote reverence among those working in churches. One such poster was directed 'To All Persons Employed in the Restoration of This Church' and pointed out that whistling or any unseemly noise was out of place in the house of God. A similar sheet was provided for those building new churches. Advice was given to bellringers in 'A Few Words to Bellringers' and to sextons in 'Hints on the Well-Keeping & Ordering of Churches, and Their Repairs, Furniture, and Ornaments'.

The influence of the Society was exerted chiefly in its larger publications. The *Ecclesiologist*, especially in its early days, was valiant in condemning unliked practices and praising those who obeyed its dictates. It did this in numerous articles and especially in some constantly recurring features, entitled 'Church Restoration', 'Church Desecration', 'Notices and Answers to Correspondents', 'Ecclesiological Notes', 'Reviews', and 'New Churches'. This last feature was one of the most interesting in the magazine, serving as a means of reviewing as many as twenty or more new buildings in every issue. The *Ecclesiologist* once remarked: 'It is really painful to us to be always finding fault' (IV, 255). But the pain must have been rather mild, for most of the buildings reviewed are condemned; very few met the Society's approval. A typical criticism is short, but to the point: 'TRINITY, POPLAR. This is a Grecian building, standing north and south; the pulpit projects *from the wall immediately over the Altar*, and is formed of Keene's cement; the galleries are

---

[1] These included 'The Interior of S. Sepulchre's Cambridge', 'Stalls and Screenwork in S. Mary's Lancaster', 'A Lithograph of the Font and Cover in the Church of S. Edward the Confessor, Cambridge' published separately and also bound in the *Illustrations of Monumental Brasses*, and 'An Exterior View' of St Sepulchre's Cambridge published separately.

[2] Cambridge, 1845. The chancel is a rich example of Decorated gothic.

supported by cast-iron columns which serve as water-drains! Comments were needless' (I, 20). In its latter years, the *Ecclesiologist* became much less outspoken and sometimes went so far as to say 'we are sorry to see' before damning a new building. By 1848 some pangs of conscience must have bothered the editors. In answer to a correspondent demanding more 'short pithy' items as in former days, the reply was made: 'There is in all sciences, just as much as in human life, a period of maturity graver and deeper than that of youth. The "short pithy" articles to which he refers were suited to our youth. . . . We shall come out with "short pithy" articles when occasion calls for them' (VIII, 326). No apologies were made in the early years, and the magazine consistently advocated the dogmas of ecclesiology with no modifications. Sometimes sarcasm provided an effective weapon as in a sketch entitled 'Rules for Churchwardens, A.D. 1810'. This commented: 'Generally, everything ancient is superstitious, and everything superstitious is popish, and everything popish ought to be annihilated forewith' (IV, 276).

Two interesting and influential volumes were issued by the Society in 1847 and 1856. These are the two parts of the *Instrumenta Ecclesiastica*, originally published serially in small sections. The 'Prefatory Notice' in the first volume describes them well:

The *Instrumenta Ecclesiastica* will be found to contain a variety of working drawings of details and fittings, appertaining to churches and their precincts. The principle of their selection has been to supply in a cheap and convenient form, some of those designs which experience has shown the conductors of the *Ecclesiological late Cambridge Camden Society* to be most generally wanted. Some of the drawings are taken from ancient examples, some are original designs, generally framed in accordance with the suggestions of the Society.[1]

It was hoped that 'with this volume in his hands, and a tolerably intelligent carpenter or mason, no parish-priest can be compelled to insert any barbarism or countenance any disfigurement of his church' (*E.* VII, 233). The two volumes of the *In-*

[1] London, 1847, pages unnumbered.

strumenta Ecclesiastica were the source of many of the Victorian church furnishings common all over the world. It was reported that 'the Society presents a copy of this series to each of the Colonial Bishops'.[1] Such accessories as lecterns, alms chests, biers, wooden porches, pulpits, roof crosses, locks, and many other items are depicted in the seventy-two plates which each volume contains (see Plates III and IV). The Second Series gave several examples of complete buildings, such as a cemetery chapel, schools, and a strange gothic iron church. William Butterfield, the Society's favourite architect, contributed many of the designs and he was assisted in the Second Series by R. C. Carpenter, W. Slater, G. E. Street, and H. Woodyer.

One of the most controversial publications of the Society was *Church Enlargement and Church Arrangement*, probably written by Neale and published in 1843. It was designed for clergymen and intended to benefit those who needed more room for accommodation in their churches. The answer was simple—get rid of pews. But it also went on to counsel 'those who are prompted by their zeal for the honour of GOD's House to take steps towards its restoration to its original beauty, but who feel nevertheless that they are incompetent to direct the work without assistance'.[2] The rest is a foregone conclusion; the full ecclesiological code is spelled out in detail. 'The first thing to be done is scrupulously to restore all the original arrangements of the church, if it be possible.'[3] But Neale admits: 'There are several practical difficulties in the arrangement of an ancient church, . . . though . . . a more self-denying age would think little of them.'[4] These include organs, ninety per cent of which, he estimates, now appear in western galleries. Of course, the galleries had to go. The building was to be filled with stained glass, encaustic tiles, a gilt roodscreen, and painted and frescoed walls. A really pressing need for more space could be satisfied by adding new aisles.

[1] *Report of the Ecclesiological late Cambridge Camden Society, MDCCCXLV–VI* (London, 1846), p. 2.
[2] Cambridge, 1843, p. 3.   [3] *Ibid.*, p. 11.   [4] *Ibid.*, p. 15.

This tract offended one of the Society's vice-presidents, John J. Smith of Gonville and Caius College, who wrote an attack, *A Few Words on the Last Publication of the Cambridge Camden Society*. Smith found *Church Enlargement* 'involving matter seriously objectionable, both in argument and opinion'.[1] The term 'catholick' was used too indiscriminately, there was no need to ' "restore all the original arrangements" ', and there was grave danger in the 'multiplication of externals'. In concluding, Smith avowed that the Committee had mixed ecclesiology 'so implicitly and so subtlely, with the points of religious controversy, as to pervert the influence of the Society to the advancement of a peculiar line of religious profession'.[2] Smith resigned as vice-president and probably no one was sorry to see him leave.

Undoubtedly the most successful publications of the Society, and probably the best means of spreading its dogmas, were the many varieties of the 'Few Words' series. Without much doubt, all four tracts came from Neale's pen. The briefest of these was *A Few Words to the Parish Clerks and Sextons of Country Parishes*.[3] It states: 'I hope that what I am going to say may help you to know your duty, and stir you up to do it.'[4] Then follows much advice about keeping the church clean, removing whitewash, ventilating the church, escorting visitors through the building (without lying to them about its history—they might be Ecclesiologists), and preventing the theft of stained glass, tiles and brasses.

This was a relatively innocuous work, but the *Few Words to Church Builders*[5] was less so. Briggs says that the third edition of this tract 'did more harm to church restoration in the next thirty years than any other publication and led to most of Sir Gilbert Scott's acts of "vandalism" '.[6] Pugin, however, called it

[1] Cambridge, 1843, p. 3.   [2] P. 19.
[3] Three editions appeared: two at Cambridge in 1843 and one in London, 1846.
[4] 3rd ed., p. 3.
[5] Three editions: first, Cambridge, 1841 (price sixpence) and another printing (price one shilling); second edition with *An Appendix* (Cambridge, 1842); third edition (Cambridge, 1844). The *Appendix* was also published separately in 1841.
[6] *Goths and Vandals: A Study of the Destruction, Neglect, and Preservation of Historic Buildings in England* (London, 1952), p. 167.

'the first distinct publication which has issued from the present Establishment, in which ecclesiastical architecture is viewed in its true light'.[1] Neale began by stating that he wished 'to bring out of the stores of the Society a larger number of examples for the illustration of his remarks, than would be easily procured by an individual'.[2] It was this that made the work so dangerous. A large portion of the second and third editions was an Appendix of 'Lists of Windows, Fonts, and Roodscreens Intended to Serve as Models'. Hundreds of approved specimens were listed and evidently copied constantly by architects. The text carried the usual ecclesiological doctrines, from the altar to western triplets. The third edition claimed credit for part of the 'spread of true principles', but conceded that 'learning while we were teaching, some of our statements were rather hasty, and it may be that our advice, in a few instances, shewed more good will than good taste'[3], an interesting apology. However, it was hoped that the 'present edition . . . has been thoroughly corrected'.

The most important publications were *A Few Words to Churchwardens on Churches and Church Ornaments: No. I, Suited to Country Parishes* and its companion tract, *No. II, Suited to Town and Manufacturing Parishes.* Fourteen editions of Part I were required and seven of Part II.[4] These pamphlets were written for even the 'most illiterate' of churchwardens. The author, who described himself as 'but a way-faring man that go about visiting churches for the love of HIM Who is worshipped in them', undertook to advise churchwardens 'of that part of your duties which has to do with the Parish church'.[5] He counsels good care of the building, keeping out the damp, ridding it of pews, ending the keeping of 'hen-coops' in the churchyard, and avoiding a great variety of other offences against propriety. Any attempt to 'beautify' the building is cautioned against: 'Indeed you cannot

---

[1] *Present State of Ecclesiastical Architecture in England*, p. 61.
[2] 2nd ed., p. 3.
[3] 3rd ed., p. 3.
[4] Part I: Cambridge, 1841 (10 editions); 1842 (2); 1843; and London, 1846. Part II: Cambridge, 1841 (3); 1842 (2); 1843; and London, 1851.
[5] Part I, 12th ed., p. 2.

be too much on your guard against every kind of change if you would not have your church spoilt. What may seem to you an improvement may be, and most likely will, the very contrary.'[1] The usual arguments against pews, galleries, and three-decker pulpits are advanced, and evidently there was no harm in changing these. The restoration of the medieval practices and furnishings is, of course, advocated. Part II was addressed to a somewhat more sophisticated audience and catalogues a number of faults actually existing in town churches. The 'falling off from the old ways of Church-worship, and thereby of Church-feeling' is blamed on pews.[2] Advice is given on singing, candles, aisles, and a vast assortment of other concerns.

It is difficult to overestimate the importance of the *Few Words to Churchwardens* in the Ecclesiologists' campaigns. Pugin 'strongly recommended' them to Roman Catholics for 'the high Catholic view in which these writers regard the material structure of the ancient churches'.[3] Both publications were an instant success. It was reported of Part I that 'About 5,000 copies have been sold in six weeks', and that '13,000 copies had been circulated in 1843'.[4] Probably a copy reached almost every parish in England. The effect was drastic and helps account for the great changes made in every part of the kingdom during the early years of Victoria's reign.

Such success brought trouble, for Neale was probably the least judicious member of the Society. On 7 December 1841 Thorp wrote Neale, then Chairman of Committees:

I feel that I have myself incurred a grave responsibility with respect to these Publications [the Society's tracts] and very imperfectly fulfilled the censorial office which has always been allowed to me. . . .

I conceive it to be my duty, in that station in which the Society has placed me, to recommend an immediate revision of the Tracts to Churchwardens and Church Builders, with a view to their publication hereafter in such amended form as, consistently with the fundamental principles of our Society, shall leave no room for com-

---

[1] *Ibid.*, p. 8.   [2] Part II, 5th ed., p. 5.   [3] *Present State*, p. 56.
[4] *Report*, 1841, p. 25, and *A Statement of Particulars Connected with the Restoration of the Round Church* (Cambridge, 1845), p. 13.

plaint on the part of our Ecclesiastical superiors. The points to which, without entering into detail, I may now advert generally as likely to come under revision, are the symbolizing tone pervading these Tracts, and the use, however innocent and I believe justifiable, of some terms and expressions which, in the present state of ignorance with respect to Church matters and even to Church principles, are calculated to excite apprehension in many honest but uneducated minds.[1]

Thorp announced that he would not attend the Committee meeting scheduled for that evening in order to insure free discussion of the matter. The result was that it was determined that Thorp and Dr Mill should rewrite the offending pamphlets. The changes in the 1842 editions of the tracts directed to churchwardens and church-builders are surprisingly minor. But they are none the less significant, for they show what gave offence. The *Few Words to Church Builders* announces the author's 'intention to dwell on the Catholick . . . principles which should influence the building of a church' in the first edition, but in the second he has become content 'to dwell on the Ecclesiastical . . . principles which are concerned in the building of a church'.[2] Instead of reading that the 'visible building symbolizes the Holy Catholic Church' we are told that in it 'ancient architects recognized an emblem of the Holy Catholic Church'.[3] Such changes evidently did nothing to endanger the popularity of the tracts but the episode was prophetic of future disturbances.

[1] Letter from Thorp to Neale, printed and preserved in the John Willis Clark Cambridge Collection in the University Library, Cambridge.
[2] *Few Words to Church Builders*, first and second editions, p. 3.
[3] *Ibid.*, p. 5.

CHAPTER V

ATTACKS, COUNTERATTACKS, AND THE CRISIS OF 1845

I

It is not surprising that the dictums of the Cambridge Camden Society, so strange and new to a generation satisfied with neat classical churches, should provoke controversy. The vigour and fervour with which these new concepts of church-building were maintained ensured disputes. Indeed, they were not long in beginning. No sooner had the *Ecclesiologist* commenced publication (November 1841), than the first issue stirred up a mutiny within the Society's membership.

The trouble was over a searing review, entitled 'New Churches', which the *Ecclesiologist* had carried regarding St Paul's Church, a building recently erected in Cambridge.[1] This structure, built in a crowded and churchless district of Cambridge, was more or less of a red brick version of St Mary the Great, the University Church. The article, which evidently had not received the approval of the entire committee, embarrassed or shocked people according to their sympathies. There was one exception; Pugin was ecstatic over the piece since it represented an affirmation of his own views and practised the same reckless denunciation of the incompetent. So delighted was Pugin, that when the *Ecclesiologist* was forced to republish the issue with a different essay substituted, he reprinted the original review in full in the *Present State of Ecclesiastical Architecture in England*. He did so for two reasons, neither of which was calculated to win the Society friends, 'on account of its being the very best description of a Protestant church that has yet appeared; and

---

[1] Built in 1841 by Ambrose Poynter, architect also of Christ Church (1839) and St Andrew the Great (1842–3), both in Cambridge.

secondly, . . . [because unfortunately] some black sheep in the society' had forced its withdrawal.[1]

The article itself reveals the full criteria of the Ecclesiologists. The style was wrong: 'The church is of no particular style or shape; but it may be described as a conspicuous red brick building, of something between Elizabethan and debased perpendicular architecture' (I, 9).[2] The architect has trespassed in 'the fearless introduction of several remarkable varieties and peculiarities of arrangement, which are strictly original conceptions' (I, 9). Details were bad, the roof being 'a kind of flat deal ceiling, . . . as gay as the roof of the saloon in a first-rate steam ship' (I, 10–11). But the real offence was the east end:

As the altar is not yet put up, and probably not yet thought of, we cannot say where it will be placed; but we have been unable, upon the closest inspection, to discover any place adapted for its reception: indeed, we are inclined to fear that it has been forgotten altogether. The elevation of the east end is rather peculiar. There is *no chancel whatever*; not even the smallest recess as an apology for one (I, 11).

In short, the building presented 'a thoroughly correct and comprehensive idea of a CHEAP CHURCH OF THE NINETEENTH CENTURY' (I, 11). It certainly was not correct according to the standards of the Society. Subsequently the Church was provided with a chancel.

This tirade was too much for several of the most prominent members of the Society. They submitted a 'Remonstrance' to the Committee. As printed in the second issue of the *Ecclesiologist*, it objected to the probable effect of the review in discouraging new church-building, and complained of the 'flippant tone' of the paper (I, 25). But the real objection was deeper—

[1] *Present State*, p. 91. Pugin continues: 'At all events the admirable remarks which drew forth this protestation will not be consigned to oblivion; they are here reproduced in full, and we hope they will be printed on a fly-sheet and circulated at architectural societies, competition committees, and church-building meetings, as Methodist sabbath-breaking denunciations are distributed in tea-gardens and steam-boats; they should be headed "*Beware of the Camden*", and hung up *in terrorem* in every church-competing architect's office, to deter those gentlemen from proceeding in the present wretched system, and lead them, if possible, into the old track.'

[2] Excerpts are from the first issue as originally printed.

we feel the more regret at observing such attempts as these to give a party character to its publications. We fear from this and other indications, that there exists in some quarters a desire to convert the Society into an engine of polemical theology, instead of an instrument for promoting the study and the practice of Ecclesiastical Architecture. We desire, therefore, to remind the Committee that it is their duty to guard against such a prostitution of its influence to purposes alien from its design . . . it is, therefore, in the highest degree improper that any school of religious belief which is by the Church permitted to exist within her body, should, in our publications, be spoken of with disrespect (1, 25).

This was signed by Professor Willis (a vice-president of the Society) and eleven others, some of them distinguished members of the University. They had raised the theological question, demonstrating the real grounds for the review's offensiveness.

In their reply, the Committee carefully avoided the real issue. Self-righteously the members of the Committee pointed out that the 'rules formed upon experience and investigation of our Rubrics and Canons, they are not at liberty to repudiate' (*E.* 1, 26). They did not bother to admit that their interpretations of the rubrics and canons were at considerable variance from the general practice of the rest of the Church of England at the time. The Committee has desired, it said, 'to make taste subservient . . . to the promotion of sound religion', fearing the noxious influence of bad examples (*E.* 1, 26). Furthermore, it is a matter of utmost significance when a new congregation 'is brought together in a place where the sacraments can scarcely be decently and rubrically administered, and which possibly presents to the unlearned parishioner no mark of distinction from some neighbouring conventicle' (*E.* 1, 26–7). The Committee members denied having a theological bias, but accused the remonstrants with 'insinuating that there is a party in the Church whose symbol is the disregard of Altars' (*E.* 1, 27). It was the Committee's intention to correct architectural mistakes, 'and if the architect has felt himself aggrieved by it [the review], the Committee are ready to make amends, . . . by offering their suggestions on the plan of a third church, which . . . he has been employed to build in this town' (*E.* I, 27).[1] As a further gesture, the Committee has 'resolved to republish the first number of *The Ecclesiologist*, omitting the article which has been objected to, and substituting for it such a description of the church . . . as in manner as well as matter shall afford no just ground of complaint or animadversion' (*E.* I, 28).

The revised version is mild only in comparison to its predecessor. The high ground of conformity to the rubrics is taken, though it is somewhat mysterious why so much space is devoted to condemning the design of the tower, the windows, and the nave parapet. Great expense, we are told, is not necessary: 'There is therefore no reason *à priori* why a church which costs £5000 should not, *so far as it goes*, be as good a design, and built with as true a feeling of the beautiful and Catholick, as Lincoln Minster itself' (*E.* I, 10, revised version). Certainly the use of 'Debased Perpendicular' is inexcusable, for Early English could have been employed as cheaply. Modern church-builders are blamed for building showy churches with towers instead of chancels. 'A cheap church', it is stated, 'is one which makes the greatest show for the least money' (*E.* I, 11). But there is yet hope 'that the sun of Ecclesiastical Architecture, after suffering a long eclipse, is again beginning to shine', and a future generation may 'emulate those glorious conceptions, the one the most sublime, the other the most beautiful that ever entered into the human mind, the West Front of Peterborough, and the Angels' Choir at Lincoln' (*E.* I, 11).

Before the controversy over St Paul's had ended, another had begun, and this was to be the pattern of the next four years in Cambridge. At the 6 December 1841 meeting of the Society, it was reported that the Bishop of London (Charles James Blom-

---

[1] The reference is probably to St Andrew the Great, Poynter's third church in Cambridge, built 1842–3. Evidently the Society's generous offer was not accepted, for the *Ecclesiologist*'s review of the building in 1843 is not exactly complimentary: 'And we deeply regret that so miserable and meagre a specimen of modern church-building should ever have been substituted for an ancient parish church in the very heart of our University. The inside could hardly be worse, if the object of the architect had been to make every thing in it as incorrect and unchurchlike as he possibly could' (II, 137).

field) had asked 'that his name should be erased from the list of patrons, on the ground of objections to one of the Society's Tracts' (*E*. I, 24). Without doubt it was Bishop Blomfield's withdrawal which prompted Thorp's letter the following day suggesting to Neale that *A Few Words to Churchwardens* and *A Few Words to Church Builders* be revised. Thorp had not been especially troubled by the objections to the St Paul's article:

But when a Bishop of our Church, . . . takes exception to matters published by us in the name of the Society of which he is a Patron; . . . the very fact of our Publications having been misapprehended in such a quarter suggests the duty of considering by what fault we have left room for misapprehensions in *any* quarter, and how they are to be removed.[1]

The year 1841 had been the Society's most active and successful to date. But it was also the year of Newman's Tract 90 and the witch-hunting had begun. Henceforth the pursuit of ecclesiology was to be anything but a peaceful pastime. A distinguished professor at Cambridge was convinced that it would 'lead to great and violent political commotion, and, it may be, to distress and bloodshed'.[2] Though the Regius Professor of Hebrew proved to be a poor prophet, the Society did become the object of many violent attacks and usually replied to its assailants vigorously. Assaults came from two directions; both architects and clergymen were upset by the activities of the Society.

II

Art historians had been among the first to feel the smart of the Society's criticism. Only a small minority of the Ecclesiologists were architects, but many of them were amateur art historians. Even the *Ecclesiologist* once admitted that it was 'an Art-journal' (IX, 209). Those art historians who did not conform to the standards of the Ecclesiologists were subject to scorn and ridi-

[1] Letter to Neale, John Willis Clark Cambridge Collection.
[2] [Samuel Lee], *A Letter to the Venerable Archdeacon Thorp, President of the Camden Society, on its Late Re-organization and Apparent Objects* (London, [1845]), p. 23.

cule. E. A. Freeman of Oxford had the impudence to advocate the condemned perpendicular style, to propose his own nomenclature for the gothic styles, and to criticize the symbolism of Durandus as one of 'merely arbitrary association'. But he was promptly taken to task for these heresies (*E.* v, 217). The case of Professor Charles Robert Cockerell of Oxford was more serious, he being an architect as well as art historian. His great sin was that although he could write important treatises on medieval architecture, he considered 'the best form and style is the Grecian, as revived by Wren!' and designed buildings in accordance with this heretical belief (*E.* III, 38). Furthermore, he had the audacity to suggest that 'the taste of the day, *which leans to the Roman Catholic form*, the *Basilica*, [is] suited to a demonstrative form of worship, rather than the auditorium required by our ritual' (*E.* III, 40). But the *Ecclesiologist* got even. A new church by Cockerell (St Bartholomew's, Moor Lane) was described as 'disgraceful to the age and city in which it is built', and declared to be 'designed in utter defiance of any art' (VIII, 54).

Professor Cockerell was not the only rogue among architects, though perhaps the most erudite one. The Ecclesiologists frequently found it necessary to censure the whole architectural profession. Neale exclaimed: 'Doubtless, we never shall have churches worthy of the name, till our architects act somewhat more in the spirit of their predecessors.'[1] The ideal architect was pictured as 'a single pious and laborious artist, alone, pondering deeply over his duty to do his utmost for the service of God's holy religion, and obtaining by devout exercises of mind a semi-inspiration for his holy taste' (*E.* IV, 277). Needless to say, few nineteenth-century architects fitted this concept. The blame was laid largely on architectural competitions: 'But whatever may be the merits of this fashion generally, yet, when applied to churches, either new or old, it becomes so dangerous and mischievous, that it is a matter of high importance to show

[1] *Hierologus*, p. 124. Pugin had come to the same conclusion years before in the first edition of *Contrasts*.

some reasons for rejecting it, and recommend some less objectionable plan for adoption' (*E.* I, 69). Scarcely less evil was the 'practice of architects to combine secular with ecclesiastical works' (*E.* v, 40). The translators of Durandus were certain that no 'Churchman should allow himself to build a conventicle, and even sometimes to prostitute the speaking architecture of the Church to her bitterest enemies'.[1]

The Society's criticism of architects became much more explicit than mere generalities. The Ecclesiologists were rarely guilty of understatement, but one occurred in the president's report in 1842: 'Till architects . . . take more generally their view of what is essential to Church Architecture from a point analogous to that assumed and insisted on by ourselves, . . . it is not to be expected but that there should be many, . . . who will indignantly repel the presumptuous intrusion into their domain of a body not exclusively professional.'[2] Certainly the actions of the Society could hardly have been less likely to produce good feelings among architects.

Without much doubt, the most provocative activity of the Society was its practice of reviewing new churches and church restorations. 'We claim', the *Ecclesiologist* noted, 'the right of freely commenting on views of churches which may fall in our way' (x, 433). Full use was made of this assumed right. In the reviews of new churches there are few kind words, but many harsh ones. One new church was greeted with the words: 'We have seldom seen a more worthless design' (VIII, 109). Another was described as being, 'even when compared with other modern churches, peculiarly miserable' (I, 141). Christ Church, Streatham, a building by W. J. Wild which has proved agreeable to modern taste, was said to 'express only the spirit of a false religion' (I, 20). Smooth words were not meted out to many church restorers either: 'We only know Mr Gough by his results, but these results justify us in asserting that we believe that in these days of architectural improvement, it would have been difficult to have found any other person who could have

---

[1] *Durandus*, p. xxii.   [2] *Report* (1842), p. 8.

so completely succeeded in doing badly' (x, 71). Some of these statements were partially justified, but they were not of the kind to win friends for the Society. Much later, Hope claimed that he wrote many of these 'anonymous critiques of bad new churches'.[1]

It is not surprising that some architects rebelled. A Mr Flint of Leicester wrote an accusing letter. It was reported: 'Mr Flint has dragged in polemical theology, as the cause of our supposed "malevolence" and "mendacity": we deny the charge in the most unqualified way. Nor should Mr Flint accuse us of "personal abuse"' (*E.* vii, 36). A certain Mr Elliott, aggrieved by the *Ecclesiologist*'s criticism of his efforts, had 'discovered that those who do not avail themselves of his services are Papists; and that long chancels ought properly to be called *transubstantiators*'. The editors took this in their stride: 'We hope that, in his next church, Mr Elliott will build a transubstantiator; and, in his next correspondence, will preserve his temper' (*E.* ix, 272).

It is most surprising, however, how successful the *Ecclesiologist*'s criticism proved. Comments frequently appear in the *Ecclesiologist* to the effect that 'we are glad to hear that the ground-plan has been altered in compliance with the suggestions of the Society' (i, 197). Even more telling are the frequent comments in issues following reviews of plans: 'We have been informed that most of the points in the proposed church at Westminster, animadverted upon in our last number, have been since altered by the architect' (i, 179). Whether such alterations came about because of changed convictions, or through sheer fear of the Society's power, it is clear that the Ecclesiologists were becoming influential.

Perhaps even more distressing to many architects was the opinion which the Society seemed to form of individual architects—sometimes, it would seem, irrespective of their work. So bold did the *Ecclesiologist* become, that in the index of its third volume it listed 'Architects approved:—Mr. Allen, Mr. Butter-

[1] *The Book of The Beresford Hopes*, p. 232.

field, Mr. Carpenter, Mr. Derrick, Mr. Ferrey, Mr. Harrison, Mr. Hayward, Mr. Kirk, Mr. Sharpe', and described as 'Architects condemned:—Mr. Barry, Mr. Blore, Mr. Carver, Mr. Cottingham, Mr. Kennedy'. 'Mr. Barry', one may assume, was no less distinguished an individual than the architect of the Houses of Parliament. With the exceptions of Butterfield, Carpenter, and Ferrey, the other 'Architects approved' have long since been relegated to the category of minor architects.

William Butterfield (1814–1900) and Richard Cromwell Carpenter (1812–55) were the Society's favourites among the chosen few. So partial did they become to these two that they were allowed the liberty to do what was forbidden to other architects—to experiment. A few others managed to retain the favour of the Ecclesiologists. These men, mostly somewhat younger, included George Edmund Street, John L. Pearson, George F. Bodley, William Slater, William Burges, and Anthony Salvin. It was inevitable that the selection of a few men on what sometimes seemed purely arbitrary grounds should offend other architects. No one resented this preference for others more keenly (and audibly) than Sir George Gilbert Scott (1811–78). Scott, who was very popular in his lifetime, built and restored literally hundreds of churches. He acknowledged a great indebtedness to the Society, admitting that previous to learning their principles 'no idea of ecclesiastical arrangement, or ritual propriety, had even crossed my mind'.[1] But about 1841, Scott met Webb:

Mr. Webb took advantage of the occasion to lecture me on church architecture in general, on the necessity of chancels, &c. &c. I at once saw that he was right, and became a reader of the 'Ecclesiologist'. Pugin's articles excited me almost to fury, and I suddenly found myself like a person awakened from a long feverish dream, which had rendered him unconscious of what was going on about him.[2]

[1] *Personal and Professional Recollections*, p. 86. This is borne out in a review of nine of Scott's earliest churches published in the *Ecclesiologist*. Five of these had 'no Chancel whatever' (I, 56). Scott admitted his 'grave idea being that this feature was obsolete' (*Recollections*, p. 86).

[2] *Ibid.*, p. 88.

Scott now had a complete architectural code supplied him, with authority ready for each detail.

But to his very pronounced chagrin, he did not receive the acceptance which he desired from the Ecclesiologists:

I may here mention that during this period [early 1840's] the Cambridge Camden Society, with many of whose views I strongly sympathized, and who had been at one time most friendly, had suddenly, and with no reason that I could ever discover, become my most determined opponents. My subsequent success was, for many years, in spite of every effort on their part to put me down by criticisms of the most galling character. No matter how strenuous my endeavours at improvement, everything was met by them with scorn and contumely.[1]

Scott was unduly sensitive to criticism and tried to rationalize about it:

I suppose that I was not thought a sufficiently high churchman, and as they fell in at the time with my very excellent friends Carpenter and Butterfield, they naturally took them under their wing. This no one could complain of: but the attempt to elevate them, by the systematic depreciation of another equally zealous labourer in the same vineyard, was anything but fair. . . . I therefore bore with their injustice patiently, chiefly grieving that the leading advocates of so great and good a cause should not act on principles better calculated to recommend it to the moral perception of the public.[2]

Scott, however, was guilty of one major offence, and evidently the Society never forgave him for it. In 1844 he entered and won a competition to build a large Lutheran Church in Hamburg, the Nicholai-Kirche. The victory of a foreign architect was a considerable honour, but the *Ecclesiologist* saw to it that Scott did not enjoy it long. Probably the Ecclesiologists knew

---

[1] *Recollections*, p. 103. This is not entirely true. A careful reading of the *Ecclesiologist's* reviews of Scott's churches reveals that his work was generally approved and frequently commended. It had too little originality to offend the Ecclesiologists very much. Scott, on the other hand, considered himself a great architect, deserving nothing but praise.

[2] *Ibid.*, pp. 104–5. Scott obviously differed in churchmanship. He accused the Society of having an excessive tendency 'towards an imitation of obsolete ritualism' (p. 105).

very little about Lutheranism, but they did know that it was heretical and schismatic.[1] Scott was severely rebuked:

But the question arises, how must we characterize the spirit that prostitutes Christian architecture to such an use? If this art means anything,—if it is not a hollow mocking of beauty,—a body without a spirit,—then it symbolizes the whole substance of Catholick teaching, the whole analogy of the Faith. How absurd then, in the first place, to apply it to those who reject that teaching and that faith! ... Truly absurd is this, in an aesthetical point of view; and what in a moral? ... We do earnestly trust that Mr. Scott's example will not be followed. We are sure that the temporal gains of such a contract are a miserable substitute indeed for its unreality, and,—we must say it,—its sin (*E.* IV, 184).

Scott could not take such criticism peacefully. He wrote 'a formal defence' which the *Ecclesiologist* refused to print, but which (with considerable theological acumen) showed that the Augsburg Confession was no less Catholic than the Thirty-nine Articles, that the Lutherans were orthodox on Baptism and the Trinity, and furthermore that they had preserved medieval church furnishings much more carefully than Anglicans.[2] The *Ecclesiologist* ignored Scott's plea and inquired: 'Is a body in separation from Christendom Catholic? Is a body in a rebellion against Bishops, Apostolic?' (IV, 243).

The Ecclesiologists, as Scott learned, demanded obedience, totally and unconditionally. When they changed their mind on any subject, architects were supposed to do likewise. Scott's objection must have been felt by many other architects: 'What I do protest against, is the custom of taking the cue from some self-elevating leader of their own, and, whatever the circumstances may be, treating with pitying scorn every one who does not chance to fall in with the new rule or opinion.'[3]

[1] Brilioth remarks that Newman 'completely escaped Lutheran influence, and all the more easily as he never knew Luther's language'. Tractarian and Ecclesiologist constantly regarded Calvinism and Protestantism as practically synonymous. Cf. Yngve Brilioth, *The Anglican Revival: Studies in the Oxford Movement* (London, 1925), p. 35.
[2] *Recollections*, p. 134.
[3] *Ibid.*, p. 207. According to Scott, 'even Pugin himself could not escape their lash, his single sin being his independent existence. ... [The Society] was

Scott's complaints, though heartfelt, were based on purely personal grievances. The entire profession, however, found a valiant defender in a publication edited and published by a London publisher, John Weale. The *Quarterly Papers on Architecture* appeared in four large illustrated volumes in the years 1844 and 1845. These were crucial years in the Society's career and Weale did what he could to make things more difficult for the Ecclesiologists. The publication spoke for all architects: 'In this age, when everybody must meddle with his neighbour's business, and fancies he knows it much better than the man does himself; no set of persons have suffered more, from the interference and dictation of their neighbours, than the architects.'[1] Had there been any doubt as to whom this referred, it would have been dispelled by an anonymous broadside in Volume II, possibly by George Wightwick, a professional architect. It launches out—

we feel it a duty, at least on the score of professional chivalry to break a lance with that grand high church champion, who, bearing on his shield the words 'DIOCESAN ARCHITECTURAL SOCIETY', assumes to himself the absolute right of critical dictation as it regards the general form and the component details of the English Christian Temple— now and hereafter—to be built.[2]

The source of these dictates was clearly perceived: 'The exact parallel growth of the Oxford Tracts and the clerico-architectural Treatises, affords at least a very plausible reason for concluding that the seed from which they have sprung is of the like quality.'[3] Such a condition, 'it is the duty of every man who values the freedom of his conscience, or who will persist in the (possibly erroneous) cry of "No Popery", to prevent'.[4] Having diagnosed the disease, the treatment it gets is severe:

naturally somewhat intoxicated by success, and [was tempted] . . . to estimate persons rather by their loyalty than by their merits' (p. 106).

[1] 'Review. Publications of the Oxford Architectural Society', *Quarterly Papers on Architecture*, IV (1845), 1. The same writer asks: 'Why are architects the only set of men who are to be stuck up to throw mud at? . . . anybody who has read Rickman, or Aunt Elinor, is qualified to criticize and dictate to them' (pp. 6–7).

[2] 'On the Present Condition and Prospects of Architecture in England', II (1844), 1.

[3] *Ibid.*, p. 10.   [4] *Ibid.*, p. 10.

Impotent incipiency of a bastard superstition! Hopeless tyranny of English church parsondom, seeking, under the banners of architecture, to revive—not the power of the Pope—but the power of Popery in its own body! Sad acknowledgement of a want of vitality in Church of Englandism,—of utter despair in its originative influence upon the noble art of architecture!

. . . we have no hesitation in saying, that if the arts are to be priest-ridden, we had rather have our arch-hierarch enthroned at Rome than at Canterbury. We trust, however, that the day is approaching . . . when the priest will be too busied with practical religion to have any time for practical architecture.[1]

The author of this violent prose, however, had a very practical solution. He simply stated that 'the grand and imperative principle of all architectural merits' was 'fitness to existing condition, not to fashions passed away'.[2] It was far more reasonable for architects to have 'a perfectly honest regard to CONVENIENCE, and a strict adherence to truth-telling EXPRESSION' than that they be subject to the 'dictation and peculiar employment of the self constituted critical conclaves'.[3] A very practical result would ensue: 'Our Protestant churches and chapels will cease to be the models of papal *spectatories*, and will assume an ecclesiastical form of *auditory*, suitable to the accommodation of not more than as many persons as can clearly see and hear the officiating minister in the pulpit, desk, or at the communion table.'[4] Clearly the author is in favour of building all churches of gothic, but he hopes that 'we shall cease to confound the *quaint* with the beautiful, and to mistake antiquarianism for art'.[5] This can be done by ceasing to imitate the medieval examples which, after all, were largely a result of superstitious piety. If this happens, in less than fifty years it will be found that 'amateurs [have been]

---

[1] *Ibid.*, p. 2. Several years later, a writer in the *Eclectic Review* reflected the same sentiments: 'This party [the Ecclesiologists], indeed, has been characterized as much by its petty pedantry, its arrogance, and ill-considered positiveness of assertion, as by its love of ancient art. . . . To the cause of architectural revival abstractedly, this pseudo-Romanism of a party aiming to forward it, cannot but have produced evil. The question is properly a purely artistic one. As such it should be viewed' ('The Literature of Gothic Architecture', *Eclectic Review*, xxv (1849), 37).
[2] 'On the Present Condition and Prospects of Architecture in England', p. 3.
[3] *Ibid.*, p. 3. [4] *Ibid.*, p. 12. [5] *Ibid.*, p. 13.

hushed into confiding and modest acquiescence . . . and Camdenism will have gone the way of other Old-womanisms'.[1]

Such criticism could not be ignored, and the *Ecclesiologist*
reviewed the first parts of the *Quarterly Papers* in 1844. Some of
the more telling criticisms were passed over as 'a disgrace to the
publication in which they are allowed to appear' (III, 122). But
many are answered most defiantly:

> The dislike of the writer towards 'the self-constituted critical con-
> claves', or Architectural Societies is most amusing. Less prejudiced
> persons, we believe, would not hesitate to attribute to them in some
> considerable degree the general spread of those truer principles of
> taste, by which the now exploded productions of the paganizing
> professors just mentioned [Nash, Soane, Vanbrugh] have been
> tested and found altogether wanting. Architects *cannot* now run riot
> in their individual fancies, because the 'treatises church gothical' of
> which the writer speaks with such contempt have done much to open
> the eyes of their employers. . . . And to the establishment of Archi-
> tectural Societies not only the existence of such treatises, but the
> guidance of the publick taste in the right direction is very obviously
> due (III, 122–3).

The *Quarterly Papers* was also condemned for evincing 'a mere
cold antiquarianism' by publishing disquisitions on such a
pagan topic as 'the flutings of Dorick columns' side by side with
an account of the restoration of the medieval Temple Church
(III, 123). The reviewer concluded: 'Architecture cannot be
viewed *religiously* (which from the very nature and origin of all
architecture is the only proper and even reasonable view of it)
by those whose judgment is thus warped and diverted from the
forms and developments with which *their* religion has alone the
smallest association' (III, 123).

The next round brought forth an article in the *Quarterly
Papers* bearing the name of George Wightwick. He admitted:
'The respect due to Antiquity is undeniable; but when . . . we
arrogate to ourselves omniscience on the strength of that respect,
we do indeed look most "saucily" upon the altered circum-

[1] *Ibid.*, p. 16.

stances and increased public intelligence of modern times.'[1] He argued that medieval churches were not suited to Protestant worship in which all must see and hear the service. Wightwick pointed out that 'the only "faithful" Gothic structures now erecting . . . are the Romish churches and chapels . . . [in which] the principles laid down by Mr Pugin are honestly carried out'.[2] In these churches everything was useful, but many of their accessories would be useless in Anglican churches.

Wightwick ridicules the Ecclesiologists' statement: '*If we must be Utilitarians, it follows of necessity that we shall never be good architects*', showing that 'the old Gothic architects' were very utilitarian.[3] 'CONVENIENCE and EXPRESSION' are the professed keynotes of Wightwick's architecture. To illustrate this, he had designed a gothic 'Protestant Cathedral' illustrated by four plates in Volume I of the *Quarterly Papers*.[4] Since he had had the indelicacy to refer to internal struggles in the Society and also to reprint a letter from Montalembert condemning the Ecclesiologists, vengeance was sure to follow. It appeared in the form of a blistering review of his articles and designs for the Cathedral. Both were treated mercilessly, and the crossing tower, with some truth, was condemned as 'the most hideous thing eyes ever beheld' (*E.* IV, 78). Despite the Society's best efforts, utility appears more important to modern eyes than correctness. Though the invectives of the *Ecclesiologist* were sharper, Wightwick would seem to have won the debate on the grounds of sheer common sense.

III

As has been shown, it was quite obvious to many architects that the Society had a very distinct theological position. Before long,

---

[1] 'Modern English Gothic Architecture', *Quarterly Papers*, III (1845), 1.
[2] *Ibid.*, p. 11.   [3] *Ibid.*, p. 5, quoting from *E.* III, 71.
[4] Although a pupil of Soane's, Wightwick was a gothicist. His cathedral design is truly remarkable. It represents a cruciform building with a short chancel and a ten-sided chapter house east of it. There are two west towers and a large crossing tower. In some respects it is a gothic version of St Paul's Cathedral, a building which Wightwick admired.

the Ecclesiologists were besieged by a variety of critics whose interests were specifically religious rather than architectural. The *Ecclesiologist* complained: 'On one side, Mr Close and the *Record* accuse us of being unfaithful sons of the English Church, because we are Ecclesiologists; on the other Count Montalembert and the *Tablet* upbraid us as unreal Ecclesiologists, because we are sons of the English Church' (v, 3). Strangely enough, some of the severest criticisms came from Roman Catholics. While at Madeira in 1843, Neale met Count Montalembert, one of the leading Catholic laymen of France. Probably through Neale's influence the French Count was made an honorary member of the Society. Montalembert's acceptance was not especially gracious, appearing as it did in a tract addressed to Neale: 'First, and principally, I protest against the most unwarranted and most unjustifiable assumption of the name *Catholic* by people and things belonging to the actual Church of England.'[1] Montalembert continued: 'I next protest against the object of this society, and all such efforts in the Anglican Church as absurd.'[2] All the efforts of the Society were vain, for 'supposing you do one day get every old thing back again,—copes, letterns, rood-lofts, candlesticks, and the abbey lands into the bargain, what will it all be but an empty pageant?'[3] He tried to prove that the Church of England was Protestant and had always been so. In conclusion, 'if the Church of England is not the only true Church on earth, then she is an apostate rebel . . . [and] one of the most awful forms of sin that have ever appeared in the world'.[4]

Surprisingly enough, Montalembert's letter was received with joy by some English Churchmen. Wightwick printed it in his article on 'Modern English Gothic Architecture' in the third volume of *Quarterly Papers*. It was also reprinted as a tract by an anonymous 'Enquirer' with lengthy 'remarks' on each paragraph. Since it was printed in Cheltenham, this may have come

[1] *A Letter Addressed to a Rev. Member of the Camden Society, on the Subject of Catholic Literary Societies, on the Architectural, Artistical, and Archaeological Movements of the Puseyites* (Liverpool, 1844), p. 3.
[2] *Ibid.*, p. 4.   [3] *Ibid.*, pp. 5–6.   [4] *Ibid.*, pp. 10–11.

from the hand of Reverend Francis Close or one of his allies. Ostensibly trying to refute Montalembert and the Roman Catholic position, the tract was really intended to condemn the Ecclesiologists. The 'Enquirer' begins by praising Montalembert for his 'open, manly, and avowed defence of Romanism, when you were assailed by a species of bland and artful sophistry, to induce you to aid with your good name and talents a species of mock Catholicism which you have justly and indignantly repudiated'.[1] This type of hypocrisy continued for eighty-eight pages, finally concluding by congratulating Montalembert because 'your frankness, when compared with the covert acting of our Puseyites, as well as that of your fellow members of the Camden Society, stands out in a commanding form'.[2]

Montalembert's remarks were duplicated by Pugin who certainly had grounds for disliking the Ecclesiologists. Pugin announced to High Churchmen that 'copes and two candlesticks are not the test of Catholicism' and accused them of affecting 'Catholic rites, without possessing one particle of Catholic feeling or principle . . . [and of assuming] the externals of antiquity the better to delude the people'.[3] He also asserted that 'it is quite impossible for any man who abides in the Anglican Church, as she is at present constituted, to *build a Catholic Church and use it afterwards*'.[4] The reason for this statement was Pugin's conviction that the Prayer Book was not Catholic in nature, rather 'it is of most Protestant origin, very Protestant in its character; and it is as utterly impossible to square a Catholic building with the

---

[1] *A Re-Print of a Letter Addressed to a Revd. Member of the Cambridge Camden Society by M. de Compte de Montalembert, Accompanied with a Few Remarks & Queries,* (Cheltenham, 1845), p. 3.

[2] *Ibid.,* p. 88.

[3] *Present State,* p. 20. Pugin, like Ishmael, had 'his hand against every man'. In the same book he speculates that if the Roman Catholics were to have the English cathedrals in their possession once again, 'it is not improbable that many choir screens would be demolished, stalls removed, and after a host of other barbarous innovations, . . . the buildings would be condemned as inconvenient and uncomfortable, and by no means to be compared to the new galleried assembly rooms used for Catholic worship at the present day' (p. 55).

[4] *Ibid.,* p. 136.

present rites, as to mingle oil and water'.[1] Anglicans were given a choice: '*Either the Common Prayer or the ancient models must be abandoned.*'[2] Of course, this was a challenge of the reasons for the Society's existence. The counterattack, in this instance, was not swift, but it was powerful when it came. In 1846 the *Ecclesiologist* found that 'Mr. Pugin, clever and enthusiastic as he is, has not answered the expectations which were formed of him; he has not realized the highest standard of Christian art which we expected from him' (v, 10).

But it was criticism from within the Church of England which really hurt. As Basil Clarke says, 'heresy does not alarm Englishmen particularly, but Popery does'.[3] The stream of attacks associating the Society with popery began in 1841 and multiplied yearly. The president's report for 1844 spoke of—

the extreme violence of the prejudices to which we have been opposed, . . . the press has teemed with productions originating mainly in our published works or operations, . . . and . . . for the most part taken the opposite side. . . . Counter publications have been got up with a rapidity . . . counter associations of the most motley and ludicrous character have been attempted, and failed; still one after another the rules and principles of Ecclesiastical Architecture . . . are successively denounced, combated, recognized, and adopted, by those who have most to do with their execution.[4]

The opening blows had begun in the controversies over St Paul's Church and the *Few Words* series. In 1842 the *Ecclesiologist* found that a contemporary periodical, the *Christian Remembrancer*, was making 'insinuations of a tendency to Romanism', charges which were vehemently denied. Without undue delicacy, it was suggested that the *Christian Remembrancer* itself 'must lie open to much of that ungenerous and ignorant imputation to which we ourselves have been exposed' (*E.* II, 12). That year an anonymous 'Member of Trinity College' pub-

---

[1] *Present State*, p. 142.
[2] *Ibid.*, p. 143.
[3] *Church Builders of the Nineteenth Century: A Study of the Gothic Revival in England* (London, 1938), p. 100.
[4] *Report* (1844), p. 11.

lished a tract of extravagant praise for the Society. He proclaimed:

It is a Society, such as the Church has long felt the want of, a
Society, which I do from my heart believe, has tended to produce
more salutary impressions, regard being had to Church responsibilities and Church privileges than any other Society existing in the
present day, or that has existed in any antecedent period of the
History of the Church.[1]

As if aware of a sensitive subject, he took pains to declare that
the Society was not concerned with the Oxford Movement but
was simply trying 'to restore *that* which too many have long
ceased to value—*that* discipline which is so characteristic of the
system prescribed in the Prayer-Book'.[2]

Others, it soon turned out, were not convinced that the
Society was quite so innocuous. The Regius Professor of Greek,
James Scholefield, started the next controversy by preaching a
sermon on 'The Christian Altar'. The subject kept local tract
writers busy for the next three years, although everything that
could be said about it had been said in the sixteenth and seventeenth centuries. The printed version of the sermon is dedicated
to Bishop Blomfield and Scholefield refers to Blomfield's recent
rebuke of the Cambridge Camden Society. Though it seems
strange today, Scholefield's chief objection to the Society was
its use of the term 'altar'. As early as the second issue of the
Ecclesiologist, an unknown correspondent had demanded to
know why 'the word *Altar* is always used in publications of the
Cambridge Camden Society, instead of *Communion-table,* as it is
called in the rubric and canons of our Church' (1, 30). Scholefield proceeded to demonstrate the danger involved in the use
of the term. He goes through the usual praises of the 'Reformers
of our own Church, in bringing us back to the simplicity of
Scripture, and clearing away the errors which had hidden the
truths belonging to our salvation' especially because they 're-

[1] *The Claims of the Camden Society Considered in Connection with the Church of England*
(Cambridge, 1842), p. 3.
[2] *Ibid.*, p. 17.

stored the Lord's Table in the place of the altar, and discontinued deliberately and authoritatively the use of [the term altar]'.[1] 'And now the question meets us,' he continued, 'Why not adhere to the practice of the Reformers and the scriptural standards they set up?'[2] Obviously the Ecclesiologists had failed to do this, partly because they had never been particularly impressed by the Reformers.

As everyone knew, more was involved than simply a matter of terminology. F. W. Collison, a very active member of the Society, was provoked to write several tracts on the subject. As he pointed out: 'Priesthood, and sacrifice and altar are terms so inseparably related to each other that the denial of one is a denial of all, and the proof of the fitness of either leads to the admission of the others.'[3] Collison, as one might expect, preferred to base his arguments upon the Fathers rather than the Reformers and condemned Scholefield's usage of Church History.[4] Charles Warren, Vicar of Over, joined the attack on Scholefield: 'I feel, in common with many others, that Professor Scholefield has attacked the chief power and privilege of the Christian Priesthood.'[5]

At stake was the doctrine of eucharistic sacrifice. Yet the controversy always seemed a little tangential, especially when it soon veered off to a discussion of the material of the altar. To some it seemed that a stone altar implied a doctrine of a repeated sacrifice in the Eucharist. The Society became involved in this controversy in a very direct way. In November 1841 the group voluntarily took over the restoration of one of Cambridge's oldest churches, the Church of the Holy Sepulchre, known locally as the Round Church. The restoration progressed smoothly

---

[1] *The Christian Altar: A Sermon Preached before the University of Cambridge, on Sunday Morning, Oct. 23, 1842* (Cambridge, 1842), p. 27.

[2] *Ibid.*, p. 27.

[3] *Some Further Remarks on the Christian Altar and Eucharistic Sacrifice: With Strictures on Vedilius and Williams* (Cambridge, 1843), p. 15.

[4] *Remarks on A Sermon by Professor Scholefield, Entitled The Christian Altar: Being A Vindication of the Catholic Doctrines Therein Impugned* (Cambridge, 1842), p. 22.

[5] *The Lord's Table the Christian Altar, in Some Remarks upon Professor Scholefield's Late Sermon* (Cambridge, 1843), p. 2.

(and expensively) for two years and was completed late in 1843. To everyone's surprise, the incumbent, R. R. Faulkner, opposed the 'consecration' of the building when he 'discovered the erection of the Stone Altar which had recently been put up in the Church. . . . [and] the Popish accompaniment of a Credence Table'.[1] The consequence was a long legal battle. Faulkner lost his case in the Consistory Court, which upheld the legality of the stone altar and issued an additional faculty for the credence table. In appealing for money to carry his case against the churchwardens (backed by the Society) to the Court of Arches, Faulkner declared that he was 'fully resolved to use every means to remove these abominable pieces of superstition and Popery from my Church' and called them 'most pernicious and soul-destroying heresies'.[2] The decision, as given by Sir Herbert Jenner Fust, upheld Faulkner on the grounds that a stone altar could not be moved:

After maturely weighing the subject, the conscientious impression on my mind is, that a structure like the present is not a Communion Table within the meaning of the Rubric, and that the Credence Table being an adjunct, must follow its principal. In coming to this conclusion, I do not go so far as to admonish the Churchwardens to remove it. All I can do is to refuse to confirm the sentence of the Court below.[3]

The Society had lost this battle. The stone altar was replaced by a wood table and one remains in the Church today. Ironically enough, Thorp later recalled that 'the erection of a stone altar was not the result of any premeditated intention of the Committee' but evidently had been the idea of the architect, Anthony Salvin.[4]

[1] *An Appeal to the Protestant Public Respecting the Popish Abominations of a Stone Altar and Credence Table, in St. Sepulchre's Church, Cambridge*, a circular (dated 29 August 1844), p. 1. Francis Close and William Goode helped sponsor the appeal though Close had himself recently erected a stone altar in his church in Cheltenham. This provided considerable merriment for the *Ecclesiologist* (iv, 86). [2] *Ibid.*, p. 2.

[3] J. E. P. Robertson, editor, *The Judgment of the Rt. Hon. Sir Herbert Jenner Fust, Kt. Dean of the Arches, &c. &c. &c. in the Case of Faulkner v. Litchfield and Stearn, on the 31st January 1845* (London, 1845), p. 61.

[4] [Thomas Thorp], *A Statement of Particulars Connected with the Restoration of the Round Church* (Cambridge, 1845), p. 28.

The Society at least had the consolation of knowing that many people sympathized with it. Faulkner resided in his other living (Havering, Essex) and had received considerable help from people outside Cambridge in making the opening of his Church a test of the Ecclesiologists' strength. During this time the Church remained closed, and a local wit published *The Widow's Lament*, inquiring about Faulkner's motives:

Is't because a stone table is set up therein
That he still takes the Rent and yet leaves us to sin?[1]

When the Church was finally opened in August 1845 the Master of Christ's College, John Graham, warned 'lest in reproducing the graces of medieval architecture, we should lay ourselves open to the suspicion of reviving medieval superstition'.[2]

The doctrinal aspects of the Stone Altar Case continued to engage the tract writers. William Goode, Rector of St Antholin in London, published a book, *Altars Prohibited by the Church of England*, maintaining that a 'communion-table' should have three characteristics: 'As to *material* that it be made of wood. . . . As to *form*, that it be a table. . . . That it be unattached, in any part to the church, so as to be a *moveable* table.'[3] J. Blackburne, of St John's College, countered that 'too much stress has of late been laid upon the use of *stone* in this question, as if wood were essentially Protestant, and stone essentially Popish: but this cannot be true historically'.[4] Collison agreed with this in a paper read to the Society in 1844: 'As I said before, I ascribe no sacramental virtue to one material more than the other; I attach no doctrine to the use of the one which will not equally consist

---

[1] 'One of the Unwashed', *The Widow's Lament, Literally Rendered into Verse and Respectfully Addressed to the Parishioners of the Parson Deserted Parish, Called the Holy Sepulchre* (Cambridge, 1845), p. 5.

[2] *A Sermon Preached at the Re-opening of the Church of the Holy Sepulchre in Cambridge; on Sunday, August 10, 1845* (Cambridge, 1845), p. 15.

[3] *Altars Prohibited by the Church of England* (London, 1844), p. 75.

[4] *A Brief Historical Inquiry into the Introduction of Stone Altars into the Christian Church; with Remarks upon the Probable Effects of the Altar and its Ornaments upon Church Architecture in General* (Cambridge, 1844), p. vi.

with that of the other.'[1] However, he clearly considered stone altars more appropriate.

Meanwhile other attacks poured in on the Society. At the Fourth Anniversary Meeting in 1843, Thorp found it necessary to deny the popular belief that the Cambridge Camden Society is 'an instrument for the diffusion of questionable opinions'.[2] He asserted that the Society was 'confined to the consideration of matters purely and practically Architectural—by which I mean the construction, style, and arrangement of a church'.[3] At least one Irish clergyman was unconvinced. The branch of the Society which had been established the previous year in the Diocese of Down, Connor, and Dromore fell victim to the attacks of 'Clericus Connorensis' and other critics who forced it to dissolve its connexion with the Cambridge Camden Society. These opponents had objected to the 'late attempt to introduce amongst us Popish novelties under the guise of antiquity— Ecclesiology, or, as it is now being denominated, Church Architecture'.[4] 'Clericus Connorensis' pointed out that 'it would not be difficult to connect historically the rise and progress of Puseyism and the new-fangled rage for Church Architecture'.[5] Bishop Mant reluctantly withdrew his support from the Cambridge Camden Society, and the Irish group broke off all relations with the parent Society.

There was no let up of attacks in 1844. At one meeting that year, Thorp complained of 'those who wished to involve the Society in the charge of Romanizing, to the effect that it had no right to employ itself in the restoration of chalices and church ornaments, without going over to the Roman Catholic faith' (*E.* iv, 25). That year the Society's arch enemy appeared in the person of the Reverend Francis Close, then perpetual curate of Cheltenham, and later Dean of Carlisle. Actually, the Society

---

[1] *On the History of Christian Altars: A Paper Read before the Cambridge Camden Society, Nov. 28, 1844* (Cambridge, 1845), p. 27.

[2] *Report* (1843), p. 6.

[3] *Ibid.*, p. 7.

[4] 'Clericus Connorensis', *Ecclesiologism Exposed: Being the Letters of 'Clericus Connorensis' as Originally Published in the Belfast Commercial Chronicle* (Belfast, 1843), p. 9.

[5] *Ibid.*, p. 11.

deserved a more sophisticated opponent, for Close's accusations were crude, blunt, and deadly effective. The war began with a book by Close, *Church Architecture Scripturally Considered from the Earliest Ages to the Present Time*. Close, who used typographical features to buttress his logic, asserted: 'ALL TEMPLES, ALTARS, CHURCHES, AND RELIGIOUS CEREMONIES, ARE THE BADGES AND PROOFS OF THE FALLEN GUILTY, STATE OF MAN!'[1] He disliked any undue interest in the church building, for this was not the true Christian temple: 'THAT TEMPLE IS THE LIVING BODIES AND SOULS OF HIS REDEEMED AND SANCTIFIED PEOPLE: HIS CHURCH! THE ONLY CHURCH OF THE NEW TESTAMENT!'[2] Close went on to say that after the time of the New Testament, 'Levitical and mythological observances were interwoven with Christian services, and the ecclesiastical structures were built with a view to accommodate the superstitions of the times'.[3] Close refers to the *Ecclesiologist* and its heresies in a pointed fashion: 'It must be remembered that this publication is authenticated by a powerful society, at the head of which are found some honoured names of distinguished persons, who it is hoped would be far from sanctioning that which is here put forth to the public as authenticated by them.'[4]

Such a book startled even the Ecclesiologists, though by 1844 they were quite accustomed to criticism:

When we meet with an author, . . . who does not content himself with the proposition that churches may be improperly decorated, or even with a sweeping veto on decoration altogether, but who spends his energy in proving that, strictly speaking, there is no such thing as a Christian church at all, we seem to have nothing left to us but to look on in amazement (*E.* III, 175–6).

But the *Ecclesiologist* recovered from its astonishment sufficiently to ask: 'Is the author grossly ignorant of the subject he has undertaken to treat, or is he wilfully throwing dust into the eyes of those "who value his opinion"?' (III, 178). It scored a 'very palpable hit' in commenting on Close's assertion that a

---

[1] (London, 1844), p. 19.   [2] *Ibid.*, p. 49.
[3] *Ibid.*, p. 75.   [4] *Ibid.*, p. 81.

church ought to ' "appear worthy to stand among the abodes of wealth or rank by which it is chiefly furnished with guests"' (III, 179). The *Ecclesiologist* suggested that this would include for 'the *élite* of Cheltenham cushioned pues, stoves, silk dress-gowns, and cambrick' (III, 179).

A Cambridge man, Thomas Kerchever Arnold, Rector of Lyndon, wrote some *Remarks* on Close's book which in a most temperate manner attempted to refute Close. Arnold's purpose, in his own words, was—'to prove two points: (1) that Mr Close has given a *very inaccurate* account of what is taught upon this subject in the Bible, or has been gathered from it by probable inferences: and (2) that some of his arguments are already answered in the Homilies, and ALL in the works of either Hooker or Taylor'.[1] The *Ecclesiologist* was quite satisfied with Arnold's demolition of Close's book (III, 180).

Close, as might be expected, was not content. He immediately published *A Reply* to Arnold, stating that 'Mr Arnold has dealt out to me hard measure; but I will endeavour not to "return railing for railing"'.[2] Close's real complaint was Arnold's 'total suppression of all notice in his remarks, of *the chief object* of the work which is thus minutely examined by him'.[3] Although Arnold had replied to each of Close's assertions, he had not refuted the idea that medieval architecture was incompatible with Prayer Book worship. Lest this be missed, Close ended his tract with a plea: 'May God in his mercy enable all who love "the truth as it is in Jesus", to see and to oppose the dark and fatal errors which are being interwoven with the national faith by means of ECCLESIASTICAL STATUARY, PAINTING, AND ARCHI-TECTURE!'[4] Arnold, of course, had to reply to this, and he did so immediately in *An Examination* of Close's *Reply*. This too contained a calm answer, the principle being: 'It is not our *intellect*

[1] *Remarks on the Rev. F. Close's 'Church Architecture Scripturally Considered, from the Earliest Ages to the Present Time'* (London, 1844), p. 3. Arnold was a member of the Society in 1844.

[2] *A Reply to the 'Remarks' of the Rev. T. K. Arnold, M.A., upon Close's 'Church Architecture'* (London, 1844), p. 3.

[3] *Ibid.*, p. 4.

[4] *Ibid.*, p. 37.

only; but our *whole* hearts *and* minds that should be dedicated to the service of the Almighty, and both strengthened and purified by that dedication.'[1] In this process, the architectural surroundings of the worshipper could play an important part.

This particular debate was replaced by a much more important one. In reviewing Close's *Church Architecture* and his *Reply*, the *Ecclesiologist* had admonished 'Mr. Close, when next he brings a charge against us, to quote from our own accredited writings, and not from the communications of our correspondents' (III, 181). This was a mistake, a very bad mistake. It resulted in Close's publishing a forty-six page pamphlet with the ponderous title, *The Restoration of Churches Is the Restoration of Popery: Proved and Illustrated from the Authenticated Publications of the 'Cambridge Camden Society': A Sermon Preached in the Parish Church, Cheltenham, on Tuesday, November 5th, 1844.*[2] This sermon nearly proved to be the undoing of the Society.

Close begins by asserting that in previous November Fifth sermons he had exposed popery within the English Church by denouncing the Oxford Tracts. This time, he intends—'to show that as Romanism is taught *Analytically* at Oxford, it is taught *Artistically* at Cambridge—that it is inculcated theoretically, in tracts, at one University, and it is *sculptured, painted,* and *graven* at the other. . . . in a word, that the *"Ecclesiologist"* of Cambridge is identical in doctrine with the Oxford *Tracts for the Times*'.[3] Close then proceeds to do exactly what the *Ecclesiologist* had enjoined, drawing his illustrations directly from the Society's 'Authenticated Publications'. He raps the Ecclesiologists severely for their references to the 'DEEPER AND MORE HIDDEN VIRTUES . . . of . . . ANGELIC HARMONY OF BELLS', for referring to a 'HAGIOSCOPE' ('a purely Popish invention'), or for speaking of the use of church-yard crosses 'TO SECURE THE PEACEFUL REPOSE OF THE DEPARTED'.[4] 'Now if we met with such writing as this in some old novel or romance,' Close maintains, 'we should simply call it rhapsody; but from the pen of this body of divines, it is

[1] *An Examination of the Rev. F. Close's Reply to 'Remarks' upon His 'Church Architecture Scripturally Considered'* (London, 1844), p. 54.
[2] London, 1844.　　[3] *Ibid.*, p. 4.　　[4] *Ibid.*, pp. 32, 33, 36.

"instinct with doctrine"—and "religious instruction".'[1] He succeeded in putting his finger on a very sensitive spot, showing
quite clearly that ecclesiology was far more than an innocuous
form of antiquarianism. The Ecclesiologists, as Close pointed
out, were interested in doctrinal changes. 'In their able hands,'
he charged, ' "adverse" rubrics are speedily turned into "allies".'[2] Thus the North position at the altar became for them
the northwest instead.

The churches which the Ecclesiologists sponsored were also
condemned: '*Such Churches* are palpably *unfit for* all the circumstances of modern worship . . . we want *Protestant Churches, not
Popist Mass-Houses!*'[3] Close warned that by such insidious means
as these new buildings, 'papists and semi-papists are dissemin-
ating their subtle errours through the length and breadth of the
land'.[4] Churchmen everywhere should be alert lest they miss 'in
these things the return of incipient, insidious, but unquestionable Popery!'[5]

Close could not expect a gentle reply from the Society and he
did not get one. Instead, the *Ecclesiologist* exclaimed: 'Against
such an airy nothing who would condescend to hazard a defence? Certainly we shall not do so' (IV, 111). It then proceeded
virtually to accuse Close of approving 'of certain avowed Nestorian heretics'. Instead of openly denying Close's charge that
the Society had a definite theological position, the reviewer
turned 'to prove that of Mr. Close's statements some are contrary to fact, and of his extracts "from the authenticated publications of the Cambridge Camden Society", some are mis-
quoted, some are misinterpreted, and some are not extracts at
all' (IV, 112). A number of minor inconsistencies are pointed
out, and an attempt is made to show that many of the items to
which Close had objected as 'popish inventions' were in use
after the Reformation. Of course, their almost complete dis-
appearance for two centuries was ignored. The conclusion
reached is that 'whether his extracts be fair or not, . . . his
pamphlet is rather silly than wise, rather slanderous than true.

[1] *Ibid.*, p. 15. [2] *Ibid.*, p. 29. [3] *Ibid.*, p. 17. [4] *Ibid.*, p. 24. [5] *Ibid.*, p. 38.

The Cambridge Camden Society need not dread such attacks'
(IV, 122).

Evidently there was some doubt about this, for the next issue
of the *Ecclesiologist* renewed the attack, devoting twenty pages to
analysing and refuting Close's specific accusations. Scornfully,
Close was told: 'All who in building churches neglect the great
object, and accommodate their structure to the conveniences of
man, must inevitably be bad architects' (IV, 153). They ridiculed his fear of such suspicious devices as the Orientator. But
they certainly did not clear themselves of Close's assertion that
their theological principles were those of the Tractarians.
Rather, they sought to discredit Close:

The Fifth-of-November sermon quotes from accredited writings, but
falsifies where it quotes. We must now recommend Mr. Close, when
next he brings a charge against us, to quote from our own accredited
writings, and to quote fairly. Perhaps upon the whole, it will be
safer for him not to bring charges at all.
'THOU SHALT NOT BEAR FALSE WITNESS AGAINST THY NEIGHBOUR'
(IV, 169).

But Close can be said to have won the war. His work went
through at least four editions, and received much attention.
Whatever its defects, it had raised the alarm. It was consoling
ten years later for the *Ecclesiologist* to point out that Mr Close
had been 'himself absorbed by the movement' (XV, 3), but by
then the damage had been done.

IV

The year 1845 was a very important one for the Church of
England. For several years, the Heads of Houses at Oxford had
been seeking a means of punishing the Tractarians. The first
part of Froude's *Remains*, published in 1838, had raised a violent
storm in the Church and Newman's Tract 90 published in 1841,
agitated matters even more. A drift towards Rome was apparent
by 1842 and it grew, abetted by W. G. Ward's *The Ideal of a
Christian Church* (1844). Ward's ideal, of course, was the Roman

Church, but he yet remained in the Church of England, boasting that he had not been censured for his position. On 13 February 1845 the Oxford authorities proceeded to exact vengeance. Ward's book was condemned, his B.A. and M.A. degrees were revoked, but an attempt to condemn Tract 90 formally was vetoed by the proctors. Newman, however, had virtually ended his career as an Anglican clergyman by the autumn of 1843. On 3 October 1845 he was received into the Roman Catholic Church and was soon followed by others.

The year 1845 was one of tension at Cambridge too, especially since Close had proved to the satisfaction of many that the *Ecclesiologist* was 'identical in doctrine' with the *Tracts* of Oxford. In the ensuing crisis, the *Ecclesiologist* was the first to suffer. Beginning with the January 1845 issue (the first of volume four), the *Ecclesiologist* was officially severed from the Society. The 'Preface' to the fourth volume announced: 'The Society, losing its organ, would also lose some obloquy, and a responsibility under which a part of it was uneasy. The ECCLESIOLOGIST, losing its former influential sanction, would gain in a greater unity of conduct more individual responsibility, more regularity of issue, greater general independence, and wider field of action' (IV, 3).

This new status made little difference in the periodical itself. 'From January 1845 for a year-and-a-half the new series of the *Ecclesiologist* was conducted by the very same writers, with few exceptions, who contributed to the first three volumes. The tone, principle, and object were identical with those volumes.'[1] Volume IV became Volume I of the new series and a dual system of numbering was continued till the end of the publication. The only real change which occurred during this interval was 'that the Society was not responsible for it; and that the editors were consequently obliged continually to keep up a kind of legal fiction, and to act and speak always in two characters' (*E.* v, vi). The editors were at the same time the Committee of the Society, though they acknowledged the help of

---

[1] Boyce, *Memorial*, p. 16.

'friends from Oxford' during the year and a half of legal separation. In July 1846 at the beginning of volume six, the magazine was once again restored to the Society's official control.

The crisis soon became much more significant. On 13 February 1845, the same day that Ward was condemned at Oxford, the Society held its Forty-first Meeting at Cambridge. The president's speech contained startling news:

The members were aware that one of their patrons, the Bishop of Exeter, had not only withdrawn, but had published his retirement and disapprobation to the world. . . . Another of their patrons, the Bishop of Lincoln, had since withdrawn his name, on grounds similar to, and brought to his notice by, those adopted by the Bishop of Exeter; and subsequently the Committee had received an intimation simply announcing the retirement of the Chancellor of the University, followed . . . by that of the Vice-Chancellor (*E.* IV, 71).

The Bishop of Exeter (Henry Phillpotts) had denounced the Society in a letter to Mr March Phillips.[1] Thorp wrote the Bishop about certain facts 'which would seem to be . . . of sufficient importance to have at least arrested his judgment' (*E.* IV, 73). The Bishop, however, mislaid Thorp's letter without reading it.

The remedy proposed for this mass exodus of patrons was drastic. The Committee suggested the dissolution of the Society: 'They feel satisfied that any advantages which might be expected from its continued operations would be insufficient to counterbalance the positive evil that must result from even an apparent disregard of the sentiments of those invested with authority. They therefore recommend unanimously that the *Society be dissolved*' (*E.* IV, 71). The announcement took the meeting by surprise. Those assembled were not satisfied with the president's assurance that it did not mean 'retiring in weakness

---

[1] It is strange that Bishop Phillpotts should have initiated the withdrawal of patrons from the Society. His actions in the Gorham case and in taking the radical step of ordering his clergy to wear surplices (November 1844), until mob violence caused him to rescind this order, mark him out as one of the very few High Churchmen on the episcopal bench. However, he was fond of controversies and participated in more than fifty lawsuits as well as refusing to hold communion with the Archbishop of Canterbury.

. . . the Society numbered nearer 900 than 800 members: not more than three ordinary members had withdrawn: and no other patrons besides those he had named' (*E.* IV, 72).

Evidently there were at least three motives behind the proposal for dissolution of the Society. The Committee did not care to offend those 'to whom a hearty deference was with *them* a principle', referring to the bishops and university officials (*E.* IV, 72). Many of the leaders had gone down from the University, and Thorp spoke of 'the prospects of that change in the condition of the Society, which had long been anticipated as the consequence of the near removal of himself, and others its founders and principal managers, from the University' (*E.* IV, 72). Although it had begun largely as an undergraduate society, most of the Society's members had long since taken their degrees. Obviously the strength of the Society was not localized in Cambridge, but spread throughout the Church. Furthermore, the members were determined to 'offer to die rather than yield', desiring '*that the Society should be what it has been, or not at all*' (*E.* IV, 85).

Philip Freeman, a member of the Committee that year, published a small tract on 5 March explaining and defending the proposed dissolution of the Society. Though it was not published by the Society, Freeman noted that it had the approval of his fellow Committee members.[1] Freeman narrated the development of ecclesiology, noting that 'from every fresh accession of facts, glimpses more and more clear were obtained of a Law capable of governing all the developments of Christian Art'.[2] Rather than compromise this, Freeman was determined that it would be better for the Society to dissolve. He took the high ground that the Committee was motivated by 'a deep sense of the obligation Christians are under to acknowledge the Word Incarnate'.[3] The Society could not change without involving itself in 'an element of *anti*-Christian principles if it limits its views to raising structures of a vague religious char-

---

[1] P[hilip] F[reeman], *Thoughts on the Proposed Dissolution of the Cambridge Camden Society Suggested for the Consideration of the Members* (London, 1845), p. 3.
[2] *Ibid.*, p. 8.   [3] *Ibid.*, p. 20.

acter, and does not attach to them distinctive Christian features'.[1]

Neale, who was not on the Committee that year since he was in poor health, evidently disagreed. He wrote Webb: 'I am more and more averse to the dissolution of the Society. I should like to be free from an University yoke, and then set going again . . . if without giving up any principle, the C.C.S. can be organized again, we should vote for that; if not (but only if not) for dissolution.'[2] The Committee pursued its plan for dissolution. Legal opinion showed that 'in strictness, no consent even of a majority of the whole Society can have the effect of wholly dissolving the Society so long as members remain who are desirous of its continuance'.[3] Accordingly, a circular and two blank forms for voting were sent to the members—

to take the sense of the Society with respect to the expediency of attempting to effect the dissolution in the manner recommended by Counsel. The following Resolution is therefore proposed in place of the one originally suggested: 'That the Committee to be elected at the anniversary Meeting be instructed to adopt measures for dissolving the Society in a legal way.'[4]

The Committee announced at a meeting on 24 April that it was also prepared to propose an alternative 'in the event of the proposition for taking steps to dissolve the Society being negatived, . . . to which they can be parties, and by which, in their opinion, the Society can continue to subsist in the spirit of its original constitution, and consistently with duty, usefulness, and honour' (*E.* IV, 173). In order to see if dissolution were possible, 'voting papers returnable on 6 May were sent to every Member who could be reached by post'.[5] The totals of the Society's poll indicated that 380 members voted, and of these 271 opposed the dissolution and 109 favoured it, many of them no doubt in the

---

[1] *Thoughts on the Proposed Dissolution*, p. 23.
[2] *Letters*, p. 84.
[3] [Circular from the Committee on the proposed dissolution of the Society, 24 April 1845], p. 3.
[4] *Ibid.*, p. 4.
[5] Boyce, *Memorial*, p. 13.

belief that the Committee desired the dissolution.[1] It was quite apparent to the Committee that most of the membership wished the Society to continue, although less than half had voted before the Sixth Anniversary Meeting. The Committee maintained that they had '*by every means in their power promoted*, the dissolution of the Society'.[2]

The climax came at the hectic Forty-fourth Ordinary and Sixth Anniversary Meeting held on 8 May 1845. So many people came to this meeting that it was necessary to hold it in the Cambridge Town Hall. The meeting began with Webb reading the Annual Report. A suggested set of twelve new laws was then offered, as retaining 'those parts of the Society's operations which are confessedly beneficial, discarding, so far as this Society is concerned, everything which brings it into contact with the University'.[3] The proposal sought to conserve most of the Society's actions except for the public 'meetings, and whatever brought its executive and resident members into so prominent a position in the eyes of the University'.[4] It was not pointed out at the time that this would give the Committee even more absolute control over the Society. The alternative of moving the Society's headquarters was not a part of the proposed scheme.

The resolution, as finally passed, read: ' "That the Committee to be elected this evening be instructed to revise the laws on the basis of the scheme now submitted to the Meeting".'[5] This was not accomplished without a major battle. The *Account* reports a speech by Thorp in favour of the resolution: 'It was because the Society had committed itself to some principles, be they right or wrong—because there *was* such a thing as "Camdenism", that they were placed in their present position (hear, hear).'[6] He did not admit that these were theological principles, but simply those of '*church* architecture'.

As might be expected, considerable discussion ensued. Al-

---

[1] *Accounts of the Sixth Anniversary Meeting of the Cambridge Camden Society, May 8, 1845* (bound at the end of volume four of the *Ecclesiologist*), p. 7. (Cited hereafter as *Account.*)

[2] *Ibid.*, p. 3. [3] *Ibid.*, p. 10. [4] *Ibid.*, p. 13. [5] *Ibid.*, p. 11. [6] *Ibid.*, p. 14.

though a determined group of dissidents were present in force they were outnumbered by young members of the Society who were fiercely loyal to the Society's principles. The dissidents were led by Professor Lee who rose to announce that 'there was something more than architecture involved in the proceedings and objects of the committee'. He continued: 'The Church had enemies enough already, what with Romanism without, and something like Romanism within, to say nothing of dissent.'[1] He proposed that the Society be dissolved completely and refounded, a step which quite possibly would have involved a change in leadership. But he was ruled out of order for provoking a 'theological discussion'; the young men laughed at him, and his amendment was rejected.

He was followed by a Mr Currey. This gentleman insisted that suspending the meetings as proposed would not solve the problem: 'The Society was established simply as an architectural Society, and for antiquarian purposes bearing on architecture. The reason why so much feeling and dissatisfaction had been expressed was that that principle had not been adhered to. . . . The present proposal [for the suspension of meetings] did not go to the bottom of the evil.'[2] Hope replied that from the first the Society had stood for 'sound principles of *church-membership*'. He quoted from a speech which Thorp had made in 1840 referring to the need of bringing ' "the esoteric spirit of our religion to illustrate the purposes and meaning of the architectural facts they rightly described" '. ' "Ecclesiastical architecture",' Thorp had said, ' "is only just beginning to be treated as an ecclesiastical thing; as a thing in which the Church, *as a spiritual body*, is concerned" '.[3]

The next challenger was Professor Sedgwick, the famous geologist who was also a clergyman. Like Professor Lee, he too was in favour of dissolution. He based his complaints on some of the members' publications: 'Every body knew that men con-

---

[1] *Account*, p. 17.   [2] *Ibid.*, p. 18.
[3] *Ibid.*, p. 19, quoting from address delivered on 28 March 1840, printed in *Report* (1840), p. 7.

nected with the Society had sent forth books, the language and principles of which no consistent member of the Church of England could possibly approve of.'[1] He referred to 'articles perfectly absurd and contrary to common sense', which had condemned Cranmer, Ridley, and Latimer as having died justly. Specifically, he condemned a publication entitled the 'Christian Calendar', which carried the identification 'by a member of the Camden Society'. This publication by S. N. Stokes, Sedgwick called 'an insult to the Church and University'.[2]

The dissidents, however, accomplished nothing. The resolution, allowing the Committee to revise the laws of the Society, was passed without amendment. Then the members proceeded to elect the Committee for the following year. As if to demonstrate their strength, Stokes was proposed and elected, as well as F. A. Paley, who soon resigned on grounds of health and eventually became a Roman Catholic. Hope became the new Chairman of Committees, and henceforth monopolized this position.

As might be expected, the dissidents were not willing to give up so easily. For several weeks the *Cambridge Chronicle* bristled with denunciations of the Society's executives. On 14 June a letter from 'Academicus' announced that the 'spirit and aims of Camdenism and Puseyism are the same, viz. the disparagement of the Reformation and the encouragement of Romish usages and doctrines'. An anonymous writer had already (31 May) mentioned that 'in giving advice when consulted upon matters

---

[1] *Ibid.*, p. 20.

[2] Sedgwick refers to *A Christian Kalendar for the Use of Members of the Established Church Arranged for the Year of Our Lord God MDCCCXLV*, 'by a Lay Member of the Cambridge Camden Society', (Cambridge, [1845]). The work is very Roman Catholic and includes a 'List of All the Saints Commemorated in the Later English Church, with Their Days Alphabetically Arranged'. This contains the names of St Fabian, Pope; St Machutus, and many others not in the Prayer Book. It advocated confession of 'our sins, as occasion is, to a learned and discreet Priest' (p. 6) and many practices then considered exclusively Roman Catholic. Stokes soon resigned from the Society and became a Roman Catholic. Thorp declared his 'sentiments of disapprobation' and announced that the work was by no means an official publication of the Society (*Account*, p. 23).

of Church architecture', the Committee, 'must have *some* principle to go upon'. He agreed that these might be the wrong principles, but there was no escaping the necessity for taking a theological position.

Professor Lee, who had been effectively throttled at the Sixth Anniversary Meeting for provoking 'theological discussion', now had his say in print. He lost no time in publishing a letter addressed to Thorp and dated the day following the Meeting. He was annoyed that he had not been heard in full and disturbed by Hope's indiscreet speech 'with the ardour common to youth and inexperience'.[1] The election of Stokes to the Committee upset Professor Lee greatly and was convincing evidence 'that the Oxford and Cambridge movements are actuated by the same *esoteric principles*, and, in the main, for the very same pious ends'.[2] He concluded with a resounding blast against such a 'development of Jesuitism'. The *Ecclesiologist*'s reply was no more subtle: 'However much he may know of Oriental literature, he knows nothing else, and less than nothing of ecclesiology' (IV, 216). Lee renewed his attack in September with another letter devoted chiefly to condemning *Durandus*. His conclusion was magnificent, if not particularly accurate. He ridiculed 'the cause which it [*Durandus*] is labouring to promote, viz. the interests of the schismatic Church of Rome, its statements are defective and deceptive; its reasonings imposing and fallacious; its piety put forth that of heathenism; its pretensions great, insolent, and groundless . . . both you and they [their 'Oxford coadjutors'] are labouring in a cause which you are ashamed openly to avow'.[3]

Another disaffected Ecclesiologist, C. A. Swainson, published a letter dated 14 May trying to show that the proposal for dissolution had been a disingenuous device. 'Deference to authority' was only a smokescreen and the Committee had no intention

---

[1] *A Letter to the Venerable Archdeacon Thorp, President of the Camden Society, on its Late Re-organization and Apparent Objects* (London, [1845]), p. 9.

[2] *Ibid.*, p. 13.

[3] *A Second Letter to the Venerable Archdeacon Thorp, President of the Cambridge Camden Society, on Symbolism* (London, 1845), p. 55.

of changing.[1] Swainson soon found a more effective way of venting his rage. This was in conjunction with C. J. Ellicott, W. Webb, A. M. Hopper, and others. A committee was formed to send a statement to each of the Society's members. The intention was to secure as many resignations from the Society as possible on the grounds that the only changes proposed at the meeting (no more public meetings) 'would throw the whole management of the Society's affairs more exclusively than before into the hands of the Committee'.[2] Signatures were invited to a statement of grievances:

Thus the Executive of the Society remaining virtually unchanged, and being supported by a majority in the determination to maintain a position which we consider still to be pregnant with evil, and alike disrespectable to the authorities of the Church and University, we deem our connection with this Society inconsistent with the duty which we owe to both these Bodies. . . . We have therefore determined to withdraw from the Society.[3]

The original statement was signed by four masters of colleges, Professors Lee, Sedgwick, and Corrie, and about thirty fellows. Shortly thereafter a longer version was published with a list of about seventy signatories including William Wordsworth, the poet, and the Bishop of St David's.

It is difficult to tell which side won the struggle. The Society left Cambridge, diminishing its influence on the younger clergy there but gaining a national scope. Membership dropped off when the Society left Cambridge and the group was never again to be so active as it had been during its agitated six years at the University. Some of the dissidents joined the Cambridge Architectural Society which was founded in November 1846. C. A. Swainson became vice-president of this group. It showed an interest in church architecture, but lacked any strong theological convictions.

---

[1] C. A. S[wainson], *A Letter to a Non-Resident Member of the Cambridge Camden Society, on the Present Position of That Body* (Cambridge, 1845), p. 5.

[2] [Statement respecting withdrawal from the Society, drawn up by C. J. Ellicott and others, 17 May 1845], p. 2.

[3] *Ibid.*, p. 2.

On the other hand, the Cambridge Camden Society had not sacrificed any of its principles. Neale had written: 'I want to protest most strongly against forming an Architectural Society out of our ruins. People will ignorantly think that our religious views are given up, and our Architectural retained—as if the two were separable.'[1] This was avoided, though the members became more discreet as they advanced in maturity.

During the ensuing year no public meetings were held. Two circulars, reporting the activities of the Committee were published on 9 December and in April 1846. The *Report* for 1846 mentions that sixty ordinary members had been received, Stokes and Paley had resigned upon becoming Roman Catholics, and some of the serial publications were continuing. Significantly, no English bishops are listed as patrons, though bishops in Wales, Scotland, the United States, and the colonies had not deserted the Society.

On the whole, the membership of the Society had remained faithful. As a result of the crisis, the Society had 'been weeded of some who never sympathized with it, and never gave it any assistance' (*E.* IV, 174). The *Ecclesiologist* published the figures on membership in September 1845, remarking that 'the only subject for wonder is the smallness of the secessions' (IV, 216). The statistics showed:

	Seceded from the Society.	Remain in the Society.
Members, not members of the University	7	125
Undergraduates	13	129
B.A.	13	124
M.A.	67	267
Of higher standing than M.A.	21	35
	121	680

(IV, 217).

It is quite obvious that most of the dissidents were men who had received their B.A. several years earlier, and were somewhat

---

[1] *Letters*, p. 84.

older than a large portion of the membership. At any rate, the majority of the members remained loyal, though their enthusiasm may have been dampened. The *Ecclesiologist* boasted: 'The real business of the Society has not been for a moment interrupted, and we sincerely trust will never be' (IV, 217). Nevertheless, the structure and activities of the Society were subsequently considerably modified because of the crisis of 1845.

CHAPTER VI

ECCLESIOLOGY APPLIED IN THE RESTORATION OF CHURCHES

I

The real measure of the Society's accomplishments became more apparent each year, despite the onslaughts of hostile critics. These achievements appeared in the large numbers of churches restored along ecclesiological principles and the new churches built according to the Society's standards. Few old churches escaped some form of restoration during this period. The efforts of the Society left their mark on a very large proportion of these buildings.

A great amount of the Society's activity was connected with restorations. By the nineteenth century, few churches retained more than a small portion of their medieval furnishings, and many buildings had been repaired or modified to some extent in one of the classical styles. Medieval features, where they remained, were frequently unused, defaced, or concealed. The restoration of these departed glories became the Society's favourite task. Even this activity was open to criticism. The *Report* for 1841 stated that 'it is ignorance alone . . . that would connect with the act [of restoration] the charge of superstition'.[1]

Much was done to encourage restorations through the publications of the Society, but it soon became apparent that the Ecclesiologists were not eager to sanction any haphazard form of repair or reconstruction. The Society found that restorations, to be worthwhile, had to be directed carefully. The Preface of *Hierugia Anglicana* asked: 'Is the church restorer at a loss (in the absence of precise or canonical guidance), how suitably to decorate the eastern wall of his chancel?' and promised, 'the Hierugia will direct him'.[2] The *Ecclesiologist* carried similar direc-

---

[1] *Report* (1841), p. 29.   [2] *Hierugia*, p. viii.

tions. One of its most significant features was a column entitled 'Church Restorations'. As might be expected, there was usually more to condemn than to approve. 'The restoration of the church of Sampford Brett, Somersetshire, has given us much pain', it was reported. 'Such a monstrous misconception of Christian ornament. . . . Huge borders of grapes, suggesting the idea of Bacchanalian merriment, ornament the east end, and seem to hang over the holy Altar' (I, 114). Incompetent architects were condemned, and the news of Professor Cockerell's projected restoration of Wells Cathedral produced the comment: 'How dare he undertake the restoration of an edifice with which he does not even pretend to sympathize; of the laws of design of which he neither has, nor cares to have, the slightest acquaintance' (II, 113).

On the other hand, partly through the intervention of the Society, a number of restorations met the *Ecclesiologist*'s approval. The restoration of St Mary, Aylesbury, Buckingham, was praised: 'We have seldom heard of a more complete and noble undertaking: and it is the more commendable and interesting from the example it sets to all parishes, . . . of the duty of fearlessly and generously resolving upon a thorough and Catholick restoration' (II, 59).

Individual members of the Society often furnished examples of correct church restoration. Beresford Hope was delighted to have an opportunity to apply his store of ecclesiological information in restoring Christ Church, Kilndown, Kent, an edifice near his family estate. The *Ecclesiologist* had its doubts as to whether the work could actually be called a restoration; the Church had only recently been built. It originated as a 'plain oblong room, with low thin roof, broad lancet windows, a mean table for the altar (not even raised on a single step), a clumsy reading-pen and pulpit, and pues' (IV, 91). Such a challenge must have whetted Hope's appetite and the building underwent a 'sea change'. Salvin, Carpenter, Butterfield, Willement, and other artists were employed to correct the building. Elimination of the pews left room for a 'moderate chancel, which is now separated from the nave by a glorious rood-screen, exquisitely designed and carved, and coloured and gilt to perfection' (*E.* IV, 91). The entire building was subjected to a similar 'most marvellous change', glass, tiles, and painting being introduced to produce 'a *whole* of colour . . . such as is to be seen, we suppose, in no other English church at the present time' (*E.* IV, 92). Christ Church, Kilndown, was considered especially remarkable 'as showing what may be done under the most unfavourable circumstances' (*E.* IV, 92). The *Ecclesiologist* concluded its review of the Church by noting that 'the chancel of Christ Church, Kilndown, lighted up for evensong, is a sight which all ecclesiologists ought to see' (IV, 92).

Neale was a very enthusiastic restorer: 'How can I but feel the most devoted affection to so noble a cause as that of Church restoration?'[1] In 1841 he superintended the restoration of St Nicholas Church, Old Shoreham, Sussex, on behalf of the patron, Magdalene College, Oxford. The work is described in detail in a paper printed in Part I of the *Transactions*. As warden of Sackville College in East Grinstead, a post which he occupied throughout the latter half of his life, Neale had at his disposal a chapel built in the seventeenth century. His attempts at adding the ornaments which he considered proper (a vested altar, benches and a rood) led to his being inhibited from 1847 till 1863 by the Bishop of Chichester, A. T. Gilbert. The Bishop wrote: ' "In consequence of what I saw in the Chapel of Sackville College, I have felt it my duty to inhibit the Rev. J. M. Neale" '.[2] It was one of the first, but by no means the last, conflict between a ritualistic clergyman and his bishop.

Many less confident souls applied to the Society for direction. The annual reports contain numerous notices of applications for advice and help. Boyce says that in the year 1842–3 'no less than 98 applications were made to the Committee for advice respecting the reparation of old churches, designs for new ones,

---

[1] *Hierologus*, p. 303.

[2] Neale, *A Statement of the Late Proceedings of the Lord Bishop of Chichester against the Warden of Sackville College, East Grinstead* (n.p., 1849), p. 24.

details in connexion with the internal arrangement of existing Churches, and designs for Church Plate and Ornaments'.[1] When possible, such information was sent. As might be expected, many such applications also requested money, and the Society occasionally made grants, especially for the restoration of fonts, roodscreens, or remarkable features of buildings.

One Church was aided by the publication of a special pamphlet. The Church of St Mary the Virgin in Stow, Lincolnshire, had all the features which the Society disliked most—pews, galleries, and plastered walls. But it was an interesting building, partly Norman and partly in the favoured Decorated style. As a result, the Society issued a special plea for aid in its restoration. Obviously the pews and galleries must be evicted, the plaster could be scraped off the walls, doorways should be repaired, and the mouldings and ornaments ought to be restored to their pristine splendour. The publication of *An Account of the Church of St. Mary the Virgin, Stow Lincolnshire in Aid of the Proposed Restoration*[2] seems, however, to have been the full extent of the Society's involvement in this particular project.

Obviously, the practice of acting as a consultant could not continue long without some canons for restoration being developed. Strangely enough, no formal consideration of such principles occurred until after the crisis of 1845 had passed. In 1842 the *Ecclesiologist* said: 'To restore, is to recover the original appearance, which has been lost by decay, accident, or ill-judged alteration' (1, 70). This was far more difficult than it might seem, for almost all medieval churches contain features of several periods, representing a number of rebuildings. What could be considered the 'original appearance' of the building? The *Ecclesiologist* had an answer:

We must, either from existing evidences or from supposition, recover the original scheme of the edifice as conceived by the first builder, or as begun by him and developed by his immediate successors; or, on the other hand, must retain the additions or alterations of subsequent ages, repairing them when needing it, or even carrying out

---

[1] *Memorial*, p. 22.   [2] Cambridge, 1841.

perhaps more fully the idea which dictated them. . . . For our own part we decidedly choose the former; always however remembering that it is of great importance to take into account the age and purity of the later work, the occasion for its addition, its adaptation to its uses, and its intrinsic advantages of convenience (I, 65).

This decision had many unfortunate consequences. The Ecclesiologists believed that the steep roofs of early gothic were infinitely preferable to those of Perpendicular. As a result, they wrote: 'We have no hesitation in urging the propriety of entirely removing late superadded clerestories, and restoring the roofs to the form they undoubtedly had when the earlier arcades of the nave were built' (*E.* IV, 104). Actually clerestories had often been added to compensate for the loss of light resulting from the addition of aisles. Since many churches have such evidence as weather-moulding to indicate the existence of a previous roof of steeper pitch, removing clerestories in favour of a high roof could be justified as recovering the 'original appearance'. The Ecclesiologists did not think of it as substituting nineteenth-century work for medieval as we do today. They were bold in their destructiveness. In the case of the Church of St James, Audley, the *Ecclesiologist* expressed 'an earnest hope that the architects . . . will not hesitate to replace the existing *late* Middle Pointed tracery of the east window with a design of an earlier character, so as to restore it to the state in which it *must* have been originally erected' (V, 77). The Ecclesiologists were determined to produce correct medieval churches, even if they had to destroy ancient features to achieve their end. There can be no doubt as to the conviction with which the Society held its dogmas of church architecture.

The Society's direct involvement in actual restoration projects was brief and disastrous. It began on a small scale: 'The first restoration undertaken by the Society was that of the Font at Coton Church, near Cambridge.'[1] This led to removing the rough cast from St Bene't's Church, Cambridge, and a restoration of the font cover at St Edward's, Cambridge, since re-

---

[1] Boyce, *Memorial*, p. 23.

placed. The one major work of restoration which the Society directed has already been mentioned. The Society published a circular, *The Church of the Holy Sepulchre or the Round Church, Cambridge*, which described its anticipations in this project. It felt that 'the recent fall of a portion [of the aisle vaulting] . . . presents an opportunity such as may never again occur, of restoring this curious and venerable fabrick to some of its former beauty'.[1] It was a rare opportunity indeed, for St Sepulchre's was one of only four medieval circular churches surviving in the kingdom. The Society resolved to use this occasion to demonstrate its principles. A restoration committee was appointed with Thorp as its chairman, and including clergy and wardens of the parish and several of the Society's members. Anthony Salvin was employed as architect. The restoration was to be both 'complete and correct', a work 'which should be a lasting, and if possible a perfect example of the principles of church-building which the Society have advocated in their various publications'.[2]

The work was not merely of local significance. It was undertaken with great expectations: 'Should the Committee for the restoration be enabled to procure sufficient funds to carry their intentions into effect, this ancient church will be one of the most interesting buildings in the kingdom, and present, it is hoped, an example of successful restoration well worthy of being imitated by others' (*E.* I, 115). After the work had begun, it was referred to as '*in Cambridge*, our workshop and training school for future church-restorers, and *to the world* our example of what can be done and how'.[3]

The restoration was to be most thorough. Even the *Ecclesiologist* admitted: 'It is now almost impossible to ascertain the original form of this ancient Church, which was consecrated in the year 1101; for the round tower is the only portion that remains of the old edifice' (I, 6). But this did not deter the

---

[1] [Cambridge, 1842], p. 1.
[2] *Report* (1843), p. 27.
[3] Circular: *The Round Church* [Cambridge, 1844], p. 1.

Ecclesiologists. Besides strengthening the walls, considered in danger of collapse, they—

proposed to take off the belfry story and surmount the original part of the tower with a conical roof; to clear away the earth, which has accumulated against the walls, to the original earth line; to restore the semi-circular Norman windows (of which fortunately one remains in the clerestory, and will serve as a model); to clear away all the pews and gallery from the circular part; to procure equivalent and more convenient, if not increased, accommodation by building a south Aisle to the present Chancel, corresponding to that on the north side; and to recast and relay the entire leaden roof of the Chancel. A belfry tower must also be erected for the reception of the peal of bells.[1]

Those familiar with the present building would hardly recognize it in Ackermann's print of 1815. The two plates in Ackermann's *A History of the University of Cambridge, Its Colleges, Halls, and Public Buildings*[2] show a building with Perpendicular windows in the circular nave. On top of this is a Perpendicular bell tower which has now disappeared. The interior is filled with pews. A gallery was introduced at a later time.

The building, as the Society left it, was radically transformed. All traces of Perpendicular disappeared from the nave. The north chancel aisle was almost completely rebuilt and a bell tower added at its northwest corner. An entirely new aisle duplicates it on the south side of the chancel. Norman windows were inserted in the nave and filled with stained glass. The original bell tower was replaced by the present conical roof. It makes a picturesque building, undoubtedly a good deal more so than it did in its unrestored state. But it has become largely a nineteenth-century building rather than a medieval structure. The same was to happen to many other ancient buildings.

This troubles moderns, but evidently no one in the 1840's was seriously disturbed about that aspect of the restoration. What did upset people was the fact that the Restoration Committee, acting without much communication with the non-resident incumb-

[1] Circular: *Church of the Holy Sepulchre or the Round Church, Cambridge*, p. 1.
[2] London, 1815, vol. II, plates 57 and 58.

ent, saw to it that no item was omitted in its work of restoration. It could not resist the temptation of installing a stone altar and credence table. The *Ecclesiologist* published a drawing of 'the unpretending altar of the Round Church, which has raised the indignation of Messrs Faulkner, Goode, and Close' (IV, 86). It consisted of three parallel stone slabs supporting a horizontal stone slab. The front was left open. Even Goode had to admit that 'the altar which has been erected at the Round Church Cambridge, . . . differs from the tomb-like altars generally seen in the Romish churches [in] . . . that it is not closed in front, (though it is on the sides)'.[1] But Faulkner found it necessary to ' "contend for the faith which was once delivered to the Saints",' and the altar and credence table were ejected. As the *Ecclesiologist* put it, the Church was 'despoiled of its altar and credence-table, which were thrown out ignominiously into the Church-yard' (IV, 194).

The Restoration Committee returned the building to the parish, 'not, indeed, in that fulness of architectural beauty which their more sanguine wishes may have contemplated, but still far beyond the extent of the engagements in virtue of which they were intrusted with the superintendence'.[2] But the worst was yet to come:

The incumbent, having sufficiently defaced its beauty, by the re-erection of monuments on the walls, the 'formation'—to use his own term,—of a reading and clerk's pue, the introduction of a table, with flimsy buttresses to its legs, and cockney spandrils,—of chocolate-coloured commandment boards, and useless benches between the piers of the nave, proceeded to give notice of its re-opening (*E.* IV, 217).

The Society's dismay was audible: 'And this humiliating spectacle was the end of so many months of labour, and thought, and expense; the termination of hopes for a church that should be the glory of the University.' (*E.* IV, 218). Not all was loss, though, for the restored building 'remains a monument of what, even in these days, Christian art can effect to the glory of God,

---

[1] *Altars Prohibited by the Church of England*, p. 56.   [2] *Report* (1844), p. 72.

and has been the mother, by the force of the example which it shows, of many other restorations'.[1] It was reported that 'many similar restorations in various parts of our country, are known to be now in progress, which but for this example, would never have been thought of'.[2] Lest the Church in its full splendour be forgotten, the Society had lithographs of the exterior and interior printed and distributed. A view of the interior was included in *Illustrations of Monumental Brasses* in order 'to perpetuate the memory of the appearance of the church immediately after its restoration'.[3] Thereafter the Society confined its efforts in matters of restoration to giving advice instead of assuming a direct responsibility.

II

It is rather strange that the Society was so tardy in enunciating rules for restoration when so many other laws were promulgated early in its career. It was not until the spring of 1847 that the work of seriously formulating principles for church restoration began. The immediate cause was a tract by Mr E. A. Freeman on the *Principles of Church Restoration*. Although the Society had frequently crossed swords with Mr Freeman before, his opinions were respected, and on this occasion favourably received.

Freeman began by pointing out the difference between the medieval builders who frequently destroyed the work of their predecessors and contemporary architects who were reluctant to do so. The medieval architect, according to Freeman, 'may sometimes have wantonly destroyed beauties, the other too scrupulously preserved defects, yet, as a general rule, they have pursued the courses most proper for them respectively'.[4] However, there were good reasons for this difference. Modern knowledge was insufficient:

[1] *Illustrations of Monumental Brasses*, p. 215.
[2] [Thomas Thorp], *The Church of the Holy Sepulchre, Cambridge* (Cambridge, 1844), p. 22.
[3] *Illustrations of Monumental Brasses*, p. 215.
[4] *Principles of Church Restoration* (London, 1846), p. 5.

But the merely imitative position of architecture at present is both an undeniable fact, and, as a moment's consideration will show, is a necessary stage in the revival of a lost art. It is only by doing for a while as the ancients did, that we can expect at some time to do better; we must thoroughly understand their principles and be able to reproduce their details before we can expect to improve upon them.[1]

Furthermore, ancient and modern architects are distinguished by 'the absence of an antiquarian spirit in the one, and in its presence in the other'.[2] Modern architects have a kind of reverence for the work produced before the Reformation, and the gap of three centuries gives an aura of sanctity to the architecture of the Middle Ages. This feeling was called 'association'.

Freeman then proceeded to make some 'practical remarks' on restoration. His cardinal rule was that the architect should 'introduce as little of his own invention as he possibly can'.[3] But supposing a client demanded that a church be restored to its 'ancient condition'? In a church built in one style this was comparatively simple. 'But in the far more abundant cases where a Church has received changes in several stages of architecture, . . . what is here to be done? It cannot be maintained that all is to be reduced to its original condition.'[4] Freeman decided:

The question then after all must be left to turn in each individual case on the extent and merit of the work of the different dates. Where one style is decidedly predominant, especially if the Church be a rich or remarkable example of that style, and the later alterations few and poor, no one would probably hesitate in restoring exclusively in the older style.[5]

As an example, he cites the splendid Norman church at Iffley, near Oxford, a building containing some Geometrical and Perpendicular windows. Freeman would not object to the removal of these later additions.

The difficulty of making a blanket rule for restoration is apparent to Freeman: 'Perhaps in most cases the best plan would

---

[1] *Ibid.*, p. 7.   [2] *Ibid.*, p. 7.   [3] *Ibid.*, p. 13.   [4] *Ibid.*, p. 12.   [5] *Ibid.*, p. 13.

be to bring back the Church to the appearance it presented immediately after the last alteration of tolerable character; but even this must be liable to many exceptions; almost everything still remains to be settled in each particular case.'[1] He praised a restoration of St Mary's, Stafford, which had involved removing a choir clerestory, replacing it with a high roof, and substituting 'a noble Lancet triplet . . . for a very poor Debased window'.[2] In any case, Freeman realized how important the 'restoration of Catholick arrangements' was and strongly deprecated instances where 'matters of architectural beauty [were] preferred to those of ritual necessity'.[3]

The Society eventually adopted principles similar to those Freeman advocated, though in practice the results offended him highly. The *Ecclesiologist* reviewed Freeman's book favourably in May 1847 and used it as a means of raising the question of the proper method for restoration. The reviewer also seized the opportunity to create labels for the different theories of restoration—the Destructive, the Conservative, and the Eclectic.

The Destructive theory was described as—'that which was universally adopted by our ancestors. It directs that in restoring any building the original style, arrangement, and proportion, be entirely left out of the question; it employs the best style of art, adopts the best conceptions which present themselves, and to these it sacrifices the work of an earlier generation' (VII, 162). Directly opposed to this was the Conservative system which would—'reproduce in repairing a building the exact details of every piece of ancient work which presents itself at the time the reparation is taken in hand; Norman, First-Pointed, Middle-Pointed, Tudor work are equally respected; and the church in its new state is a mere *facsimile* . . . of the old building unchurchwardenized' (VII, 162). Somewhat of a compromise is indicated by the third theory, the Eclectic—'in certain cases it would simply restore, in others it would re-model: but the unfortunate thing is, that no one who has hitherto written on the subject has been able, or has even endeavoured to lay down any definite

---

[1] *Principles of Church Restoration*, p. 14. [2] *Ibid.*, p. 15. [3] *Ibid.*, p. 16.

rule, when we are to be content with the one and when we may venture on the other' (VII, 162–3).

The reviewer then commented on the three systems. It could be said in favour of the Destructive that it was 'the only system which offers the logical possibility of working a building into a state of abstract perfection; for it logically follows upon the theory of architectural development that there can be only one perfect period of architecture, all others tending to or declining from it' (VII, 163). But this has the disadvantage of ignoring all 'feeling of association', an item of importance, particularly in view of the revived reverence for the past. Undoubtedly the Conservative system is the 'safest', but that is its only advantage. 'There is no use in believing or asserting one style of Christian art to be superior to others, if nevertheless we are not to employ it because it happens to have been removed to make way for another' (VII, 167). The *Ecclesiologist* boasted: 'We take some credit to ourselves for having been among the first to advocate what we esteem a sounder course, as for example, when we advised the removal of late clerestories' (VII, 167). The Eclectic system received enthusiastic approval, but it had one difficulty which only time could cure: 'To lay down any principle for such Eclecticism would not only be a task beyond our own power, but—we are too much afraid—beyond that of any architect, professional or unprofessional, of the present day. Yet that principles exist we are certain; that they will be discovered we firmly believe' (VII, 167). The Eclectic system seems to be primarily the absence of any clear system, but the *Ecclesiologist* committed itself to this method.

The stage was now set for the great discussion of restoration, an event which occurred at the Eighth Anniversary Meeting, held in London on 18 May 1847. As reported in the June 1847 issue of the *Ecclesiologist* it must have been a very interesting occasion. Hope noted, in introducing the debate, that 'the question had been lately brought before public notice in an able pamphlet by a member of the Oxford Architectural Society' (*E.* VII, 237), referring to Freeman's tract. Most of the

Society's prominent members were present as well as several architects. Each theory of restoration found its supporters.

Neale, always the radical, 'took up the Destructive side of the question, and announced his readiness to see Peterborough Cathedral pulled down, if it could be replaced by a Middle-Pointed cathedral as good of its sort' (*E.* vii, 238). Pressed on this point, Neale 'observed that the ancient architects only destroyed the works of their predecessors in the belief that their own were better. He himself, could he know that a better style than Middle-Pointed was discovered, would destroy every Middle-Pointed building.' Other advocates of the Destructive system were found. 'The Rev. J. L. Patterson announced himself a Destructive, still he did not think all previous stages ought to be obliterated. In practice he would keep up all the intermediate steps of architectural developement' (vii, 238). A Mr Parkins agreed with this, stating that 'the destructive was the right *theory*, but untenable in practice' (vii, 239). To these men, Rev. W. Scott quite sensibly pointed out that if previous generations had abided by this method, no medieval churches whatsoever would have remained, and it 'would have left us absolutely nothing by this time but such churches as All Souls, S. Marylebone, for example' (vii, 238). This was a shocking statement, for few churches were as sincerely despised by the Ecclesiologists as this building by Nash.

The Conservative school had few adherents, though today almost all church restorers would claim allegiance to it. Mr W. C. Luard admitted he was one, believing that 'churches were not only temples of GOD, but historical monuments, and as such ought to be preserved' (vii, 238). Another Conservative, Mr J. D. Chambers, mentioned the importance of a 'sense of what was due from us to the intentions of the founders of religious edifices' (vii, 239). Rev. W. Dodsworth was also a Conservative.

The Eclectic theory was clearly the most popular among those present.[1] Hope belonged to the Eclectics, and pointed out

---

[1] Sir Kenneth Clark's assertion that 'the members were almost unanimously in favour of this last course [Destructive] and it was decided that, should funds permit,

that 'all arts called out invention and imitation' (vii, 238). On the grounds that it was the 'least of two evils' and that 'we were speaking, not a living, but a dead language', Mr W. T. Parkins joined the Eclectic party. Mr A. H. Burford felt that the 'Eclectic theory had quite gained the day in point of argument' (vii, 239). Webb likewise was an Eclectic, though he felt it necessary to ascertain 'what limits should be fixed to the value of association as attached to styles or details in any restoration' (vii, 239). Street was a manly Eclectic, feeling that 'Eclecticism might sometimes even require the destruction of Middle-Pointed work' (vii, 240). The Dean of Chichester, the chairman of the debate—

wound up the discussion in favour of the Eclectic theory; considering Conservatism a Chinese principle, and Destructiveness a most dangerous experiment. Variety, he thought, should pervade art, as it does nature. By adopting the Eclectic theory, we might hope to develope something more beautiful than ever yet known. In the meantime we are not to keep up nor copy deformity, but aim at advancing and developing the ideal of beauty (vii, 240).

Eclecticism won the day, though, being such a flexible principle, it could be extended to embrace the other theories. The extreme forms of conservatism and destructiveness were ruled out. The following year, the *Ecclesiologist* announced: 'The only principle which can be universally and satisfactorily maintained is what may be termed "*Eclectic Conservatism*". Merge the mere reverence for existing things and the too great regard for historical record in the Conservative, with the innovating (so to speak) tendency of the Eclectic, and a principle will be the result, which may be universally adopted' (viii, 85).

The Eighth Anniversary Meeting was an important occasion because an increasing number of architects and clergymen were looking to the Society for guidance. The Society had condemned enough restorations to make architects realize what a hazardous

it would be a worthy object of the Society to pull down Peterborough Cathedral and rebuild it in the style of the best period' (*Gothic Revival*, p. 249) is quite contrary to the report of the meeting carried in the *Ecclesiologist*.

occupation restoring churches was. The month of the great
debate, the *Ecclesiologist* had published 'a specimen of letters
which we are constantly receiving and to answer which satisfactorily involves the determination of a question which has as
yet received no satisfactory and philosophical answer' (VII, 161).
The sample letter asked for 'advice as to the style of the restoration: whether the old work is to be exactly copied, or whether
it might be advisable to replace it by details of a better date'
(VII, 161). It was the type of question the Society had certainly
provoked through its stress on the superiority of Decorated.
Evidently many architects took the prevailing opinion of the
Eighth Anniversary Meeting as the answer.

Scott, who considered himself a Conservative though the
twentieth century thinks of him as a leading destroyer, felt that
this discussion had had a very baleful influence. In his *A Plea
for the Faithful Restoration of Our Ancient Churches*, Scott wrote:

It is much to be regretted that so highly influential a body as the
Ecclesiological Society should have given an indirect sanction to
this system of *radical restoration*, by the very unhappy discussion which
took place at their annual meeting in 1847, in which the different
members severally announced their adherence to what had been
rather whimsically distinguished by a very talented writer in the
'Ecclesiologist' as the 'Conservative', the 'Destructive', and the 'Eclectic' systems of restoration. If such unguarded conversations must
take place, it would be better that they should be *in private*.[1]

Scott added in a footnote:

The unlucky conversation . . . was, probably, so far as the 'destructive' opinions went, intended in a semi-jocose sense; but the pro-
pounders of such notions must have underrated the influence of what
passes at their meetings;—what they said has by many been taken
in earnest, and their jokes have thus become *no laughing matter*. I
believe that no such opinions are now for a moment entertained by
any of the gentlemen I refer to.

It would appear that Scott's assumption about the mood in
which the Destructive method was introduced was correct. At

---

[1] London, 1850, pp. 21–2.

a similar discussion at the Twenty-sixth Anniversary Meeting, G. E. Street stated that Neale had adopted the Destructive position in order to challenge discussion. 'He did not for an instant mean to say that Mr Neale held those sentiments. He merely threw them out as a suggestion in order to raise a discussion. He would be as much horrified as anybody to propose destructive restoration' (*E.* xxvi, 246). Whatever Neale's intentions had been, the Society was rarely accused of being too conservative, but those criticizing it for destructiveness are legion.

There were occasions, especially as restorations multiplied, that the Society did condemn work for being too radical. One correspondent argued with the Society about Ferrey's destruction of medieval frescoes in St Laurence, Reading, in order to insert triple lancets. To the argument that such frescoes were exceedingly rare, he replied: 'This is an argument fitted rather for the "*Archaeological Journal*" than the "*Ecclesiologist*". It goes simply on antiquarian, not on artistic grounds; the fresco is to be retained, to the prejudice of the building, merely as a curiosity. I say merely as a curiosity, because careful copies, . . . would answer every purpose of study' (*E.* ix, 127). The *Ecclesiologist* disagreed: 'Were we absolute Conservatives in our views of church restoration, or absolute Destructives, our course would be very clear; but, Eclectics as we are, we must decide according to the circumstances of the peculiar case' (ix, 129). It condemned Ferrey's work of destruction in this instance, but excessively conservative restorations were also subject to harsh criticisms.

III

The Society's enthusiasm for restoration continued, and the number of restorations increased throughout the land. In 1854 the *Ecclesiologist* reported that calculations showed 'that one fourth of the parish churches of England have been restored within the last twenty years' (xv, 4). Probably even more were subjected to restoration in the next two decades. Many of the cathedrals were restored at this time, occasionally undoing the restorations of the eighteenth century. Scott was a favourite with cathedral authorities, no fewer than eighteen cathedrals being committed to his mercy. In general, the *Ecclesiologist* approved of Scott's restorations. His book, *A Plea for the Faithful Restoration of our Ancient Churches* received a favourable review from the *Ecclesiologist*. The 'great difficulty' Scott had written, 'is to know where to stop'.[1] But as he himself admitted, 'while I venture forward as a champion of conservatism, I cannot boast of having my self carried out its principles to my own satisfaction'.[2] The *Ecclesiologist* was pleased to 'be sure that his type of arrangement was not that which we took the liberty some years ago to term semi-Catholic', of which Scott had obviously been suspect (XI, 12). The reviewer declared: 'Mr Scott belongs in Church Restoration to the conservative party, but he words his dogmas so very moderately, that in point of fact, we can discover but little difference in him from that shade of the *Eclectic* theory of which we are the professors' (XI, 12).

One of the most unfortunate developments of the restoration mania was what the Society named 'recasting'. In 1867 the *Ecclesiologist* reported:

Recasting has become so much a phenomenon as contrasted with restoration, that we have often thought of making a separate head of those churches which have been operated on, not with the intention of bringing them back to mediaeval excellence of architecture, but of conferring a religiosity of aspect and arrangement, above their genuine nature, to the buildings of the last two centuries (XXVIII, 231).

Under the pretext of satisfying 'the purer religious sentiment of this age, which has learned the more excellent way of Church architecture' (*E.* XXI, 153), many seventeenth- and eighteenth-century churches were recast. Wren's churches were frequently victims of such efforts. The *Ecclesiologist* cheerfully reported Scott's 'recasting' of St Michael's, Cornhill: 'He fuses the vaulting into something transitional between Pointed and Italian.

[1] P. 29.   [2] P. 6.

And he inserts tracery in all the round-headed windows, and the great ugly stable-like circles of the clerestory become roses under his plastic hand' (xvII, 107).

Such efforts did not satisfy all of the *Ecclesiologist*'s readers. 'J. C. J.' wrote an indignant letter on 'Sir Christopher Wren Turned Goth'. He complained that recasting amounted to a 'cruel barbarism', and that 'we have no earthly right to tear this page out of our history, or to make a poor palimpsest of it' (*E.* xxv, 13). The *Ecclesiologist*, however, was eager to improve Wren's work and longed to begin painting the interior and installing stained glass in St Paul's Cathedral. 'Colour is what is most needed in S. Paul's' and a chancel screen came next. Without the screen 'we reduce our S. Paul's to that level [St Peter's in Rome]' (*E.* xxII, 104).

The Society considered its work in encouraging and directing restorations to be highly useful; yet none of its activities have been so offensive to succeeding generations. The encouragement which the Ecclesiologists gave to replacing medieval features by more 'correct' details was abused by many architects. But the Society must bear the responsibility for the wholesale destruction of great quantities of medieval art. Sir Kenneth Clark remarks: 'It would be interesting to know if the Camden Society destroyed as much medieval architecture as Cromwell. If not it was from lack of funds, *sancta paupertas*, only true custodian of ancient buildings.'[1] In 1879 an English writer lamented:

And now, what has been the actual result of thirty years of church 'Restoration'? Briefly this,—that in by far the greater number of our lesser country churches there scarcely survives a *single point of interest*. In the case of our more considerable structures—with a few bright exceptions—the merest wreck remains of what did once so much delight and interest the beholder.[2]

Most such denunciations of the restorations of the 1840's and

[1] *The Gothic Revival*, p. 237.
[2] John William Burgon, Introduction to Scott's *Personal and Professional Recollections*, p. xii.

1850's came after the original Society ceased to exist (and when the damage had been done). Even in its time, though, the Society did not escape all criticism. In 1853 E. A. Freeman produced a very pointed tract *On the Preservation and Restoration of Ancient Monuments*. He asserted:

'There are persons calling themselves admirers of ancient art, lovers of ancient churches, who have sent forth, in a style which would not have disgraced King Harry himself, a solemn mandate for the entire destruction of Peterborough Cathedral and King's College Chapel, with the single proviso that buildings supposed to approach more nearly to some fancied ideal may be erected in their place.

'This view was put forth with sufficient plainess of speech in a discussion among the members of the Ecclesiological Society, of which I am sorry to say that a former pamphlet of mine was the indirect occasion' (*E*. xiv, 40–1).

The *Ecclesiologist* replied that Neale, 'as a private member of the Ecclesiological Society', had simply suggested 'that, were it possible to rebuild our present cathedrals in a higher style, he thought that association ought to give way to beauty'. It added: 'The supposition was confessedly an *ex impossibili* one: and Mr. Neale may very possibly be mistaken' (xiv, 41).

Certainly the most eloquent opponent of restoration was John Ruskin. His *The Seven Lamps of Architecture* appeared in 1849 and left little doubt as to Ruskin's opinion on restoration:

Neither by the public, nor by those who have the care of public monuments, is the true meaning of the word *restoration* understood. It means the most total destruction which a building can suffer: a destruction out of which no remnants can be gathered: a destruction accompanied with false description of the thing destroyed. Do not let us deceive ourselves in this important matter; it is *impossible*, as impossible as to raise the dead, to restore anything that has ever been great or beautiful in architecture.[1]

The *Ecclesiologist*, in reviewing the book, approved of Ruskin's 'high-toned standard of taste, his perception of the real dignity of art, his abhorrence of the sordid and unreal' (x, 111). But

---

[1] *Seven Lamps of Architecture*, 2nd ed. (London, 1956), p. 199.

when it came to restoration, the periodical admitted: 'For our-selves, while we own that we tremble every time we hear of a Church-restoration—however many of them we commemorate in our pages—yet we cannot go to the same length as Mr Ruskin.' Righteously, it added: 'We are not *artists* only: we have a duty to consult, the comeliness and decency of GOD's house' (x, 118).

Ruskin and the Society were in considerable accord on artistic principles; on religious grounds they were miles apart. In the first volume of his *Stones of Venice*, Ruskin showed his hatred of Catholicism:

But of all these fatuities, the basest is the being lured into the Rom-anist Church by the glitter of it, like larks into a trap by broken glass; to be blown into a change of religion by the whine of an organ-pipe; stitched into a new creed by gold threads on priest's petticoats; jangled into a change of conscience by the chimes of a belfry.[1]

The *Ecclesiologist* could not ignore such an oblique reference to its own activities. In reviewing volume one of the *Stones of Venice* it commented: 'Fortunately we may adopt, almost without re-serve, Mr. Ruskin's principles of criticism without in the least degree sharing his hatred of Catholicity. . . . His speculations concerning questions of art lead him to one conclusion; his religious principles drive him to another, wholly irreconcilable' (xII, 216). Suffice it to say, Ruskin could approve of neither the method nor the purpose of the restorations which the Society promoted. He did, however, appear at the Twenty-second An-niversary Meeting of the Society (13 June 1861) and joined a discussion on the 'destructive character of modern French re-storation' and in condemning 'the utter want of a sound artistic feeling among the French clergy and the general French laity' (*E.* xxII, 251).

Ruskin led the way in condemning the restorations of Scott. In 1874 he rejected the medal of the Royal Institute of British Architects in annoyance with its approval of restorations, a very pointed gesture since Scott was then President of the

[1] *Stones of Venice* (New York, 1865), Appendix 12, 1, 378.

Institute. In a speech on this occasion Scott blamed the Society: 'More than half of our ancient churches . . . have been so dealt with by ignorant and sacrilegious hands that one is ready to curse the day when the then youthful Cambridge Camden Society, all too sanguine and ardent, adopted for their motto the ominous words so sadly realized, "*Donec Templa refeceris*".'[1] Scott's method of restoration, applied to hundreds of buildings, often meant the destruction of many medieval features. 'This seems to us appalling,' Sir Kenneth Clark remarks, 'for we forget one great difference between Gilbert Scott and ourselves: he believed that he built very good Gothic, we that he built very bad. As long as the Gothic revivalists had faith in their movement they thought of restoration merely as the substitution of one good thing for another.'[2] Much of the blame rests upon the Society for it frequently rejoiced in Scott's undertaking restorations as at Ely in 1847 (*E.* VIII, 117) or at St Alban's in 1856 (*E.* XVII, 253).

In 1877 William Morris and others founded the Society for the Protection of Ancient Buildings. A statement issued at its formation summarized what had occurred:

'We think that these last fifty years of knowledge and attention have done more for their destruction [ancient buildings] than all the foregoing centuries of revolution, violence, and contempt.

'But those who make the change wrought in our day under the name of Restoration, while professing to bring back a building to the best time of its history, have no guide but each his own individual whim to point out to them what is admirable and what is contemptible; while the very nature of their task compels them to destroy something and to supply the gap by imagining what the early builders should or might have done.'[3]

The twentieth century has not yet seen fit to reverse this judgement and contemporary feeling finds the Ecclesiologists largely responsible for the destruction of much medieval art. It is indeed

[1] *Recollections*, p. 404. [2] *The Gothic Revival*, p. 251.

[3] Quoted by Briggs, *Goths and Vandals*, pp. 208–9. The Society numbered among its members, Carlyle, Ruskin, Bryce, Stephen, Patmore, Keene, Hunt, and Burne-Jones. It was sometimes referred to as the 'Anti-Scrape'.

ironical that modern opinion regards the Ecclesiologists in much the same light as William Dowsing, the Puritan iconoclast whom the Society hated so fervently.

Possibly we are more sentimental about ancient buildings than the nineteenth century was, though we like to think of it as being the century of sentiment and feeling. So sensitive have Englishmen become to the damages wrought by nineteenth-century church restorers, that the twentieth century, thus far, has distinguished itself by being the first not to add contemporary art to medieval churches. The French have made many interesting experiments in adding contemporary stained glass to such cathedrals as Amiens and Beauvais, and have considerably modified the liturgical arrangements in many ancient churches. French churches likewise suffered from much ill-advised restoration in the nineteenth century, but this has not prevented the twentieth century from making its own contribution to French religious art.

CHAPTER VII

ECCLESIOLOGY APPLIED IN
BUILDING NEW CHURCHES

I

The tremendous expansion of urban areas in the nineteenth century necessitated the building of hundreds of new churches throughout England. This provided a golden opportunity for the Cambridge Camden Society to exercise a creative role in guiding those directly responsible for the new buildings. The Society never undertook the responsibility for erecting a new church, perhaps having been warned through the unfortunate experience with the Round Church. At one of the Society's meetings in 1841 mention was made of a 'contemplated scheme for erecting by national subscription a Model church' (*E.* i, 8). Neale announced in *A Few Words to Church Builders*: '*Another method of proof is in contemplation by the* CAMBRIDGE CAMDEN SOCIETY . . . *it is intended to exhibit, in a church to be dedicated in honour of* S. ALBAN THE PROTOMARTYR OF ENGLAND, *and in Decorated as the most beautiful style, the nearest approach we can make to a perfect model of a Christian temple.*'[1] This early project was never realized.

Although the Society did not duplicate the work of the various church-building societies, it made its influence felt most keenly on their officials. Mention has already been made of the petition which the Society addressed to the Incorporated Society for Promoting the Enlargement, Building, and Repairing of Churches and Chapels, requesting that it revise its *Suggestions and Instructions*. If such an institution could be persuaded to revise its standards, it is not surprising that churchwardens in numerous parishes could be awed into submission. The situation has hardly changed today; inexperienced building committees

[1] 2nd ed., p. 31.

seem peculiarly susceptible to the guidance of any 'authority' in fulfilling their responsibilities.

Whatever else it possessed, the Society had absolute confidence that it knew what was correct. Nowhere was this more apparent than in the Society's publications which reiterated the same laws constantly. The *Few Words to Church Builders* contained an appendix listing 'Windows, Fonts and Roodscreens Intended to Serve as Models'. *Church Enlargement and Church Arrangement*, though intended primarily for those seeking greater accommodation in an old building, dictated how the building should appear. Similar instructions were issued in the *Few Words to Churchwardens*. Drawings ready for copying of a cemetery chapel, a lichgate, and a school appeared in the Second Series of *Instrumenta Ecclesiastica*.

The *Ecclesiologist* provided another kind of weapon through its continuing series of reviews entitled 'New Churches'. In the course of its existence, the periodical must have examined well over a thousand buildings. As already indicated, the *Ecclesiologist*'s tactics were not of the gentle variety. A notice of some work by the architect Edward Blore suggested: 'For his competency let the curious go to see that truly contemptible building, Christ Church, Hoxton, to select one of this gentleman's enormities.' And with proper gentility it added: 'We have no wish to be disrespectful to Mr. Blore, or to detract from any merits which he may really have' (III, 99).

The Society's criticism was anything but subtle. Frequently comments appear on various individuals which are by no means restricted to an objective appraisal of their work. The *Ecclesiologist* pointed out for the benefit of the 'many who have really felt it a stumbling-block that a person of Mr. Rickman's religious persuasion [he was a Quaker] should be regarded as a benefactor to Christian Art', that after all, 'he did very little . . . and his churches are monuments of extreme ecclesiological ignorance' (VII, 91). Rickman was dead when this appeared (1847), but Pugin was very much alive. Pugin's sole fault, one feels, is that he was a Roman Catholic. Otherwise he might have been accorded the favours granted to Butterfield. But Pugin's work was propaganda for both the gothic revival and for the Roman Catholic Church. He delighted in publishing engravings of his projected buildings 'as in a state of ideal perfection'. This annoyed the *Ecclesiologist* considerably, and it inquired: 'We appeal to our readers, if they ever visited a church of his, after having studied it in his engravings, and were not disappointed' (v, 11). The verdict was damning: 'Mr. Pugin, clever and enthusiastic as he is, has not answered the expectations which were formed of him; he has not realised that highest standard of Christian art which we expected from him; he has not improved in the degree which we should have hoped for, while all about him were in breathless progress' (v, 10–11). After his death, the *Ecclesiologist* admitted: 'his genius, had it ever had full scope, would have manifested itself in works infinitely superior to those, which, as a fact it has left behind' (XIII, 353). Presumably such scope would have been given in the Church of England.

Pugin's case was hopeless, but generally such bullying was successful. The Society made its demands of architects and they responded, either out of fear or conviction. There were, however, exceptions. In 1856 two English architects, Henry Clutton and William Burges, won a competition for Lille Cathedral in France with a design from a period earlier than Middle-Pointed. Scott claimed:

This was really the first occasion on which the Ecclesiological Society's law, as regards the 'Middle Pointed', was set at nought. . . . Clutton and Burges certainly had the credit of overthrowing the old tyranny, and even some of its most rigorous abetters soon found it necessary to outvie each other in setting at nought their former faith, and in trying who could be *earliest* in the style of their buildings. One thing, however, never changed, the intolerance shown by them [the Ecclesiologists] for all freedom of thought on the part of other men. Every one must perforce follow in their wake, no matter how often they changed, or how entirely they reversed their own previous views. Nor was anything more certain than this, that however erroneous their former opinion might have been, their views for the time being were right, and that every one who differed from them was a heretic, or an old-fashioned simpleton. It had many years before been a saying of mine, that there was no class of men whom the Cambridge Camden Society held in such scorn, as those who adhered to their own last opinion but one; and this sentiment has been the great inheritance and heirloom of their imitators.[1]

Scott, of course, was bitter because the Society did not prefer his churches to those of Carpenter and Butterfield. But there is much truth in what he says about the power of the Society's opinion.

It became obvious, as time went on, that the Society's ideas were being accepted in many places. An unexpected success was found in the mission field where new churches were a constant necessity. It was reported that the Society's 'intention to select and adopt certain ancient churches, of which working drawings might be sent to colonies of a climate not unlike England . . . has been found very successful'.[2] Butterfield and Place had contributed some drawings for this purpose. Even architects working overseas could not escape criticism since many foreign churches, especially in the United States, were discussed on the basis of drawings received by the Society. In the *Ecclesiologist*'s opinion, the Chapel of the Cross, Chapel Hill, North Carolina, was 'as bad as bad can be' (x, 198).[3]

It was noticed that Dissenters were also building gothic churches, sometimes in correct Middle Pointed. Few went so far as the Unitarians of Leeds who, '*horribile dictu*, are building a meetinghouse in florid Middle-Pointed. We hear that they intend to establish in it a kind of choral service, with vestments

[1] *Recollections*, p. 206.   [2] *Account of the Sixth Anniversary Meeting*, p. 9.
[3] Ecclesiology in the United States was promoted by the New York Ecclesiological Society. In 1846 the *Ecclesiologist* announced: 'We understand that it is proposed to establish an Ecclesiological Society in the United States' (vi, 160). Twelve years later, it was necessary to declare 'our regret at the premature extinction of our daughter Society of New York. We have heard that it had become a mere Church Building Association, and had ceased to concern itself with theoretical ecclesiology' (xix, 30). The New York Society published the *New York Ecclesiologist* from 1848 to 1853. It also issued an *Annual Report* and *Transactions* for several years. An interesting tract by Walker Gwynne, *The Beginnings of Church Architecture in America*, (n.p., [1917]), speaks of the New York Society as the 'beginning in America of real Church architecture, liturgical science, and their allied arts of ornamentation and music' (p. 3).

for their ministers' (*E.* IX, 144). Such a testimony to their own influence did not please the Ecclesiologists. In 1847 the *Ecclesiologist* included a report on 'The New Independent Meeting-House at Manchester'. The building, it said, was—

in imitation of an old Catholic church, in the style transitory between First and Middle-Pointed, with a lofty spire, and will . . . be able to vie in ecclesiastical effect with many a well-intentioned Church of the 'Movement'.

. . . It will, according to the temperament of various persons, be either set down as a hopeful sign, . . . or as a piece of mere unreal pageantry, a proof of deadness of heart, and obtuseness of sense, a hollow and sickening thing, like the laughter of idiotcy, or a drunken revel in a charnel-house (VII, 171).

With admirable consistency, the *Ecclesiologist* admitted that such good architecture permitted it to say of modern Dissenters 'what we cannot say of the earliest leaders of the body, that they may be to any conceivable extent, and in any conceivable proportion good men and good Christians' (VII, 172). Irvingism was a more 'subtle antagonist' but it was hoped that the Church would successfully grapple 'with the novel delusion' (*E.* XV, 88).

If one can believe the word of the Society, Roman Catholics were much less successful as Ecclesiologists. The *Ecclesiologist* admitted that if it failed to review Roman Catholic churches, 'our Roman brethren' would assume 'we had absolutely nothing to say in criticism of them, that they were so much superior to what we could produce, that we prudently passed over them' (IX, 151). This certainly was not the case, as the writer proceeded to show. Pugin's St George's, Lambeth, was too large, Catholics (despite Pugin) lacked 'tangible appreciation' of chancels, roodscreens were ignored, and many other mistakes were apparent. Subsequently, the *Ecclesiologist* reported with horror that at a Roman Catholic cathedral built by Pugin in Ireland, 'the altar has been brought down from the eastern end, and placed under the tower: the great arch, at the entrance of the choir, is now being blocked up: the choir itself, thus cut off, is boarded over, and made the site of *confessionals*!' (XI, 271). On numerous occasions, the *Ecclesiologist* returned to condemn the 'ritual shortcomings' of the Roman Church. There was some justice in this, for Roman Catholics in England (especially, it seems, some of the bishops) had little interest then in medieval art and ceremonial. But certainly the Society was not disinterested. By attacking Rome it demonstrated its loyalty to Anglicanism.

Of course, it was within the Church of England that the Society's principles had their greatest success. The Society was never modest about this. As early as 1843, Webb boasted: 'The calm and steady diffusion of the views and principles advocated by the Society, and especially the growing adoption of them by professional architects, are highly satisfactory and encouraging' (*E.* II, 88). Six years later, it was reported that the 'proper arrangement and use of the chancel and sanctuary, and the nature and employment of decorative colour and general ornament have been, during the past year, very generally diffused and extensively acted upon'.[1] At the Twenty-sixth Anniversary Meeting, Hope asserted: 'We have turned minds upside down as to the outside and general fabric of the church, . . . and so we have given a new life, a new character, a new significance to the Prayer Book and to the worship of the Church of England' (*E.* xxv, 209).

Evidence of the change was everywhere. In 1872 Eastlake could make the statement: 'At the present day an architect would as soon think of building a church without a chancel, as of building one without a roof.'[2] This certainly could not have been said twenty-five years previously. In 1852 the *Ecclesiologist*, with obvious delight, reported on Pearson's Holy Trinity Church, Westminster:

With the one single exception . . . of the absence of [a] chancel screen, Holy Trinity church exhibits every distinctive feature of that system of church arrangement which it has been the constant and primary intention of our pages to advocate, as the embodied mind of the Church of England, for which we have often been laughed at and

---

[1] *Report* (1849), p. 19.   [2] *History of the Gothic Revival*, p. 220.

often taken to task, and in which we have triumphed. Such a triumph of these principles as the church now before us, is far more striking . . . than would be manifested in a structure of even superior merit erected under our own more immediate influence. The founder of this church . . . is personally unknown to us (*E.* XIII, 409).

Such acceptance, though, was not universal. In 1851 during the controversy over the 'Papal Aggression', the Archdeacon of Middlesex charged that ecclesiology ' "which under happier circumstances would have been safe and harmless, had a tendency to heighten . . . this Romanizing fever" '. His colleague, the Archdeacon of London, denounced ' "chancel worship" ' (*E.* XII, 190). Architects occasionally found themselves caught between the demands of the Society and the restrictions of Church authorities. 'An Architect' complained to the Society as late as 1867:

I may also mention that the bishop will not pass any plan which has more than one step at the entrance of the chancel, or more than two at the communion rails. . . . No 'super-altar' will be sanctioned. Nor should the prayer-desk face north or south, but west.

In an adjoining diocese, 'No footpace is allowed, the table is to stand on four legs, no reredos or super-altar is allowed. The prayer-desk is to be in the nave facing west'.

In another diocese, 'No credence is permitted'.

The question is, How can we build even *decent* churches with such arbitrary rules? (*E.* XXVIII, 64).

There were also the incorrigibly classical architects. Thomas Goodchild spoke for them in 1857 while defending classical architecture:

It has never been properly understood and practised in this country but by the few, and, indeed, by them in most cases as servile copyists of the details of old Greek and Roman buildings—the same course as that pursued in the present day by 'Gothic architects' in churches, even to the reproduction of useless papistical piscinas, obsolete screens, and disease-engendering sedilia.[1]

But Goodchild spoke for a losing cause, and even the classicists had learned to design buildings with chancels. Hundreds of

[1] 'Gothic and Classic', *The Builder*, xv (1857), 25.

gothic churches were built all over England in the 1850's and 60's.

II

The Society was never troubled by undue modesty about its accomplishments. After ten years of activity, the *Ecclesiologist* paused to reflect on what had been achieved:

When our Society first started, just ten years ago, we seemed to be fighting a desperate battle against overwhelming odds. . . . Had our cause not been that of the Catholic Church, in its external manifest-ation, we should have most assuredly been shipwrecked. . . . We were neither grave ecclesiastics nor practical architects—but simply un-dergraduates of Cambridge, bringing to our work no little of the petulance of youth and the ignorance of tyros. . . . We can . . . affirm, that our principles have triumphed. . . . The scope of our exertions has already been twice shifted. It is no longer to fight the battle of architectural reality against barbarous conventionalism—of roofs and aisles, and legitimate windows, against the weak contrivances of Soanes, and Burtons, and Elliotts—It is hardly even to press the higher claims of Middle-Pointed. The old type of church seems to have been absolutely expunged, except from some few remote local-ities—Southwark or the Colonies—or Kemp Town—and to have given place to a craving, which is really dangerous, from its rapid growth, for the external shape and form, and dignity, of the stateliest churches of the Edwardean age—with just an opening for 'Early English' in villages (x, 204).

This unexpected success brought a number of refinements in the architectural code championed by the Society. None of the revisions affected the liturgical arrangement or the type of floor plan advocated by the Ecclesiologists, but they did materially alter the appearance and decoration of the buildings them-selves. Some of these changes were the result of the Society's move to London; others were the result of continental travel and further study on the part of the membership. Theologically little had changed; architecturally many features were com-pletely altered.

The most significant change came several years after the

185

Society had moved its headquarters to London. The ideal church, as originally conceived by the group, was an exquisite village church, set in a spacious churchyard far away from the shadows of other buildings and the smoke of the city. At first the members seemed to assume that a city church need only be a larger version of the perfect country church. But in 1850 it was objected that the new church of St Barnabas', Pimlico, was 'too little like a town church' and that St Stephen's, Westminster, had 'too much of a country-church look'.

The distinction between village and town churches was spelled out in detail later that year by George Edmund Street in a communication 'On the Proper Characteristics of a Town Church'. Street began:

I think our failure in the production of good town churches of distinctive character must have struck you often, as it has me, when contrasted with our comparative success in country churches. The fault seems to me to have been that men have taken ancient country churches as their models and have failed to discover that between them and churches in towns there ought to be a most distinct and marked difference (*E.* xi, 227).

Village and town churches were distinguished, not merely by a difference in size, but by 'an absolutely different and distinctive character'. For examples of the type of church suitable for towns, 'we must go to such towns as Bristol, York, and Norwich; and here almost all, if not all, are of Third-Pointed date, and . . . there does seem to me to be something in this late work which essentially fits it for the neighbourhood of houses' (xi, 229).

Street then proceeds to lay down six points 'as of essential importance in town churches which are not at all equally necessary in the country'. First of all, 'it is most necessary to avoid rusticity in any way, whether in material, design, or execution'. On these grounds St Barnabas', Pimlico, and St Matthew's, City Road, were condemned and the heretical suggestion made that brick was better than rough stone in the city. Street went on to question the need for steep roofs and to advocate the use of clerestories as 'in a town church the right

place for the admission of light' (xi, 230). 'Regularity of parts'
was essential, but he questioned 'the invariable use of the spire'
since they were much less effective in the city. The final characteristic was height which was 'of immense importance, and to
be obtained at all costs' (xi, 231). Though Street admitted he
would not like to see the Perpendicular town churches copied,
he did wish 'that the truths which they teach should be made
applicable (as they may be) to our new Middle-Pointed buildings' (xi, 233). These suggestions evidently were taken to heart
by the *Ecclesiologist* for its reviews of town churches became
flexible on these points.

The use of colour in churches became an increasingly prominent part of the Society's programme. As early as 1843, Neale
pleaded for the use of colour:

A church is not as it should be, till *every* window is filled with stained
glass, till every inch of floor is covered with encaustic tiles, till there
is a Roodscreen glowing with the brightest tints and with gold, nay,
if we would arrive at perfection, the roof and walls must be painted
and frescoed. For it may safely be asserted that ancient churches in
general were so adorned.[1]

The *Ecclesiologist,* in reviewing Pugin's *Glossary of Ecclesiastical
Ornament and Costume* in 1844, stated: 'Colour however in
churches is to us a novelty, and as such, alarms the prejudices
of many.' But, the review went on to say: 'It is impossible to
look through the illustrations of this volume without admiring
their splendid effect . . . and . . . without longing to introduce
them into our churches' (iii, 143). This longing was soon fulfilled. The following year, a writer in Weale's *Quarterly Papers*
announced: 'Public favour has been gained for Polychromy by
that most powerful of all arguments, an appeal to public sympathy; and the practice of it, at first regarded as an experiment
is rapidly spreading as a fashion.'[2]

If the Society could not claim the credit for originating the

[1] *Church Enlargement and Church Arrangement*, p. 12.
[2] John Whichcord, 'Observations on the Polychromatic Decorations of the
Middle Ages', *Quarterly Papers on Architecture*, iv (1845), 3.

fashion of polychrome, at least it did its best to propagate the use of colour. In 1845 an article in the *Ecclesiologist* 'On Decorative Colour' referred to 'the living foliage of an Early-Pointed capital, and the mysterious intricacy of a late Pointed rood-screen'. 'These things', it maintained, 'are not perfect till suitably painted and gilded' (IV, 199). The Bristol Architectural Society had gone on record claiming that colour should be used only in stained glass. The *Ecclesiologist* replied: 'Indeed, if the modern ideas on the subject be correct, mediaeval architects were completely wrong. And if wrong in so very important a question of ecclesiology, how can we trust them in any other?' (IV, 200). It was, to say the least, a good question. The same writer boasted: 'We are consistent; we would have every inch glowing. Puritans are consistent; they would have every inch colourless' (IV, 201).

The use of flowers in adorning churches, a practice now almost universal, owes some of its popularity to the Society's championship of floral decoration: 'A grey Protestantism of hue still opposes us; and though we are gradually overthrowing it, we wish to take every fresh opportunity . . . [using] the simplest method of decorative colour,—the spontaneous offering of external nature to the Church of GOD,—we mean flowers' (*E.* VI, 215). Greens and blossoms were common enough at Christmas and Easter but the Society advocated flowers on every Sunday and saint's day.

But the Society was also interested in much more permanent decoration than flowers. Increasingly, the *Ecclesiologist* devoted space to reviews of the minor arts. Such stained glass makers as Willement, Winston, Willis, or Clayton and Bell were frequently discussed. One of the Society's publications insisted 'that the study of ancient models is the only way by which they can hope to raise their glorious art to that state of perfection in which it existed four hundred years ago'.[1] Confidence in contemporary work was high, and it was stated 'that *the art of staining glass is now thoroughly understood*' (*E.* III, 16). Glass makers were

[1] *Churches of Cambridgeshire*, p. 118.

cautioned against antiquating glass as it was mere deception now but the glass would look right in five hundred years. The Society did not anticipate the Blitz.

The prevalence of encaustic tiles in churches built or restored in the nineteenth century is partly due to the Society which promoted their use vigorously. The *Ecclesiologist* gave instructions on their use, advocating that red tiles be used mostly, mingled with black. Patterned tiles were to be used sparingly (IX, 81). Frequent reference was made to the tiles manufactured by Minton. Hardman's metal work, the mosaics of Powell, and the embroidery of Miss Blencowe were also frequently mentioned. Another opportunity for adding colour was advocated in a letter from John H. Sperling 'On Polychrome As Applied to Organ Pipes'. Sperling suggested foliage on small pipes and saints arranged 'one above another' as on the orphreys of copes in ancient brasses for larger pipes (X, 377).

Increasingly the Society relaxed its attitude on the subject of foreign architecture. Scott claimed: 'The introduction of the foreign element in a systematic way, may, perhaps, have been due to Mr. Ruskin, certainly it came on shortly after the publication of his "Seven Lamps". This, undoubtedly, set people upon Italian Gothic. For my own part, I never fell into this latter mania.'[1] But fall into it the Society certainly did. The Society's early dictum: 'What principle can be so reasonable as the adoption in each country of its own peculiar and national variety of architecture?' (I, 161) seems to have been forgotten. The *Ecclesiologist* increasingly turned its attention to describing foreign art. Frequent articles appeared on foreign ecclesiology, largely the products of travelling Ecclesiologists. Comments on churches built in the foreign varieties of gothic became more and more frequent, particularly as Neale's influence in the Society became less and Hope's became greater. In a letter to the *Ecclesiologist* written in 1846, E. A. Freeman commented that the periodical had once shown 'a degree of narrowness of

[1] *Recollections*, p. 204. The first edition of *Seven Lamps of Architecture* appeared in 1849.

conception with regard to English and Foreign buildings. This latter charge, I rejoice to say, the later numbers of the *Ecclesiologist* have entirely taken away, as far as it is concerned' (*E.* v, 178).

In 1861 Hope, by this time President of the Society, published an important book entitled *The English Cathedral of the Nineteenth Century*. This book shows how far at least one prominent member of the Committee had come in modifying his views:

I am unable to find an intelligible standing ground in the absolute antiquarianism which is involved in the literal revival of any past style. At the same time the 'progression by eclecticism', on which this inability lands me, must be conservative and not destructive, retrospective no less than prospective, national rather than cosmopolitan, and yet enriching its native tradition by the imported and assimilated contributions of other lands.

. . . We have outgrown the literal reproduction of the particular phase of Gothic which prevailed in England between 1250 and 1370, but we need not have outgrown making that our point of departure, if it is in itself worthy of the selection. We need not be afraid of adopting it as the platform upon which we are to construct our own superior style, which it will be in our power to enrich by the teachings not only of its own counterpart and contemporaneous styles on the Continent, . . . but by those of the Lancet varieties at home and abroad . . .—all moulded together and modified so as to combine in a style which should be emphatically northern and emphatically English, yet not narrowly northern nor narrowly English.[1]

Hope made great concessions to such an unworthy motive as utilitarianism: 'The Chapter-house, . . . is an apartment in the arrangement of which archaeology must bend to practical sense.'[2] Perhaps even more radical was his proposal for the cathedral system, for it was to be the nucleus of evangelism in the large towns, Hope having lost confidence in the results of 'relying on the parochial system' alone in this endeavour. He proposed: 'The religious institution which will undoubtedly grow out of rational and business-like endeavours to evangelize

---

[1] London, 1861, pp. 31–2.   [2] *Ibid.*, p. 204.

large populations, whether it is called so or not, will, in every large town, virtually be a cathedral, and it had therefore best be moulded openly and honestly into a cathedral shape.'[1] Hope wanted such a building to include rooms for administration, assembly halls, and classrooms, in short, those adjuncts which since have developed into the parish house or church hall. He argued both as a churchman and as 'an architecturalist', maintaining that 'these two off-shoots of Christianity, co-operative evangelization and hallowed art, make up that which I concisely designate as the cathedral system'.[2] In the past hundred years, the type of church Hope advocated, with rooms for a variety of purposes besides worship, has become very common in cities. Hope's contribution to this development has never been sufficiently recognized.

III

After the Society's removal to London in 1846, an especial interest was taken in certain buildings being built in the metropolis. By no means did the Society limit its attention to these pet projects. The accounts of 'New Churches' in the *Ecclesiologist* form a very valuable catalogue of buildings projected and erected during the Society's existence, though frequently the periodical disdained to notice classical buildings. At times it had reasons for doing so, as in the case of the Church of St John Evangelist, Clapham Rise, Surrey: 'This is a pagan structure, and therefore beyond our province; but we notice it with a view to expose the abominable arrangement of the altar' (IV, 284). As might be imagined, this was done most thoroughly. In addition to the notices of churches, throughout the 1850's and 1860's reviews appeared entitled 'New Schools' and 'New Parsonages', perhaps a reflection of the parochial responsibilities of the editors.

The Society took a special interest in a number of new churches which were centres of Ritualism or built by the group's

---

[1] *Ibid.*, p. 261.   [2] *Ibid.*, p. 280.

favourite architects.[1] Richard C. Carpenter was an especial favourite of the group. His design for St Paul's, Brighton, was warmly greeted in 1846. The *Ecclesiologist* printed a 'perspective' of the east end (see Plate V), and had only a few minor criticisms (v, 156). The only serious blemish in the completed work was 'a prayer-desk looking west in the nave', a feature forced upon the architect (x, 207). The project for Carpenter's All Saints' Church, likewise in Brighton, pleased the reviewer, though he remarked that 'the very high opinion which we have of Mr. Carpenter's talents makes any praise on our part of his works suspicious in many quarters' (viii, 56).

Carpenter's Church of St Mary Magdalene, Munster Square, London, was one of the Society's favourites. (The interior is shown in Plate VI.) A writer in the *Ecclesiologist* linked it to Butterfield's All Saints', Margaret Street, saying: 'We take a peculiar interest in these churches, from their metropolitan locality, and from the desire of their founders and of their architects to embody in them those principles of church arrangement which we have always enforced, as the natural developement of the catholicity of our communion' (x, 64–5). St Mary Magdalene was begun in 1849. A view of the proposed building appears in the *Ecclesiologist* (x, 353). It was a Decorated building of three aisles with an imposing tower and spire (never erected). The reviewer objected to the absence of a pronounced chancel arch and the number of stalls (five on a side) was considered insufficient. In the building, as completed in 1852, the Society found little to condemn aside from the absence of a suitable screen, but there was a great deal to praise (xiii, 167). Carpenter and the incumbent, Edward Stuart (likewise a member of the Society), were highly commended for the building.[2] Unfortunately Carpenter died young in 1855.

[1] Many of the important Victorian churches are illustrated and described in Henry-Russell Hitchcock's *Early Victorian Architecture in Britain* (New Haven, 1954), 2 vols. and Basil Clarke's *Church Builders of the Nineteenth Century: A Study of the Gothic Revival in England* (London, 1938).

[2] Cf. Tom E. Sedgwick, J. T. Micklethwaite, R. Norman Shaw *et al.*, *Description and History of the Church of St. Mary Magdalene, Munster Square, London, N.W.* (London, 1902).

A number of buildings directly interested the Society because they exemplified its rules about ritual propriety. St Andrew's, Wells Street, London, was erected in 1847 according to the designs of an architect named S. W. Dawkes. The *Ecclesiologist* appraised the building: 'It is not too much to say that, considered in a ritual point of view, it is the most satisfactory church which has yet been built in London, and this is a matter of no slight importance' (VII, 80). Nevertheless, it was necessary to 'protest most vehemently against the style, which is Third-Pointed', though 'good of its sort'. The presence of galleries and the design of the altar, 'an attempt . . . after an original developement', were quite objectionable. 'The arrangement of the chancel however is the feature which gives us most satisfaction' (VII, 79), following as it did the dictates of the Society. In 1862 Webb was made vicar and the church became noted for its music. The building was subsequently moved to Kingsbury, a suburb of London.

The Church of St Barnabas, Pimlico, fascinated the Ecclesiologists, chiefly because of 'its fittings, decorations, and general effect'. 'In brief,' the *Ecclesiologist* commented in 1850, 'S. Barnabas' is the most complete, and, with completeness, most sumptuous church which has been dedicated to the use of the Anglican communion since the revival: and this fact . . . would far more than compensate for even greater architectural shortcomings than those which we have felt it our duty to touch upon' (XI, 112). Mr Cundy, the architect, had transgressed in using a rough stone unsuited to the city and in adopting First-Pointed gothic under the mistaken impression 'that this is the style most suited to the poor man's church'. But the chancel was very richly decorated, creating an 'aesthetic triumph of colour and design' (XI, 113). Furthermore, the chancel was 'separated from the nave by screen and parcloses, and duly fitted for the services of the Anglican Church' (XI, 112). It was reported with pleasure that 'the services are most satisfactory; the daily sacrifice, and matins and even-song duly sung' and 'the sexes are separated' (XI, 114).

Another building, consecrated the same month (June 1850) and likewise 'a church to make the heart of the Catholic Christian rejoice', was St Stephen's, Westminster, designed by Benjamin Ferrey. St Stephen's was superior architecturally since Ferrey has used the 'Flowing Middle-Pointed' but St Barnabas' came first in 'ritual completeness'. 'The great fault of S. Stephen's, both internally and externally, is the disproportionate lowness of the chancel compared with the nave, which gives it, particularly inside, too much of a country-church look' (xi, 119). This made the east window too low. An interesting comment appears in the statement: 'There is nothing in which we can better afford to improve on the Middle Ages, than in the height of the reredos' (xi, 119).

No one delighted the Ecclesiologists as much as did William Butterfield. A man of strong principles, he built little else but churches, and refused to build any for Roman Catholics. Even Neale was puzzled by his principles: '*Why* should Butterfield find it contrary to his conscience and principles to restore this Chapel [the seventeenth-century chapel at Sackville College] ?'[1] Summerson calls Butterfield a 'devout adherent of the narrowist Anglicanism' and says that 'church building and worship were the whole content of his life'.[2]

Yet Butterfield broke many of the Society's firm rules. In a church he built in West Lavington, Sussex, the *Ecclesiologist* reported:

We think we detect a growing use of Third-Pointed forms—disguised, of course,—but not made really more tolerable by their being presented in Middle-Pointed detail. . . . We can enter into the temptation an architect must feel to depart from the beaten track in design: but we must anxiously watch any such departure. In this case we have an interesting and excellent design deprived of much of its beauty by what we can consider little better than *crotchets* of its author (x, 68).

If the Society had any reservations about Butterfield in 1849

[1] *Letters*, p. 131.
[2] Sir John Summerson, *Heavenly Mansions and Other Essays on Architecture* (London, 1949), pp. 160–1.

(when this review was written), it soon got over them. The following year E. A. Freeman complained that Butterfield's innovations did not receive the 'same just severity as those of other architects, though I am sure there is no one whose perpetual and ineffectual strivings after originality more constantly deserve it' (*E.* xi, 210). Butterfield was allowed to experiment, a privilege denied other architects.

The design for Butterfield's highly unorthodox St Matthias, Stoke Newington, was considered 'grave and stately' by the *Ecclesiologist* though Freeman found it 'one of the very worst designs I have seen for a long time' (*E.* xi, 209). The building was vigorously defended in a later issue as an instance of 'legitimate development' (xi, 234). Of the finished product, a reviewer stated: 'It would be difficult to speak too highly of the genius and power shown in the design of this fine church, and the admirable adaptation of its plan and arrangements to the proper performance of Divine Service is equally conspicuous' (xiv, 268–9). An interesting qualification was made regarding the woodwork, 'than which we have seldom seen anything more positively ugly' (xiv, 269). The writer pointed out that 'natural as is the reaction from the prettiness and frippery of much modern design, it would be almost equally reprehensible to go into the opposite extreme'. This is the reaction of many people today to Butterfield's work. The deliberate avoidance of mere prettiness seems to be more agreeable to moderns in music than in architecture.

By their own confession, the Ecclesiologists were more 'intimately concerned' and 'deeply interested' in Butterfield's All Saints' Church, Margaret Street, London, than in any other single building. (The interior is shown in Plate VII.) All Saints' was an extraordinary church from the start. It broke as many of the Society's rules as any gothic building could, especially the old edict that 'brick ought never to be used'.[1] All Saints' was built of red and black brick with coloured marble and tiles thrown in for good measure. The result was eagerly awaited as

---

[1] *Few Words to Church Builders*, 3rd ed., p. 10.

it was to be 'a practical example of what we are very anxious to see tested, viz. constructional polychrome' (x, 432).

Hope was very much involved in the project, donating several thousand pounds of money and assuming responsibility for guiding the undertaking. He later wrote that 'it was my object to work out a higher and more minster-like type of parish church than previously existed in modern English architecture'.[1] All Saints' had a clergy house and a choir school attached. The project was indeed a difficult one. As Hope soon realized, Butterfield could be exceedingly stubborn. 'Butterfield', he wrote, 'already has the stuff of a heresiarch in him, he is of the stamp of Tertullian, Eutyches, etc. stiff, dogmatic, and puritanical, and pushing one side of Catholicism into heresy.'[2] At another time Hope complained: 'I am certain that I am co-originator with him of the Church. He will, I fear, get more and more wild, and will not stop till he finds himself Butterfield against the world, not as Athanasius. I have often imagined he might be tending to Irvingism.'[3] The difficulties were compounded by Bishop Tait who interposed a number of objections and found the consecration of the Church (28 May 1859) a good occasion to urge the worshippers 'not to be carried away with the decorations of All Saints''.[4] Even then, the difficulties did not end. Though a High Churchman, Hope believed in setting definite limits to Ritualism. When he suspected the vicar, Upton Richards, of burning incense Hope was greatly offended. Difficulties multiplied and Hope eventually wrote of All Saints' 'I very likely may never go there again'.[5] Fortunately St Andrew's, Wells Street, was just around the corner, and when the more moderate Webb was installed there in 1862 Hope became a very active churchwarden.

Whatever the difficulties, the Society's anticipation grew in the ten long years in which All Saints' was abuilding. Nor was it disappointed. At its completion in 1859, All Saints' was

---

[1] *English Cathedrals of the Nineteenth Century*, p. 234.
[2] *The Book of the Beresford Hopes*, p. 175.
[3] *Ibid.*, p. 177.   [4] *Ibid.*, p. 167.   [5] *Ibid.*, p. 191.

hailed as the church—'in which the embodiment and the success of our principles find their best illustration. If All Saints', Margaret Street is not in all respects that "model-church" which was one of our earliest anticipations, it is at least the nearest approach to that ideal which the ecclesiological movement has yet produced' (xx, 262). The *Ecclesiologist* admitted in 1859 that it had some 'defects', but then, 'it is not fair to criticize it as a work of to-day. All Saints' church was begun ten years ago' (xx, 184). 'Upon the whole, however,' the reviewer continued, 'we have never had occasion to notice a more suitable and dignified adaptation to the Anglican ritual than this magnificent church presents' (xx, 188). The Society admitted that Butterfield had taught it the virtues of brick (as exemplified by Plate VII), and that 'in this impressive church . . . he has approached to the sublime of architecture' (xx, 185). With considerable truth, it was asserted 'that our generation has seen no greater or more memorable work, or any more pregnant with important consequences to the future of art in England' (xx, 189).

CHAPTER VIII

THE MATURE YEARS OF THE ECCLESIOLOGICAL SOCIETY

I

During the year following the crisis of 1845 the Society suspended its more conspicuous activities. The *Ecclesiologist* appeared regularly, though no longer officially connected with the Society. No public meetings were held until 12 May 1846, when the Seventh Anniversary Meeting was held. A precedent was established by convening in London. At this very important meeting, the Society was completely reconstituted. A resolution, passed at the Sixth Anniversary Meeting in 1845, had instructed the Committee to alter the laws of the Society in accordance with a scheme submitted at that time. This plan had suggested suspending the public meetings at Cambridge, but had not mentioned moving the Society elsewhere.

Even though the Committee may have exceeded its commission, the eighteen laws submitted at the Seventh Anniversary Meeting were soon accepted. (The Revised Laws appear in Appendix B.) Most of the old laws of the Society were retained. The specified objects of the Society were only slightly modified, making it quite obvious that the Ecclesiologists had no intention of sacrificing any principles. The name of the Society was changed to Ecclesiological late Cambridge Camden Society, a name abbreviated in 1852 to Ecclesiological Society. Neale wished to keep the original name (Cambridge Camden Society) but was defeated. It was determined that all members must be 'in communion with the Church of England' except for foreign Catholics. Trustees were provided for, Hope and the Earl Nelson being the first chosen. This office was considered necessary because of the large collection of drawings, models, schemes, and books belonging to the Society. It was also decided that the annual meetings should henceforth 'be held in London in the month of May' (*E.* v, 256). Those present expressed their pleasure at this indication that the Society had become national in its scope, having only the vestigal evidence of its name to link it with the University.

One of the most important actions taken at this meeting was the unanimous adoption of the resolution: 'The Proprietors of the *Ecclesiologist* having proposed to restore the copyright of that periodical to the Society,—Resolved that this offer be accepted, and that the *Ecclesiologist* be in future published by the Society under the editorship of the Officers' (*E.* v, 257). The officers elected at the meeting, Hope, F. H. Dickinson, Webb, and Neale, were all prominent members of long standing. Apart from moving the centre of the Society's activities to London and restoring the *Ecclesiologist* to its official position, very little of significance was changed. The crisis had acted as a purge. Once the dissidents had left and the Society had moved away from the University, a remarkable unanimity prevailed, and the rift between Neale and Hope never disrupted the Society's activities. Nor had any principles been sacrificed. Perhaps the Society had retreated from the scene of the battle, but it had made no concessions as far as its dogmas were concerned.

This was expressed in a Preface added to the fifth volume of the *Ecclesiologist*:

When therefore the Cambridge Camden Society at its anniversary meeting on 12 May, by varying its name and revising its regulations, took up a somewhat different and a more secured position, it was made manifest both that the Society would continue to maintain the principles which it had always held in common with the *Ecclesiologist*; and also that the members generally of the Society reposed confidence in its executive, which had virtually never ceased . . . to conduct also the periodical. It seemed then altogether expedient to formally re-unite the two (v, vi).

This reunion was indeed fortunate, for the *Ecclesiologist* bound the group together. Three years later, at the Tenth Anniversary Meeting, it was remarked 'that the publication of the *Ecclesi-*

ologist is the most natural and the most beneficial method of operation for a society like our own—the members of which are dispersed throughout England, being no longer bound either by an academical or a diocesan tie' (*E.* IX, 376–7).

Both the *Ecclesiologist* and the Society itself changed in the years following the reorganization of the Society. In 1846 the *Ecclesiologist* announced that in its early days—

> our principal aim was to be a channel of communication between the Cambridge Camden Society's Committee and its absent members, and we took but little pains, comparatively, to obtain general Ecclesiological information, none certainly as to what was doing out of England. We were, in short, a sort of newspaper. . . . Now our position is rather that of a magazine . . . we claim to be considered as offering a repository of *general* Ecclesiological intelligence (v, 1).

Increasingly the magazine devoted space to long and scholarly discussions of a wide variety of subjects. In 1848 it noted: 'Several correspondents reproach us with the learned heaviness of some of our papers' (IX, 79). A great many of the articles dealt with continental ecclesiology or even the churches of such remote spots as central Syria, Dalmatia, and Georgia. The *Transactions* were not published after 1845 and many an essay which would have appeared in them found a place in the *Ecclesiologist* instead. The Oxford Architectural Society also made 'arrangements . . . that . . . papers read before the Society [Oxford] might be more frequently published in that [*Ecclesiologist*] periodical' (*E.* x, 52).

The *Ecclesiologist* had come a long way from the time when it called itself 'a work strictly *practical*' (IV, 260). In many issues there is little that could be called '*practical*' except for the 'New Churches' and 'Church Restorations' features. More restraint was apparent in denunciations of disapproved buildings, writers often merely showing surprise that 'in this day' such a disfavoured thing might be done. This general moderation in tone certainly did not please Neale. In 1859 he wrote Webb, respecting the possible appearance of an article on the riot at St George's in the East: 'Your article comes simply to this: let us give the people as much Ecclesiology as they will bear without howling. Had we said that twenty years ago, there would have been none in England now.'[1]

Much of the change in the tone of the *Ecclesiologist* can be accounted for by the fact that the editors considered their efforts to have been so successful that they need not be as 'rough' as in the past. In 1854 the *Ecclesiologist*, having become a bi-monthly publication, published its hundredth issue. Its introductory essay, 'Our Centenary Number', contains an interesting bit of reflection:

When . . . we commenced our studies and appeals, it must be borne in mind that the vast field of Ecclesiology, now smiling with so rich a harvest, was an uncultivated wilderness. We may admit that we did a rough work in rough fashion. . . .

It is really amusing to turn back to the *Ecclesiologist* of 1842. What solemn proses about the inexpediency of pews; what edifying hints about the desirableness of chancels of some sort; what timid homilies about attempting to decorate Churches; what halting and hesitating preference for Middle-Pointed. . . . At the present moment there is not a Church erected in Islington or Cheltenham—nay, there is scarcely a meeting house in Manchester which is not far purer in many details, and which aims at, and generally attains, a more Ecclesiastical spirit than the very best of the Churches which were built by the very first architects fifteen years ago (xv, 2–3).

Progress was indeed evident, and perhaps the editors felt justified in being more moderate in tone.

Changes were likewise apparent in the Society itself. Its activities are harder to trace, but can be glimpsed in the reports of the anniversary meetings. The earlier rapid growth in membership (almost nine hundred in six years) came to a sudden halt after the Society's removal from Cambridge. At the Tenth Anniversary Meeting, it was reported that there had been a few resignations during the past year but that fifteen new members had joined (*E.* IX, 375). Two years later, sixteen new members

---

[1] *Letters*, p. 310. Shortly before, in objecting to the fact that the *Ecclesiologist* was not willing to pay him for scholarly articles (though other magazines were), Neale wrote Webb: 'The *Ecclesiologist* makes me sad too. You must feel what perfect trash two-thirds of it is' (p. 309).

were mentioned as exceeding the number lost during the year (*E.* xii, 217). The budget of the Society was much smaller than in past years, and in 1850 the Society decided it could no longer afford the expense of maintaining exhibition rooms for its collections. Three years later, the collections were given to the Architectural Museum, an independent organization which the Society encouraged. The number of publications dropped off significantly. All of the Society's new works published after the move to London were rather scholarly and limited to one edition each, in sharp contrast to the earlier days. The first series of *Instrumenta Ecclesiastica* appeared in 1847. The following year saw *Hierugia Anglicana* and *The Hand-Book of English Ecclesiology*, but after these the only publications (besides the *Ecclesiologist* and an occasional *Report*) were *Funerals and Funeral Arrangement* (1851), the seventh edition of *Few Words to Churchwardens, Part II* (1851), the Second Series of *Instrumenta Ecclesiastica* (1856), and the *Hymnal Noted* (1852 and 1854). The chief activities of the Society seem to have been the annual meetings and the meetings of the Committee to examine the plans for new churches and restoration projects. However, this last activity was a very influential one and the number of churches affected was very large.

A quite pronounced change in the nature of the Society became apparent. An unfriendly writer in an independent journal, the *Eclectic Review*, commented in 1849:

The Ecclesiological party is a party narrowing the study of mediaeval architecture to its ecclesiastical bearings . . . discoursing of this partial study under the style of Ecclesiology as a *science*; and with the most conspicuousness and purity represented by that Society, once, for a brief interval, so prominent and active, and widely known, as the Cambridge Camden, now leading a quieter existence under the title of the Ecclesiological. This party has actually done *something* for the increase of our knowledge in this direction, much alloyed with exaggerated pedantic emphasis on specialities, and general Puseyistical religious leaven.[1]

It is quite apparent that the Society led a 'quieter existence'

[1] 'The Literature of Gothic Architecture', *Eclectic Review*, xxv (1849), 36–7.

after moving to London. At the Eleventh Anniversary Meeting, 16 May 1850, Thorp 'opened the proceedings by remarking that it was a gratifying fact to know that the Society was going on successfully, without making any noise, at least without making more than was absolutely necessary' (*E.* xi, 51). Certainly the Society had changed from the days of its youthful vigour when it had been very eager to make 'noise'. By the time of the Twentieth Anniversary Meeting, 21 June 1859, it was admitted that 'comparatively few persons assembled at their anniversary meetings, . . . they were going on quietly, but still they were effecting a great work' (*E.* xx, 272-3). Although their success became increasingly apparent, there was still work to do, and members were warned at times to be vigilant for 'in many quarters the ancient Paganism had not been eradicated' (*E.* xiv, 277). But the battles against 'the ancient Paganism' had long ago ceased to be noisy conflicts. The Society had lost much of its pristine energy by the end of the 1840's and seemed ready to settle down for a productive middle age.

If the Society as a whole had acquired a new restraint, there were times when the old crusading zeal reappeared. Many of these occasions were in connexion with a new factor which held the attention of the Church of England throughout the second half of the century, the movement known as Ritualism. This extremely amorphous phenomenon had no organization or constituency, though its adherents seem to have been chiefly clerical. Ritualism represented the extension of the Oxford and Cambridge Movements beyond the University quadrangles into the parish life of the country. Storr says that 'the fundamental motive of the movement has been dogmatic, and is to be traced to Tractarian teaching'.[1] Basically, Ritualism involved a return to a more elaborate ceremonial in worship, but practices varied with the convictions and situation of the clergy.

Ritualism did not necessarily involve a return to medieval architecture and furnishings. Frequently priests simply bought the necessary articles abroad since they could be purchased

---

[1] *The Development of English Theology in the Nineteenth Century*, i, 269.

very cheaply from French or Belgian Catholics. This often resulted in a rather heterogeneous collection of styles. Certainly the basic inclination of Ritualism was dogmatic and not artistic. Hope made an effort in 1879 to distinguish between Ritualism and ecclesiology:

The science of Ecclesiology was that of worship carried out in all its material developments. They had heard a great deal lately of that newer movement, which was called Ritualism, but which ought more properly to be called Ceremonialism. Ecclesiology was Ceremonialism, and a good deal besides. The defect of Ceremonialism was that it merely started from the book; it was merely a development of the rubric, and of the book of which the rubric was a running index. Ecclesiology had taken a further stride, and said that, not only must worship consist in forms of words and in rules whereby those forms of words were put in action, but that there must be the place, the building itself, the details of its construction, and the provision of all the necessary ornaments. Therefore, Ecclesiology was the science of worship.[1]

The history of Ritualism extends far beyond that of the Society. In brief, it can be said that in the 1840's and 1850's certain London churches, several of them in very poor areas, became the centres of Ritualism. Among these were the Margaret Street Chapel; St Paul's, Knightsbridge; St Barnabas', Pimlico; St Mary Magdalene's, Munster Square; St Andrew's, Wells Street; St Matthias', Stoke Newington; St Alban's, Holborn; All Saints', Margaret Street; St Peter's, London Docks; and St George's in the East. The Society was very influential in the design of several of these buildings. The clergy of these churches suffered frequent abuse, especially when, after the formal reconstitution of the Roman Catholic hierarchy in England in 1850 Prime Minister John Russell attacked Ritualism. Riots broke out in a number of churches, sometimes over such small items as the appearance of crosses on book-markers. The result was a long series of lawsuits, lasting almost till the end of

[1] Report of the Inaugural Address of A. J. B. Beresford-Hope as vice-president of the St Paul's Ecclesiological Society, *Transactions of the St. Paul's Ecclesiological Society*, 1 (1879), 1.

the century, testing the legality of candles and a fixed cross on the altar, the mixed chalice, incense, wafer-bread, vestments, the eastward position and other new ritualistic practices. The courts occasionally supported the Ritualists, but frequently upheld their opponents who were often well organized and militant. The Public Worship Regulation Act was passed in 1874 in an effort, as Disraeli said, to end 'mass in masquerade'. Under it, four clergymen were sent to jail for refusing to stop ritualistic practices now common throughout the Church of England.[1]

Probably no group could have given leadership to so formless a movement. But the Ecclesiological Society was a steadfast supporter of Ritualism and some of the leading Ritualists were Ecclesiologists. On the other hand, the names of some of the leading Ritualists such as W. J. E. Bennett, Bryan King, and A. H. Mackonochie never appear among the Society's lists of members as published in each annual *Report*. As early as the Eighth Anniversary Meeting (18 June 1847), it was announced that the *Ecclesiologist* was to be 'a periodical which shall occupy a distinct ground, and one which has never been taken up by any other among those of the day which are devoted to the service of the Church'. It was explained that this meant 'the scope of the *Ecclesiologist* is not Church Architecture merely, but the general science of Ecclesiology, under which they [the Society] consider that Ritualism is legitimately included' (*E.* VII, 234).

The publication of the complete *Hierugia Anglicana* in 1848, after appearing in serial form for five years, was a major contribution. The Preface contained what amounted to a manifesto of Ritualism:

Let us endeavour to restore everywhere amongst us Daily Prayers, and (at the least) weekly Communion; the proper Eucharistick vestments, lighted and vested altars, the ancient tones of Prayer and Praise, frequent Offertories, the meet celebration of Fasts and Festi-

[1] Good brief summaries of the important cases appear in Gordon Crosse's article 'Ritual Cases', in the *Dictionary of English Church History* (London, 1948), pp. 536–8, and in Peter Anson's *Fashions in Church Furnishings 1840–1940* (London, 1960), pp. 213–14.

vals . . . but let us be careful not to retard the general return of the Clergy to Rubrical regularity, by attempting as individuals, and by the adoption of isolated practices, to do more than our Church sanctions in the ceremonial departments of Divine Service.[1]

The chief value of the book, as far as the Ritualists were concerned, was that it cited many Anglican sources to show that various practices were retained after the Reformation. Those who referred to Hooper and Grindal as authorities could now be confronted by the evidence of Andrewes, Laud, and Cosin. Since the ritualistic controversies were based on the interpretation of sixteenth- and seventeenth-century rubrics and canons, it was a major asset to be able to draw ammunition from prominent churchmen of these periods.

Two points were of particular interest to compilers of *Hierugia*: the arrangement of chancels and the vestments of the clergy. The Preface insists—

the Book of Common Prayer says nothing, *totidem verbis*, of the distinctness and separation of the chancel from the nave, of roodscreens, stalls, etc.: in this case, the *Hierugia* attests that, according to our best ritualists, the first rubric in the Prayer Book (*i.e.*, *the chancels shall remain as they have done in times past*) requires the retention of all these features of catholic arrangement, so dear to the lovers of primitive order and Christian symbolism.[2]

In considering the eucharistic vestments, the editors remark with surprise 'that the ecclesiological movement of the last ten years has accomplished little or nothing towards their restoration'.[3] The chasuble was at the time (1848) almost unknown in the Anglican Church, though a footnote adds the information 'that a chasuble was worn by an English priest, at the celebration of the Holy Eucharist, on a recent festal occasion; and . . . a priest in the diocese of Exeter has, for some time past, officiated at the altar similarly apparelled'. The *Hierugia* is full of extracts which show that the vestments were retained by some of the Caroline divines.

[1] *Hierugia Anglicana or Documents and Extracts Illustrative of the Ritual of the Church in England after the Reformation*, p. v.
[2] *Ibid.*, p. viii.   [3] *Ibid.*, p. ix.

A review of the book, published in the *Ecclesiologist*, tried 'to remove the suspicion which we know has been felt in some quarters, of a wish on the part of the Hierugists to excuse and even suggest the revival of extra-rubrical and Romish observances. It is not, then, as giving a license for illegal and uncanonical innovations that the precedents above alluded to are valuable' (IX, 237). Evidence was presented from Anglican sources on many of the issues which were later contested in the law courts:

Dedication feasts, rogation, and other processions, the separation of the sexes at public worship; the mixed chalice at the Holy Eucharist; the use of the credence-table; flowers, crosses, incense, pictures, and imagery in churches; feretories, herses, banners, escutcheons, and the Holy Communion at funerals; have the sanction of the Church of England; the *Hierugia* will convince him [a parish priest] that the maintenance of all these is perfectly compatible with her obedience, —at least, has been so regarded by her staunchest and most dutiful sons.[1]

By 1859 the *Ecclesiologist* had become more cautious. The *Directorium Anglicanum* by John Purchas[2] was greeted with the words: 'We cannot but think that a sounder judgment would have kept back much that is here given to a scoffing and irreligious public. We are bidden to be "wise as serpents", and are warned against throwing pearls before swine' (XX, 32). The 'swine', of course, were the opponents of Ritualism who by this time were very active in their opposition. Neale, Philip Freeman, and other Ecclesiologists had assisted the author. However, the reviewer had one major criticism: 'We must record our regret, that the old English use of Sarum has not been more religiously followed in the matter of precedent' (XX, 33), a cry echoed a number of times later in the century. Failure to do this 'entirely evacuates our legal standing ground in matters of

---

[1] *Ibid.*, p. viii.

[2] *Directorium Anglicanum; Being a Manual of Directions for the Right Celebration of the Holy Communion, for the Saying of Matins and Evensong, and for the Performance of Other Rites and Ceremonies of the Church According to Ancient Uses of the Church of England* (London, 1858). The book was another attempt to show that many medieval practices and ornaments were legal in the Church of England.

ritual. We inherit the old English traditions, and none other' (xx, 33). The book, nevertheless, was considered very useful and informative.

The persecution endured by the Ritualists frequently evoked the old militancy of the Ecclesiologists. The *Ecclesiologist* rallied its forces in 1851:

> We have been very successful, and our success has borne a common fruit. . . . We are a 'large party', and the world fears us. We find ourselves no longer in conflict with the foes of our tenderer days. The Prime Minister has pronounced the ritualism of the Anglo-Catholic Church to be the 'Mummeries of superstition'.
>
> . . . .
>
> Hitherto we have avoided the strife of tongues, almost to an excess. Henceforth we will speak out like men, and fight as our fathers fought against commission, if need be, and against Parliament, for the ritual of the English Church (xii, 1–3).

The same issue carried news that at a special meeting on 16 December 1850 the Committee had resolved 'to express their cordial sympathy with the Rev. W. J. E. Bennett [vicar of St Paul's, Knightsbridge], under the trials which he is suffering from his zeal to restore the Ritualism of the English Church' (xii, 59). Later a contribution was made to the Knightsbridge Church's Defence Fund. A subsequent issue announced the Society's determination 'to defend the right, and to encourage those who were in various ways suffering persecution for their steady adherence to the express laws of the Church' (xii, 219). Frequent references were made to the lawsuits of the 1850's and 1860's, and the adverse decisions were usually roundly condemned.

One of the ironies of the time was the fact that, although the entire Tractarian movement placed emphasis on the importance of the Apostolic Succession, no group was so consistently opposed to Tractarianism and Ritualism as the bishops. Many of the Ritualists were harried by their diocesans.[1] In an essay on

---

[1] Neale was constantly annoyed by his diocesan, A. T. Gilbert, who referred to Neale as an 'infatuated man'. In writing to Webb about the Denison Case (on the

'The Present State of the Rubrical Question', the *Ecclesiologist* denounced the bishops' caprice on ritual questions and asserted that 'the time has come when it is absolutely necessary to define the episcopal authority' (xII, 84).

The Bishop of Manchester, James Prince Lee, denounced ' "symptoms" in the English Church "encouraging to Rome" ' such as the sedilia, piscina, credence shelf, and altar tomb (xII, 46). The *Ecclesiologist*'s reply to his lordship was not particularly respectful: 'Could it have been conceived that a man in his senses could ever even talk, we say nothing of writing, such trash, the nonsense of which is only equalled by the falsehood?' (xII, 48). But then, the Society had special reasons for disliking Bishop Lee. An account of the Bishop's visit to a church in which the late incumbent, Rev. T. V. Bayne, had added a chancel in correct Middle-Pointed, shows how seriously the Victorians took their piscinae and sedilia:

The Bishop's fury, on occasion of the visit to which we have been alluding, is described to us as having been perfectly *maniacal*. We hear on authority which we cannot doubt, of cushions and altar-cloths flung down, carved ornaments screwed off and dashed on the pavement, and this by the Bishop's own hands . . . he also there and then expressed the wish, that the 'boys would break the stained glass windows of the church' (*E.* xII, 48).

The Society accepted the challenge: 'Now we beg leave to tell the Bishop, very quietly, but very decidedly, that these outrages shall not be borne. We are a strong party; we know our strength; we have right on our side; and no court, civil or ecclesiastical, but must be with us' (xII, 48). The old militant spirit had not entirely vanished.

A major portion of the Society's contribution to Ritualism came through the practices of its individual members. Webb was vicar from 1862 to 1885 of St Andrew's, Wells Street, London. His son referred to Webb as 'a man of conspicuous moderation, whose avoidance of extreme practices and disinclination

Real Presence), Neale referred to the Archbishop's actions as proving 'what we knew before, namely that J.[ohn] B.[ird] C.[anterbury] is a fool and a heretic' (*Letters*, p. 279).

to insist upon extreme doctrines was as marked as his resolute adherence to what he regarded as the essential principles of High Churchmanship'.[1] The evidence of his letters to Neale shows that in his early years Webb was more inclined to Roman practices than Neale. In later days Webb was more moderate, never wearing vestments at St Andrew's, but celebrating from the eastward position and using the mixed chalice. Under his leadership St Andrew's became famous for its choral services. At Webb's death, it was said: 'Neale with all his genius was not judicious, and how much the worship movement owes to Webb's wise, tolerant judgment cannot be overstated.'[2]

Hope described his religious position as 'an Anglicanism with maybe more of toleration, perhaps from foreignism of temperament, than that of other Anglicans of my age, strong in Sacramental doctrine and aesthetic in worship'.[3] There were limits, though, as to what degree Hope would condone ritualistic practices. When Richards began burning incense at All Saints', Hope had had enough and left the parish. Hope always regarded Neale with suspicion, and once stated: 'His historical lore, which is great, is altogether subservient to his own one-sided propagandism.'[4]

Hope had grounds for his suspicion of Neale. Perhaps realizing that his fragile health could not long endure (he was forty-eight when he died), Neale at Sackville College was consistently in the forefront of Ritualism. As early as 1843 he had remarked: 'I am sure that when once churches are built or restored to be equal to those of olden times, . . . the poverty of our present vestments will become intolerable.'[5] Having added a rood and

[1] Clement C. J. Webb, 'Benjamin Webb', *Church Quarterly Review*, LXXV (1913) 330.
[2] *Sermons Preached in the Church of St. Andrews, Wells Street on St. Andrew's Day and on Sundays in Advent 1885 after the Death and Funeral of the Rev. Benjamin Webb, M.A. Vicar and Prebendary of Portpool in St. Paul's Cathedral together with Other Published Notices of His Life and His Work*, ([London], 1886), p. 21.
[3] *The Book of the Beresford Hopes*, p. 133.   [4] *Ibid.*, p. 146.
[5] *Hierologus*, p. 71. In 1846 Neale wrote Webb: 'The great use of a Cope is, it strikes me, to accustom our people to coloured vestments; once do that and do it on such irrefragable Anglican grounds as we have, and the Chasuble follows without difficulty' (*Letters*, p. 94).

other accessories to the College Chapel, Neale began wearing
the chasuble in 1850. Only one or two other Anglican priests
elsewhere had preceded him in this. He was outspoken against
the decision on the Gorham Case concerning baptismal regeneration.[1] Neale's teachings concerning the Holy Communion
were unpopular with several bishops.[2] Like most of the Ecclesiologists, Neale was a fervent believer in daily services and open
churches, especially in poor districts. In 1855 he took the mo-
mentous step of founding a religious order for women, the Sisters
of St Margaret. The original house was devoted to nursing in
the vicinity of East Grinstead. As might be expected, Neale
received a considerable amount of persecution. Besides being
inhibited by his Bishop, he was subjected to mob violence on
several occasions. In 1851 a mob tried to burn Sackville College
and a few years later a riot broke out in Lewes at the funeral of
one of the sisters. Neale was an extremely courageous man and
never retreated from any of his ritualistic practices.

II

The mature years of the Society were characterized by an expanding range of interests. Its activities extended to many new
subjects, especially music. Some of these concerns were passing
affairs, provoked by current events. The national exhibitions of
the time caught the interest of the Ecclesiologists, and the
Society offered suggestions on the Great Exhibition of 1851.
According to the *Ecclesiologist*, the Crystal Palace was 'engineer-
ing—of the highest merit and excellence—but not architecture'

[1] Neale felt that 'the formularies of the Prayer Book not only assert the doctrine
of Baptismal Regeneration, but do so expressly, definitely, dogmatically' (*A Few
Words of Hope on the Present Crisis of the English Church* (London, 1850,) p. 6). Neale
contemplated secession and drew up a 'Protest and Declaration of Suspension of
Communion' in the event that the Church (rather than just the Privy Council)
should sustain Gorham. If it did, he declared, he would join the Episcopal Church
in Scotland rather than the Roman Church (*Letters*, p. 142).

[2] In 1849 Neale wrote Webb: 'What we both wish to express is this: the Bread
and Wine are in the Liturgy changed into the Body and Blood of our Lord, as much
as one thing can be changed into another; but how it is done we don't decide: it
may be by Transubstantiation, or by Impanation, or by Hypostatical Union'
(*Letters*, p. 123).

(XII, 270). The Great International Exhibition of 1862 included a display entered by the Society. Much pride was shown in the exhibit's success, especially in the tangible evidence of progress in the gothic revival since 1851. At the Twenty-third Anniversary Meeting (1 July 1862) the Exhibition was discussed and Hope referred to 'that type of art, . . . which though called mediaeval, is still modern and progressive'. He added: 'There are many things which make mediaeval art the most serviceable to the present nineteenth century' (*E.* XXIII, 229). In 1866 the Society prepared an exhibit for an international exhibition in Paris.

During the early 1860's the Society departed from ecclesiastical architecture to enter into the fray over the new Foreign Office building. Although Scott had managed to secure the appointment as architect, the Prime Minister, Viscount Palmerston, would have none of '*your damned* Gothick'. Since Scott was unwilling to relinquish the appointment, he finally agreed to design an 'Italian' building, a decision which the *Ecclesiologist* announced with 'unfeigned regret'. 'Let us hope', it said, 'that this ill-omened meddling with the principles of the rival style will not affect the purity of Mr. Scott's Gothic design' (XXII, 222). Thereafter, secular buildings were occasionally reviewed, it being obvious that the struggle for gothic was not solely an ecclesiastical one.

Besides the passing tide of contemporary events, many varied subjects consistently held the Society's attention. In the 1850's ecclesiastical embroidery caught the Society's fancy. A Miss Agnes Blencowe took the lead and published some 'working patterns' under the Society's sanction. An exhibit was held in 1848 of 'numerous specimens of ancient embroidery, chiefly belonging to the Society's collection, . . . [and] some beautiful modern imitations, especially some worked by Miss Agnes Blencowe' (*E.* IX, 48). After this, there are frequent references in the *Ecclesiologist* to the Ladies' Ecclesiastical Embroidery Society, sometimes referred to as the Society for the Advancement of Ecclesiastical Embroidery.

Bell ringing was a subject often discussed in the *Ecclesiologist*. Churchwardens were advised that 'the more you encourage ringing, I mean good ringing, the better; but I hope you will never let the bells be rung at an election, or any thing of that kind'.[1] Frequent instructions for careful and suitable ringing occur in the *Ecclesiologist*, but none so interesting as 'Successful Tactics of a Country Curate with an Ungodly Set of Ringers'. The author, 'A Warwickshire Curate', had attempted to interfere with the rather rowdy crowd ringing the church bells:

But the men, not understanding my motive, did not appreciate my presence, and gave me several hints that they preferred my room to my company. The fact was, they had never been accustomed to have a 'gentleman' come amongst them, and the parson's presence was decidedly an uncomfortable check upon their usual free and easy mode of proceeding (*E.* xxvi, 172–3).

All ended well, however, for on one Christmas Eve he invited the ringers to dinner, lectured to them afterwards, and persuaded them to form an association with their parson a member. The result was gratifying: 'Our belfry which was once the resort of the idle and profane, has now become regarded as it should be—a holy place.'

It is rather strange that the Ecclesiologists took so little interest in painting, although concerned with every other form of church decoration. Neale wrote Webb: 'You know I don't generally take much to pictures.'[2] But like many others, the Ecclesiologists knew what they liked. And what they liked was best typified by a rather minor German painter by the name of Johann Frederick Overbeck (1789–1869) of the German-Roman school. One of his paintings, 'Religion Glorified by the Fine Arts', received an enthusiastic review:

The design is so vast, its treatment so masterly, . . . herein symbolized by the first Christian artist of the age, is so true and noble and inspiring, embodying so much our own feelings on the subject, that we think no one interested in the revival of Christian art in England

[1] *Few Words to Churchwardens, Part I*, 12th ed., p. 13.
[2] *Letters*, p. 228. On this occasion (a visit to Belgium) he was, however, very much taken with the Van Eyck altarpiece in Ghent.

ought to delay making himself acquainted with this great work (*E.* III, 83).

The *Ecclesiologist* was also fairly certain as to what it did not like. In its early days it reviewed Mrs Jameson's two-volume work, *Memoirs of the Early Italian Painters*:

In the first volume Mrs. Jameson seems pervaded with a true enthusiasm for the early Christian painters of Italy: she overflows with love for Giotto, B. Angelico, and Francia, &c. We open the second volume, and equal exstacy [*sic*] is still in store for the Paganisers of the unholy court of Leo X; and yet our authoress is not without her qualms of conscience, her self-accusing gleams of deeper feeling (v, 145).

The decorations of All Saints', Margaret Street, brought to the Society an awareness of the importance of painting. The chancel of this building was adorned with frescoes by William Dyce, himself a High Churchman. Hope, who paid for much of the decoration, declared:

Mr. Dyce has shown us what fresco can do to the glory of God, at All Saints' Margaret Street, while the groined chancel-roof of the same Church, adorned by his learned and skilful fancy, is a work no whit inferior to the vault of S. Jacques at Liège, or Sta. Anastasia at Verona and produced by a far more durable process.[1]

Shortly after the consecration of All Saints', the Twenty-first Anniversary Meeting (11 June 1860) was devoted to a discussion of 'The Tendencies of Praeraffaellitism, and Its Connection with the Gothic Movement' (*E.* XXI, 247–9). It must have been an interesting occasion. Holman Hunt's 'The Awakened Conscience' was praised. Some felt that the best accompaniment of gothic architecture was the work of Dyce, Overbeck, and Herbert. Others liked the 'naturalism' of Hunt, Rossetti, and Millais and considered their work in accordance with gothic. During the early 1860's, the Society offered an annual 'Colour Prize' for painting casts of various pieces of sculpture. Evidently there was a growing appreciation of the importance of painting in church decoration.

[1] *English Cathedral of the Nineteenth Century*, p. 250.

214

For many years the Society showed concern about the conduct of funerals, perhaps a reflection of the parochial concerns of the editors. In 1851 it expressed this concern in the form of a tract, *Funerals and Funeral Arrangements*, consisting of a series of papers which had appeared in the *Ecclesiologist*. The genuine religious feeling with which the subject was approached is evident:

> Their bodies, which were temples of the HOLY GHOST, must be treated as His temples still; and since it is by the grave and gate of death that they must pass to their resurrection, it is ours to make the grave honourable, and the gate of death as reverend a thing as they should do who believe it to be the porch of life.[1]

Several means were advocated in effecting this. 'Let us get rid of the expensive trash of a modern funeral,'[2] the tract suggests. The end of intramural interment was frequently demanded by the *Ecclesiologist*. In order to secure more respect for the dead, the Society decided to introduce '*dead-houses*' though the word 'Lich-House' was invented as less offensive. The Second Series of *Instrumenta Ecclesiastica* carries Butterfield's drawings for a Lich-House. It was to be a circular gothic building with projecting chancel, designed so as not to resemble a church. The *Instrumenta* also carried designs for a hearse, coffins, and tombstones, all properly gothic. The Society was careful about every detail. *Funerals and Funeral Arrangements* strongly advocated the use of biers and hearses (for supporting the pall). Some mention was made also of the recent government scheme for large municipal cemeteries. Part should be consecrated by the Church, the rest left for dissenters, 'but the two parts should be as distinct as if they were two separate grounds'.[3] A step forward was announced in 1852: 'Mr. H. R. COOKSEY . . . will shortly, we trust, supply sets of coffin furniture from designs approved by the Society, at at least as cheap a rate as the vile and heathenish designs now almost universally prevalent' (*E.* XIII, 444). The organization of a burial guild was attempted, but with little success.

[1] London, 1851, p. 2.   [2] *Ibid.*, p. 10.   [3] *Ibid.*, p. 27.

Many other topics held the Society's attention during the 1850's and 1860's. In 1858 the discussion of the purpose of lychnoscopes was reopened after lying dormant for several years. A discussion on 'The Proper Position of the Pastoral Staff in an Episcopal Effigy' continued for years. Papers appeared repeatedly in the *Ecclesiologist* on such varied subjects as 'Modern Iron Work', 'Worcestershire Ecclesiology', 'Painted Glass', 'Organ Building', and 'Use of Colour in Church Architecture'. For many years, 'Foreign Gleanings', 'Secular Buildings', and 'Aphorisms Respecting Christian Art' were regular features.

There was one topic of great importance introduced in the 1850's. This was music, a subject which the Society suddenly realized it had been neglecting. In late 1849 the *Ecclesiologist* carried an anonymous communication on 'Ecclesiastical Music'. The writer claimed: 'There is one branch of Ecclesiology which has scarcely kept pace with the rapid advances made in other departments. We mean Ecclesiastical Music . . . it is obvious that no efforts have been made adequate to the emergency, or proportionate to the means placed in our hands, for the due study of the genuine music of the Church' (x, 208). Several years later, the *Ecclesiologist* announced: 'Not forgetting that architecture is our first work, we have associated Church Music as a parallel branch of ecclesiology' (xv, 3).

The first step was a decision in 1850 to—

add certain additional members to the committee, who need not of necessity be members of the Society, for the exclusive consideration of musical questions; and the Rev. J. L. Crompton, W. Dyce, Esq., R.A., and Sir John Harrington, Bart., were so appointed. The Rev. T. Helmore accepted the office of honorary secretary of the committee of music (*E.* xi, 135).

Two years later, the Society merged with the Motett Society and in turn was promised three concerts each year. In the following years, the *Ecclesiologist* notes various concerts with the music of Palestrina, Gibbons, Vittorio, Gregorian chant, and plain song as favourites. After ten years together, it was decided to dissociate the Motett Choir from the Ecclesiological Society.

The Society developed some very definite ideas about church music. At an early date it was decided 'that Church Musick is abstractedly and originally, vocal, and that no instrumental accompaniment is necessary for its perfection' (IV, 4–5). In the 1840's organs were unpopular with the Society, especially in small country churches, both because of the architectural problems of their placement (damage to the structure and lack of medieval authority) and because they became too dominant in the service. The complaint was made that 'people, generally, and still more organists in particular, are quite unable to conceive the organ as a mere subsidiary and unessential appendage to the Divine offices' (*E.* IV, 7). There was no objection, however, 'to the use of a violoncello or horn to steady the chant in some cases' (*E.* III, 2).

The Society knew what it desired in vocal music:

It is needless for us to repeat, what we have so often urged, that, in our opinion, the Plain Song of the Church is not only the most right, and the most beautiful method, of praising God, but also practically the most easy, and, in the long run, when time is given to remove prejudices, the most successful and most popular kind of ecclesiastical music (*E.* XIII, 365–6).

It was also decided that 'we must seek, not to introduce the popular music of the modern Roman Church, but to revive the ancient grave styles of the ecclesiastical music of the Church of England from the Reformation to the Great Rebellion' (*E.* XIV, 193). Evidently this would include the music of Merbecke, Tallis, Byrd, and Gibbons in addition to plain song. Pugin was disgusted that the Church of England was reviving plain song while Roman Catholic music remained at a low ebb, though Abbé Guéranger was then busy reviving Gregorian chant in France.

Various proposals were made for improving music. A Mr F. R. Wegg Prosser read a paper, 'On Modern anthems', to the Society in 1850. He noted: 'At a time like the present, when efforts are being made to improve the music in so many of our churches, and when the metrical psalms are being generally

discarded, it is quite necessary to determine what we shall substitute for them' (*E.* xi, 28). The Society did much to encourage
church choirs. The cathedral services had enjoyed a continuing
popularity and Hook had shown the feasibility of introducing
choral services into the parish churches. The singers, whom
Neale had once described as 'often the pest of the parish', were
quite welcome in the chancel now as a surpliced choir.

But choir music alone was not considered sufficient by some
members of the Society. Thomas Helmore contributed a paper
in 1850 on 'The Cantus Collectarum', advocating the encouragement of congregational singing (*E.* xi, 110). This led to an
agreement in the same year with the Musical Committee 'to
extend the sanction of the Society to a series of translations of
ancient hymns, noted according to the ancient music, and accompanied by separate organ harmonies' (*E.* xi, 185). This was
a much more radical step than might be imagined. Hymns were
not generally sung in many English Churches, being considered
'Methodistical'. Neale found it necessary to defend their introduction. He personally did not favour a vernacular liturgy and
offices, but he argued that 'while we have prayers in English,
why are we not to have hymns? Did ever any Church, or any
body of religious whatever, do without them? Surely, the language that can bear to be used in the prayers, can be sufficient
for the hymns of the Church.'[1] Webb, who encouraged chanting
the Psalms and Canticles at St Andrew's, Wells Street, was a
staunch opponent of hymns. Neale wrote him at an early date:
'Why should hymns be less Catholick than prayers? and, therefore why English hymns less Catholick than English prayers?
We may wish to restore Latin in both if you like. But till we can,
surely English Hymns, if good, are better than none.'[2]

Evidently Neale prevailed, for a volume soon appeared entitled *Hymnal Noted* and bearing on its title-page the words
'Published under the Sanction of the Ecclesiological Society'.

[1] *Letters*, p. 125.
[2] *Ibid.*, p. 58. Webb's objection was based on his doubt as to 'the possibility of
the language of common life, in such an age as this, being fit for this sort of composition' (*Letters*, p. 126).

Two parts were printed, dated 1851 and 1854. In 1850 the *Ecclesiologist* had carried an article, probably by Neale, stating: 'The proposed Hymnal, it need not be said, will be entirely from ancient sources. The hymns will be taken from those in general use through the Western Church, before the so-called Reform of Urban VIII. And the melody will be that of the best books, and the most correct Churches' (XI, 175). The *Hymnal Noted* contains more than a hundred hymns and several antiphons. It was intended, as the Preface indicated, to remedy 'the omission, at the Reformation, of one entire portion of the ancient ritual treasured up in the Latin devotional books of Western Christendom'.[1] Accordingly, its contents were drawn entirely from medieval offices, especially the Sarum service books. W. H. Frere states:

> The *Hymnal Noted* marks the extreme point in the swing of the pendulum in the direction of Latin office-hymns. As a practical hymn-book its contents were too much of one type for it to earn a lasting position; but it impressed once for all on the minds of churchmen the importance of the old office-hymns, and the impression has gone on deepening, though the *Hymnal Noted* survives now in only a few places.[2]

The musical editor was Rev. Thomas Helmore, identified on the title-page as 'Priest in Ordinary to Her Majesty's Chapels Royal, Precentor of St. Mark's College, etc.' The music was drawn from medieval sources, particularly that used at Salisbury. Canon Douglas says 'the music was barbarously distorted, for Plainsong notation was then but little understood'.[3]

Neale was responsible for the translations, a field in which he excelled. Indeed, it can be said that Neale's greatest contribution was made in his work of translation. A master of twenty languages, he translated many well known hymns, including

[1] *Accompanying Harmonies to the Hymnal Noted* (London, 1852), p. i.
[2] 'Introduction', *Hymns Ancient and Modern for Use in the Services of the Church with Accompanying Tunes; Historical Edition with Notes on the Origin of Both Hymns and Tunes and a General Historical Introduction* (London, 1909), p. ci.
[3] *Church Music in History and Practice: Studies in the Praise of God* (New York, 1937), p. 252.

'O come, O come, Emmanuel' (twelfth century Latin), 'All glory, laud and honour' (Theodulph of Orleans), 'Good Christian Men, rejoice' (medieval Latin), 'Come, ye faithful raise the strain' (John of Damascus), 'Jerusalem the golden' (Bernard of Cluny), and 'Of the Father's love begotten' (Prudentius). Throughout the 1850's and 1860's the *Ecclesiologist* printed a series of 'Sequentiae Ineditae', the texts of medieval sequences which Neale discovered in old service books while travelling in England and on the Continent. He also published several works such as *Hymns, Chiefly Medieval, on the Joys and Glories of Paradise*[1] and *Hymns of the Eastern Church*.[2] Probably no one else contributed as many hymns of lasting popularity during the nineteenth century as Neale. The 1950 edition of *Hymns Ancient & Modern* contains far more translations and hymns by Neale than it has from any other individual. Brother George Every says of him: 'Neale was not a great poet, but he was soaked in the Medieval breviaries and in the Fathers. Medieval hymnody had far more influence on his own thoughts about poetry than any modern romanticism whatever.'[3]

Evidently the Society was pleased with Neale's work as a translator. In 1852 it decided that it was not 'compatible with the objects and professions of the Society to undertake the selection or recommendation of any modern hymns as supplemental to the Hymnal Noted' (*E.* xiii, 236), though obviously the suggestion had been made. The *Ecclesiologist* had some reservations about *Hymns Ancient and Modern* (1861), but felt that 'a work which contains so many Catholic hymns is a precious boon to every Christian soul' (xxii, 345). It clearly preferred the ancient hymns, finding the modern ones too subjective for its taste.

---

[1] London, 1865.

[2] 3rd ed. (London, 1866). Neale was a historian of the eastern churches and wrote some of the first important works in English on eastern orthodoxy.

[3] *Christian Discrimination* (London, 1940), p. 53. Neale's facility at translation was remarkable. He wrote Webb: 'Now I reckon that a hymn takes me an evening to do: some may take less: but others take more' (*Letters*, p. 192).

III

In its old age, the Society continued to function smoothly though quietly. It was gratifying for it to see the success of its endeavours on every side. Old enemies, including Close, had been reconciled and the Society ceased to give offence to many people. This is not because the Society itself had changed—its principles only underwent minor modifications—but because its ideas were being accepted on every side. Gothic was employed by all parties in the Church, and by the 1860's chancels were no longer a theological trade-mark. A mark of the new respectability of the Society can be seen in the fact that in 1854 three bishops (outside of England) became patrons. In 1865 the Archbishop of Canterbury (C. T. Longley) agreed to be a patron, a step taken previously by the bishops of Ely (probably Edward H. Browne) and Salisbury (Walter Kerr Hamilton, one of the few high church bishops). As a crowning mark of acceptance, the Society's secretary, H. L. Jenner, was made Bishop of Dunedin (New Zealand) in 1866.

The passing of the years brought many changes in the membership. 'Some who have for many years been among our most trusty friends', according to the *Ecclesiologist*, 'only began to take a special interest in our organization after we had removed from Cambridge to London' (xxix, 316). At the Twentieth Anniversary Meeting in 1859 Thorp resigned because of his ' "duties in this parish [Kemerton] and diocese" ', having served the Society as its president since its beginning (*E.* xx, 260). The end of another era was marked by the early death of Neale in 1866, a few months after Keble. The *Ecclesiologist* carried a significant eulogy of Neale:

But he lived long enough to see the complete triumph of the great principles for which he had laboured so zealously. Indeed, when the victory of the true principles of ecclesiastical design, of correct church arrangement, and of ritual propriety, had been won, his interest in the cause sensibly abated. . . . Accordingly he tacitly withdrew some years ago from any very active concern in the management of the Ecclesiological Society. He continued indeed to contribute to our pages. . . . But for some time he had ceased to attend Committee Meetings, though he did not discontinue to share the editorial responsibility of our pages. . . . [his work at East Grinstead] engaged latterly nearly his whole time and energy. He died, worn out with incessant work at the early age of forty-eight; leaving behind him the reputation of being one of the most learned theologians, one of the most erudite scholars, one of the best linguists, one of the sweetest hymnodists, and perhaps the foremost liturgicist of his time (xxvii, 265).

Evidently not every battle had been won, for his friends were forced to abandon their plan of erecting a monumental cross over his grave in the churchyard at East Grinstead (*E.* xxviii, 368). Neale's responsibilities at East Grinstead were probably not the only reason for his withdrawal from active involvement in the affairs of the Society. He despised Hope for being too willing to compromise and Hope condemned Neale for 'ultraism', the animosity reaching its highest pitch in 1862. Webb managed to mediate between the two men, though Neale's connexion with the Society became more and more remote as Hope came to dominate it. Webb's son remarks that 'Webb has symbolized his own position by a balance, in one of the scales of which is Neale's name and in the other Beresford Hope's'.[1]

The Society did not long survive Neale. After the triumph of the group in the International Exhibition of 1862, it was felt by many that the Society had really accomplished its mission. Hope's enthusiasm kept the group going and he persuaded Webb to continue editing the *Ecclesiologist*, though Webb was anxious to terminate the Society.[2] The Library of the Royal Institute of British Architects contains several bound volumes of the Society's publications, evidently its own set, inscribed 'Presented by the Ecclesiological Society, 6 November 1865'. The disposal of these books was probably in anticipation of the Society's dissolution. The Twenty-seventh Anniversary Meeting (26 July 1866) consisted of the Committee resolving 'itself

---

[1] Clement C. J. Webb, 'Benjamin Webb', *Church Quarterly Review*, lxxv (1913), 344.   [2] *Book of the Beresford Hopes*, pp. 218–19.

into a *pro forma* Annual Meeting', which just heard reports and did necessary business (*E.* xxvii, 240). The *Ecclesiologist* has no report of a Twenty-eighth Anniversary Meeting and mentions no Committee meeting later than 2 April 1867. Since a new member was admitted at this meeting, it does not seem that it was intended to be the last meeting of the Society.

The *Ecclesiologist* came to a rather abrupt end. The December 1868 issue, the final one of volume twenty-nine, began with an address 'To Our Readers':

It is with genuine regret that we make the announcement that the present number of the *Ecclesiologist* is the last, as the one published in the November of 1841 was the first. The reasons which have led us to terminate its existence are very simple—namely, the growing preoccupations of those whose pens have for so long chiefly kept it alive. The continuance of the *Ecclesiologist* has been (to make an honest confession) in some respects a struggle from the first. It began, not as a periodical proper, but as the occasional fly-sheet of the (then) Cambridge Camden Society. As such it achieved so much success, that we gradually built it up into the shape which has for many years been familiar to our readers. . . . Our object has all along been propagandism—in the inoffensive sense of the term. . . .

At this point we feel that the stress and obligation of other— though not alien—occupations, against which we have long been contending, have overmastered our bark; and the balance of duty, which up to this date leant to the continuance, has now shifted to the discontinuance of the *Ecclesiologist* (xxix, 315).

The same issue stated: 'When we announce that the *Ecclesiologist* is to cease, we do not say that the Ecclesiological Society is to be dissolved. The Society has done much; it may still—if the opportunity should arise—do something more, to redeem the pledge which it gave when it assumed the daring motto "donec templa refeceris" ' (xxix, 316). The Society also collapsed at this time, to Hope's dismay. In 1879 it was resurrected in a rather different body. A prospectus for the new St Paul's Ecclesiological Society announces it to be a successor of the Ecclesiological Society which is mentioned as 'dissolved'. This new group centred its activities about St Paul's Cathedral and

Dean Church was its first president. From 1879 until 1937 it published a series of *Transactions*. The first volume describes the object of the Society as 'The Non-Professional Study of Ecclesiology'.[1] Hope was an early vice-president. This Society was reorganized in 1937, resuming the name Ecclesiological Society under which title it has remained active in London. The publication of the *Transactions* has been continued.

In 1859 Hope made a safe prediction. He said that 'the future historian of the Church would, some two or three hundred years hence, perhaps, render due justice to the ecclesiological movement' (*E.* xx, 269). Actually, the Ecclesiologists wrote their own obituary. The last issue of the *Ecclesiologist* announced:

We have the satisfaction of retiring from the field victors. Our mission has from the first had an ecclesiastical and also an artistic side. Our ecclesiastical position has been that of sons of the Church of England, working out from the teachings alike of our own Communion and of the Church Catholic laws of Church arrangement and Church service. The principles which we enounced in days when we were set upon as fanatics and incendiaries for their promulgation, have now made good their footing, not as the prescript rule of the Church of England—such a success would be next to impossible in these days of free inquiry—but as an acknowledged phase of the English Church, which one section gladly welcomes and another is compelled to submit to, and a large intermediate body accepts with more of liking than aversion . . . the great improvement in the general framework of worship, in which we have been permitted to take our part, will, we believe, not be reversed. The Judgment of the Privy Council of 1857 in Liddell *v.* Westerton substantially established the Catholic character of English worship.

We shall not insult our readers by recapitulating the successes of the school of art chiefly, but not exclusively, drawing its inspirations from the Middle Ages, which we have continuously vindicated. It may expect sharp conflicts in the coming time, but it will be the fault of its champions if it ever suffer a rout (*E.* xxix, 315–16).

There is much truth in this statement. The Society retired victorious. The extent of its victory can be found today in almost every parish church of the Anglican Communion.

[1] *Transactions of the St. Paul's Ecclesiological Society*, i (1879), iii.

LAWS OF THE
CAMBRIDGE CAMDEN SOCIETY

(From *Report of the Cambridge Camden Society
for MDCCCXLII*, pp. 44–46)

I. The object of the Society shall be to promote the study of Ecclesiastical Architecture and Antiquities, and the restoration of mutilated Architectural remains.

II. The Society shall consist of a President, Vice-Presidents, and Ordinary Members, who are or have been members of the University, or who, not being, or not having been, Members of the University, shall be approved of by the Committee.

III. The names of Candidates shall be proposed in the form following:—

> I, the undersigned, do hereby recommend
> _____, of _____
> College, to be a Member of the *Cambridge Camden Society*, believing him to be disposed to aid its designs.
>
> (Signed)
>
> _____
>
> _____ College.

and shall be suspended (for at least a week) in the Society's Rooms; and the Candidates so proposed shall be balloted for at the next General Meeting. One black ball in five to exclude.

IV. Honorary Members may be elected in the same manner, having been first recommended by the Committee.

V. The Chancellor of the University, the High Steward, and such of their Lordships the Bishops, and of the Heads of Houses, as shall signify their pleasure to become Members of the Society, shall be admitted as Patrons without ballot.

VI. Every Member shall pay an annual subscription of One Guinea, to be due on the First of January in each year. It shall be competent to any Member to compound for all future subscriptions by one payment of Ten Guineas.*

VII. If any Member's subscription be in arrears for one year, he may be removed from the Society, after due notice, at the discretion of the Committee. No Member shall be considered entitled to his privileges as a Member, whose subscription is in arrear.

VIII. The affairs of the Society shall be conducted by a Committee, composed of the President, Vice-Presidents, and six Ordinary Members, who shall be elected at the Anniversary Meeting in the Easter Term of each year, and of whom three at least shall have been Members of the Committee of the preceding year.

IX. The Committee shall elect out of their own body, so appointed, a Chairman, Treasurer, and Two Secretaries: and may subsequently add to their number.†

X. Two Ordinary Members, not being members of the Committee, shall be chosen annually by the Society at the same time with the Committee, to audit the Society's accounts.

XI. The Society shall meet twice a Term: the days of meeting to be appointed at the beginning of each Term by the Committee.

XII. The chair shall be taken at half-past seven by the President, or in his absence by one of the Vice-Presidents, or other officers of the Society; and the Meeting shall adjourn not later than a quarter to ten.

XIII. The day of meeting may be changed, or a special meeting called by the Committee, due notice being given.

XIV. The officer in the chair shall be sole interpreter of the Laws, and shall have unlimited authority on every question of order.

XV. The Secretaries shall have charge of the records of the Society, and shall keep a minute-book containing the reports of the Meetings, and particulars relative to all matters of interest to the Society.

XVI. No motion or communication shall be laid before the Society

* This Law only applies to Members elected after January 1st, 1842.

† The President, and such of the Vice-Presidents as are pleased to attend, are members of the Committee.

until it has been approved by the Committee. No alteration shall be made in any Law of the Society, without notice having been given at the previous Meeting.

XVII. The Society invites its Members to examine every church in their power, to furnish reports and drawings thereof to the Secretaries, and to contribute original papers on any subject connected with its designs.

XVIII. The Society shall from time to time admit such Associations, formed on Church principles for the study of Ecclesiastical Architecture and Antiquities, as shall desire it, to the privilege of attending the meetings of the Society, and purchasing its publications on the same terms as are granted to its Members.

N.B. Members of the Oxford Society for Promoting the Study of Gothic Architecture, or the Exeter Diocesan, Lichfield, and Durham Architectural Societies, are admitted to attend the meetings of the Cambridge Camden Society, and have the privilege of purchasing the publications of the Society on the same terms as are granted to the Members of the Society.

The Society trusts that its Members, while pursuing their antiquarian researches, will never forget the respect due to the sacred character of the edifices which they visit.

APPENDIX B

LAWS OF THE ECCLESIOLOGICAL
LATE CAMBRIDGE CAMDEN SOCIETY

(From *Report of the Ecclesiological Late Cambridge Camden
Society, MDCCCXLVII–VIII–IX,* pp. 40–41)

I. This Society shall in future be called the "ECCLESIOLOGICAL LATE
CAMBRIDGE CAMDEN SOCIETY". Its object shall be to promote the study
of Christian Art and Antiquities, more especially in whatever relates
to the architecture, arrangement, and decoration, of churches; the
recognition of correct principles and taste in the erection of new
churches; and the restoration of ancient ecclesiastical remains.

II. The Society shall consist of Patrons; a President; Vice-Presidents;
Honorary, and Ordinary, Members.

III. The property of the Society shall be vested in Trustees, to be
chosen by the Society. The Trustees shall be not more than five nor
less than three; and they shall hold and dispose of the property of the
Society for such purposes and in such manner as the Society shall
from time to time direct.

IV. The election of the President and Vice-Presidents is vested in the
Society.

V. The Ordinary Members shall be elected by the Committee, on
the nomination of a Member, according to the following form:—

I, the undersigned, do hereby recommend

_____, of _____
being in Communion with the Church of England, to
be a Member of the "Ecclesiological late Cambridge
Camden Society", believing him to be disposed to aid
its designs.

VI. Honorary Members shall be elected in the same manner, the
clause "*being in Communion with the Church of England*" of the form of

recommendation being omitted in the case of foreigners, members of Catholic Churches.

VII. Bishops of the English Church or of Churches in Communion with the Church of England, who shall signify their pleasure to become Members of the Society, shall be admitted Patrons.

VIII. Every Ordinary Member shall pay an Annual Subscription of One Guinea, to be due on the first of January in each year. It shall be competent to any Member to compound for all future Subscriptions by one payment of Ten Guineas.

IX. If any Member's Subscription be in arrear for one year, he may be removed from the Society after due notice, at the discretion of the Committee. No Member shall be considered entitled to his privileges as a Member, whose Subscription is in arrear.

X. The affairs of the Society shall be conducted by a Committee, consisting of six Members, who shall be elected at the Anniversary Meeting in the month of May in each year; and of whom three at least shall have been Members of the Committee of the preceding year. The Committee so elected may subsequently add to their number.

XI. The Committee shall elect out of their own number a Chairman, Treasurer, and not more than three Secretaries. The President, and such of the Vice-Presidents as are pleased to attend, are Members of the Committee.

XII. Two Members, not being Members of the Committee, shall be chosen annually by the Society at the same time with the Committee, to audit the Society's accounts.

XIII. The Annual Meeting shall be held in London in the month of May, at a place and time to be appointed, and of which at least a fortnight's previous notice by circular to each Member shall be given by the Committee. At this Meeting the audited Accounts shall be produced, the Report of the Committee read, any necessary alterations made in the Laws, the new Committee elected, and Papers read, if any have been prepared and approved by the Committee. The Meeting may be adjourned.

XIV. A Special Meeting may at any time be called by the Committee, due notice being given; and the Committee, on receiving a requisition from fifteen Members, stating explicitly the object for which a Special Meeting shall be required, is bound to call one.

XV. The Officer in the Chair shall be sole interpreter of the Laws, and shall have unlimited authority on every question of order.

XVI. No communication shall be laid before the Society until it has been approved by the Committee.

XVII. The Society invites its Members to examine every church in their power, to furnish reports and drawings thereof to the Secretaries, and to contribute original papers on any subject connected with its designs.

XVIII. The Society shall from time to time admit other Associations for the study of Ecclesiastical Architecture and Antiquities to the same privileges with respect to any meetings and publications of the Society as are granted to its own Members, the right of voting being excepted.

[The Societies admitted into union under Law XVIII. are the Oxford Architectural Society, the Exeter Diocesan Church Architectural Society, the Yorkshire Architectural Society, the Bristol and West of England Architectural Society, the Northamptonshire Architectural Society, the Lichfield Architectural Society, the Cambridge Architectural Society, the Buckinghamshire Architectural Society, and the New York Ecclesiological Society.]

A CHURCH SCHEME

(From *Report of the Cambridge Camden Society for MDCCCXLI*, folio
sheet inserted between pages 80 and 81)

No.

Cambridge Camden Society

*The Society trusts that its Members, while pursuing their Antiquarian re-
searches, will never forget the respect due to the sacred character of the edifices
which they visit.*

Date. | Name of Visitor.

Dedication. | Diocese.
Parish. | Archdeaconry.
County. | Deanery.

I. Ground Plan.

1. Length ⎱ of   Chancel {   } Nave {   } Aisles {   }
2. Breadth ⎰   Transepts{   } Tower {   } Chapel {   }
3. Orientation.

II. Interior.

1. *Chancel.*

1. East Window.
2. Window Arch.
3. Altar.
   α. Altar Stone, fixed or
      removed.
   β. Reredos.
   γ. Piscina.
      (1) Orifice.
      (2) Shelf.
   δ. Sedilia.
   ε. Aumbrye.

4. Apse.
5. Windows, N. S.
6. Window Arches, N. S.
7. Piers, N. S.
8. Pier Arches, N. S.
9. Chancel Arch.
10. Stalls and Misereres.
11. Chancel Seats, exterior or
    interior.
12. Elevation of Chancel.
13. Corbels.

ζ. Niches.
η. Brackets.
θ. Easter Sepulchre.
ι. Altar Candlesticks.
κ. Altar Rails.
λ. Table.
μ. Steps—number and arrangement.

14. Roof and Groining.

II. *North Chancel Aisle.*
　1. Windows, E. N. W.
　2. Roof and Groining.

III. *South Chancel Aisle.*
　1. Windows, E. S. W.
　2. Roof and Groining.

IV. *North Transept.*
　1. Windows, E. N. W.
　2. Transept Arch.
　3. Roof and Groining.

V. *South Transept.*
　1. Windows, E. S. W.
　2. Transept Arch.
　3. Roof and Groining.

VI. *Lantern.*
　1. Windows.
　2. Groining.

VII. *Nave.*
　1. Nave Arch.
　2. Panelling above Nave Arch.
　3. Rood Screen.
　4. Rood Staircase.
　5. Rood Door.
　6. Rood Loft.
　7. Piers, N. S.
　8. Pier Arches, N. S.
　9. Triforia, N. 1st Tier,
　　　　　　2nd Tier.
　　　　S. 1st Tier,
　　　　　　2nd Tier.
　10. Clerestory, N. S.
　11. Windows, N. S.

　12. Pulpit (position and
　　　　description).
　13. Hour-Glass Stand.
　14. Reading Pew.
　15. Eagle Desk.
　16. Lettern.
　17. Pews.
　18. Poppy-heads.
　19. Western Arch.
　20. Parvise Turret.
　21. Roof and Groining.

VIII. *North Aisle.*
　1. Windows, E. N. W.
　2. Chantry Altar,
　　α. Piscina.
　　β. Aumbrye.
　　γ. Niche.

IX. *South Aisle.*
　1. Windows, E. S. W.
　2. Chantry Altar,
　　α. Piscina.
　　β. Sedilia.
　　γ. Aumbrye.

δ. Bracket.
3. Roof and Groining.

δ. Niche.
ε. Bracket.
3. Roof and Groining.

x. *"Ornaments"*.
1. Parclose.
2. Shrine, fixed or movable.
3. Niches.
4. Brackets.
5. Mouldings.
6. Arcades.
7. Benatura.
8. Corbels (date of headdress, &c.).

9. Arches of Construction, (etc.).
10. Interior Surface of Arch towards Aisles.
11. Spandril Spaces.
12. Vaulting Shafts.
13. Woodwork.
14. Pavement.

xi. *Belfry*, E. S. W. N.

xii. *Font*.
1. Position.
2. Description.
3. Cover.

iii. Tower.
1. Form.
2. Stages.
3. Spire Lights.
4. Lantern.
5. Parapet and Pinnacles.
6. String-Course.
7. Belfry Windows.
8. Window of Tower, N. W. S. E.
9. Buttresses.
10. Construction and age of Woodwork and Floors of the Tower and Spire.
11. Bells.
   α. Number.
   β. Tone.
   γ. Inscription and Legendal History.

12. Beacon or Belfry Turret.
   α. Situation.
   β. Form.
   γ. State of Defence.
   δ. Line of Beacons.
13. Staircase.
   α. Construction.
   β. Doorways.
   γ. Spiral Bead.
14. Defensive arrangements of Tower (Machicolations, &c.).
15. Thickness of Walls.
16. General Character of Tower as peculiar to the district, or adapted to scenery and situation.

δ. Chime.

ε. Remarkable Peals rung.

ζ. Saint's Bell.

IV. Exterior.

  1. West Window.

  2. Window Arch.

  3. West Door. (Extramural Decoration)

  4. Porch, N.   Porch, S.

    α. Outer Doorway.   α. Outer Doorway.

    β. Inner Doorway.   β. Inner Doorway.

    γ. Windows, {E. W.   γ. Windows, {E. W.

    δ. Benatura.   δ. Benatura.

    ε. Groining.   ε. Groining.

  5. Parvise.

    Windows, E. W., N. or S.

  6. Doors in

    α. Chancel or Chancel Aisles, N. S.

    β. Nave or Aisles, N. S.

    γ. Transepts, &c.

  7. Niches.   18. Lych-Gate.

  8. Buttresses.   19. Coped Coffins.

  9. Pinnacles.   20. Rood Turret.

10. Arcades.   21. Masonry.

11. Parapet.   22. Nature of Stone.

12. Mouldings.

13. Pinnacle Crosses.   23. Composition and age of Mor-

14. Gurgoyles.   tar.

15. Eave Troughs, and general 24. Joints in Arches.

    arrangements of Drains. 25. Door and Stanchions.

16. Crosses in Village or Church- 26. Roof.

    yard.   α. Present pitch.

17. Sancte Bell Cot.   β. Nature.

V. Crypt.

  1. Form.   6. Windows.

  2. Arrangement.   7. Door.

  3. Vaulting.   8. Stairs.

  4. Piers.   9. Altar Appurtenances.

  5. Dimensions.   10. Lavatory.

VI.

  1. Evangelistic Symbols.   22. Antiquity of Registers.

2. Confessional.
3. Hagioscope.
4. Painted Tiles.
5. Texts, (Canon 82).

6. Church Terriers, (Canon 87).
7. Homilies, &c. (Canon 80).
8. Chest for Alms, (Canon 84).
9. Commandments, (Canon 82).
10. Church Plate.
11. Church Chest.
12. Fald Stool.
13. Reliquary.
14. Oratory.
15. Sun Dials.
16. Royal Arms—Date and Position.
17. Paintings on Wall or Roof.
18. Tradition of Founder.
19. Connection of Church with Manor.
20. Time of Wake or Feast.
21. Conventual Remains.
   α. Situation of Church with respect to other buildings.
   β. Situation and Description of Cloisters.
   γ. Situation and Description of Chapter-House.
   δ. Abbat's or Prior's Lodgings.
   ε. Gate-House.
   ζ. Other Buildings.

23. Funeral Achievements, viz. Banners, Bannerets, Pennons, Tabard, Helm, Crest, Sword, Gauntlet, Spurs, Targe.
24. Remains of Embroidered work.
25. Images of Saints.
26. Stone Sculptures.
27. Merchant's Marks.
28. Library attached to Church.
29. Well connected with Church.
30. Heraldry.
31. Brasses.
32. Monuments.
33. Epitaphs.
34. Lombardics.
35. Stained Glass.
36. Chapel.
   N. α. Dedication.
      β. Sides, N. E.
            W. S.
      γ. Roof and Groining.
   S. α. Dedication.
      β. Sides, N. E.
            W. S.
      γ. Roof and Groining.

GENERAL REMARKS

General state of repair.
Late alterations—when—by whom—and in what taste.

Notice to be taken of any recess E. or W. of the Sedilia; of any peculiarity in the S. W. or N. W. Windows of the Chancel, especially

Appendix C

in Early English Churches; and of the capping of Norman and Early English Towers.

Published for the CAMBRIDGE CAMDEN SOCIETY, by T. Stevenson, Cambridge; J. H. Parker, Oxford; and W. H. Dalton, Cockspur-Street, Charing-Cross, London. Price per score—to Members of the Cambridge Camden and Oxford Architectural Societies—1s.; to Non-Members 2s. 6d.

[Seventh Edition]

BIBLIOGRAPHY

PUBLICATIONS OF THE CAMBRIDGE CAMDEN SOCIETY

1839
[Church Scheme.] First to Fourth Editions. (Cambridge: for the Society.)

Laws, &c. of the Cambridge Camden Society. (Cambridge: for the Society.)

[Neale, John Mason and John F. Russell.] *A Few Hints on the Practical Study of Ecclesiastical Antiquities for the Use of the Cambridge Camden Society.* (Cambridge: for the Society.)

1840
Few Hints. (Second Edition; Cambridge: University Press.)

Circular: *Report of the Auditors.* (London: J. B. Nichols and Son.)

Report of the Cambridge Camden Society for MDCCCXL together with the Address Delivered by the President on Saturday, March 28, 1840 and a List of the Members, Laws, &c. &c. (Cambridge: for the Society.)

Additions and Corrections to the Report for 1840. (n.p.)

[Thorp, Thomas.] *Address Delivered at the First Evening Meeting of the Cambridge Camden Society, March 28, 1840.* (n.p.)

1841
An Account of the Church of St. Mary The Virgin, Stow, Lincolnshire, in Aid of the Proposed Restoration. (Cambridge: University Press.)

The *Ecclesiologist*, vols. I–xxix. (Cambridge: 1841–45; London: 1846–68.)

The *Ecclesiologist*, first issue. (Cambridge: November 1841.) Bound volume contains a revised edition of this issue.

Circular: [List of laws, officers, and patrons]. (n.p.)

[Neale, John Mason.] *A Few Words to Church Builders.* Two versions: one marked 'price sixpence' with four plates, and another, 'price one shilling' with no plates but short appendix. (Cambridge: University Press.)

[Neale, John Mason.] *Appendix to a Few Words to Churchbuilders Con-*

taining Lists of Fonts, Windows, and Roodscreens Intended to Serve as Models. (Cambridge: University Press.)

[Neale, John Mason.] *A Few Suggestions to Churchwardens on Churches and Church Ornaments; No. I. Suited to Country Parishes.* (Cambridge: University Press.)

[Neale, John Mason.] *A Few Words to Churchwardens on Churches and Church Ornaments; No. I. Suited to Country Parishes.* Second to Tenth Editions. (Cambridge: University Press.)

[Neale, John Mason.] *A Few Words to Churchwardens on Churches and Church Ornaments; No. II. Suited to Town and Manufacturing Parishes.* First to Third Editions. (Cambridge: University Press.)

[Neale, John Mason.] *The History of Pews: A Paper Read Before the Cambridge Camden Society on Monday, November 22, 1841, With an Appendix Containing a Report Presented to the Society on the Statistics of Pews on Monday, December 7, 1841.* (Cambridge: University Press.)

Report of the Cambridge Camden Society for MDCCCXLI. (Cambridge: for the Society.)

Thorp, Thomas. [Letter to John Mason Neale regarding some publications of the Society dated 7 December 1841 and reply by Benjamin Webb, dated 9 December 1841.] (n.p.)

Transactions of the Cambridge Camden Society, Part I. A Selection from the Papers Read at the Ordinary Meetings in 1839–41. (Cambridge: T. Stevenson.)

[Webb, Benjamin.] *An Argument for the Greek Origin of the Monogram IHS: A Paper Read Before the Cambridge Camden Society on Tuesday, May 25, 1841. With Illustrative Notes.* (Cambridge: T. Stevenson.)

1842

The Church of the Holy Sepulchre or the Round Church, Cambridge. Three versions, one dated 14 July 1842. (Cambridge: University Press.)

Circular: *Church of The Holy Sepulchre or The Round Church Cambridge.* (n.p.)

Few Hints. (Third Edition; Cambridge: University Press.)

A Few Words to Church Builders with an Appendix Containing Lists of Windows Fonts and Roodscreens Intended to Serve as Models. (Second Edition; Cambridge: University Press.)

A Few Words to Churchwardens Part I. Eleventh and Twelfth Editions. (Cambridge: University Press.)

A Few Words to Churchwardens Part II. Fourth and Fifth Editions. (Cambridge: University Press.)

Bibliography

History of Pews. Second Edition with Additions. (Cambridge: University Press.)

A Supplement to the History of Pues. (Cambridge: University Press.)

Report of the Cambridge Camden Society for MDCCCXLII. (Cambridge: for the Society.)

Circular: *The Round Church*, dated 31 October 1842. (n.p.)

Transactions of the Cambridge Camden Society. Part II. A Selection of Papers Read at the Ordinary Meetings in 1841–1842. (Cambridge: T. Stevenson.)

1843

The Church of the Holy Sepulchre or The Round Church Cambridge. (Cambridge: University Press.)

A Few Hints on the Practical Study of Ecclesiastical Architecture and Antiquities for the Use of the Cambridge Camden Society. (Fourth Edition; Cambridge: University Press.)

Few Words to Churchwardens Part I. (Thirteenth Edition; Cambridge: University Press.)

Few Words to Churchwardens Part II. (Sixth Edition; Cambridge: University Press.)

History of Pues. Third Edition Containing the 'Supplement' with Additions. (Cambridge: University Press.)

[Neale, John Mason.] *Church Enlargement and Church Arrangement.* (Cambridge: University Press.)

[Neale, John Mason.] *A Few Words to the Parish Clerks and Sextons of Country Parishes.* First and Second Editions. (Cambridge: University Press.)

Report of the Cambridge Camden Society for MDCCCXLIII. (Cambridge: for the Society.)

1844

Circular: [Announcement that the Society is no longer responsible for the *Ecclesiologist*]. (n.p.)

Few Words to Church Builders. Third Edition, entirely rewritten. (Cambridge: University Press.)

The Orientator. A Simple Contrivance for Ascertaining the Orientation of Churches. (Cambridge: Thomas Stevenson.)

Circular: *Publications of the Cambridge Camden Society.*

Report of the Cambridge Camden Society MDCCCXLIV. (Cambridge: University Press.)

Bibliography

Circular: *The Round Church*. Two versions, one dated 13 March 1844. (n.p.)

[Thorp, Thomas.] *The Church of the Holy Sepulchre*. (Cambridge: T. Stevenson.)

1845

Account of the Sixth Anniversary Meeting of the Cambridge Camden Society, May 8, 1845. (From the Newspaper Report.) (Cambridge: Warwick and Co.)

Churches of Cambridgeshire and the Isle of Ely. (Cambridge: T. Stevenson.)

[Collison, F. S.] *On The History of Christian Altars: A Paper Read before the Cambridge Camden Society, Nov. 28, 1844*. (Cambridge: T. Stevenson.)

Circular: [Letter from the Committee on the proposed dissolution of the Society, dated 24 April 1845]. (n.p.)

Place, George Gordon. *Plans, Sections, and Elevations of the Chancel of All Saints Church, Hawton, Nottinghamshire. With Descriptive Account.* (Cambridge: John Thomas Walters.)

Circular: [Proposal to pay off the debt on the Round Church, dated 8 May 1845]. (n.p.)

Circular: [Report from the Committee on the present state of the Society's operations and prospects, dated 9 December 1845]. (n.p.)

[Thorp, Thomas.] *A Statement of Particulars Connected with the Restoration of the Round Church*. (Cambridge: Deightons, Stevenson, and Walters.)

Transactions of the Cambridge Camden Society. Part III. A Selection from the Papers Read at the Ordinary Meetings in 1843–44–45. (Cambridge: John Thomas Walters.)

1846

Circular: [Call to the Seventh Anniversary Meeting]. (n.p.)

Illustrations of Monumental Brasses. (Cambridge: J. T. Walters.)

Circular: [List of revised Laws to be submitted to the Society for adoption]. (n.p.)

Circular: [Report of the Committee, dated April 1846]. (n.p.)

Undated circulars and sheets:

[Advice to Workmen Employed in Restoring a Church.] (Cambridge: Stevenson.)

Bibliography

[Advice to Workmen Employed in Building a Church.] (Cambridge: Stevenson.)

[Church Schemes.] Fifth to Sixteenth Editions.

'A Few Words to Bellringers'

'The Interior of S. Sepulchre's Cambridge'

'An Exterior View of the Same'

'A Lithograph of the Font and Cover in the Church of S. Edward the Confessor Cambridge'

'Hints on the Well-keeping & Ordering of Churches, and their Repairs, Furniture, and Ornaments.' (Cambridge: Stevenson.)

'Stalls and Screenwork in S. Mary's Lancaster'

'Twenty-three Reasons for Getting Rid of Church Pews (or Pues).' (Cambridge: Stevenson.)

'Twenty-four Reasons for Getting Rid of Church Pews (or Pues).' (Cambridge: Stevenson.)

PUBLICATIONS OF THE ECCLESIOLOGICAL LATE CAMBRIDGE CAMDEN SOCIETY

1846

Few Words to Churchwardens Part I. (Fourteenth Edition; London: Joseph Masters.)

Few Words to Parish Clerks and Sextons of Country Parishes. (Third Edition; London: Joseph Masters.)

Circular: [Laws as settled at the Seventh Anniversary Meeting, dated 15 May 1846]. (n.p.)

Report of the Ecclesiological late Cambridge Camden Society MDCCCXLV–VI. (London: Joseph Masters.)

1847

Instrumenta Ecclesiastica. (London: John Van Voorst.)

1848

A Hand-Book of English Ecclesiology. (London: Joseph Masters.)

[Russell, J. F.] *Hierugia Anglicana or Documents and Extracts Illustrative of the Ritual of the Church in England after the Reformation.* (London: J. G. F. and J. Rivington.)

1849

Report of the Ecclesiological late Cambridge Camden Society MDCCCXLVII–VIII–IX. (London: Joseph Masters.)

1851
Few Words to Churchwardens Part II. (Seventh Edition; London: Joseph Masters.)
Funerals and Funeral Arrangements. (London: Joseph Masters.)
Hymnal Noted. Part I. (London: J. Alfred Novello.) ('Published under the Sanction of the Ecclesiological late Cambridge Camden Society.')

1852
Helmore, Thomas. *Accompanying Harmonies to the Hymnal Noted.* (London: J. Alfred Novello.) ('Published under the Sanction of the Ecclesiological Society.')

1853
Report of the Ecclesiological late Cambridge Camden Society MDCCL–LI–LII–LIII. (London: Joseph Masters.)

PUBLICATIONS OF THE ECCLESIOLOGICAL SOCIETY

1856
Hymnal Noted. (London: J. Alfred Novello.)
Instrumenta Ecclesiastica. (Second Series; London: John Van Voorst.)
Report of the Ecclesiological Society MDCCCLIV–V–VI. (London: Joseph Masters.)

1857
Report of the Ecclesiological Society MDCCCLVII. (London: Joseph Masters.)

1858
Report of the Ecclesiological Society MDCCCLVIII. (London: Joseph Masters.)

1859
Report of the Ecclesiological Society MDCCCLIX. (London: Joseph Masters.)

1864
Report of the Ecclesiological Society MDCCCLXIII–MDCCCLXIV. (London: Joseph Masters.)

Bibliography

A SELECTION OF RELATED WORKS

Ackermann, R. *A History of the University of Cambridge, Its Colleges, Halls, and Public Buildings.* (London: R. Ackermann, 1815; 2 vols.)

Addison, Agnes. *Romanticism and the Gothic Revival.* (New York: Richard R. Smith, 1938.)

Addleshaw, G. W. O. and Frederick Etchells. *The Architectural Setting of Anglican Worship: An Inquiry into the Arrangements for Public Worship in the Church of England from the Reformation to the Present day.* (London: Faber and Faber Limited, 1950.)

Anson, Peter F. *Fashions in Church Furnishings, 1840–1940.* (London: Faith Press, 1960.)

Arnold, Thomas Kerchever. *An Examination of the Rev. F. Close's Reply to 'Remarks' upon His 'Church Architecture Scripturally Considered'.* (London: Francis and John Rivington, 1844.)

Arnold, Thomas Kerchever. *Remarks on the Rev. F. Close's 'Church Architecture Scripturally Considered, from the Earliest Ages to the Present Time'.* (London: Francis & John Rivington, 1844.)

Bartholomew, A. T. *Catalogue of the Books and Papers for the Most Part Relating to the University, Town, and County of Cambridge Bequeathed to the University by John Willis Clark, M.A.* (Cambridge: University Press, 1912.)

Blackburne, J. *A Brief Historical Inquiry into the Introduction of Stone Altars into the Christian Church; with Remarks upon the Probable Effects of the Altar and Its Ornaments upon Church Architecture in General.* (Cambridge: T. Stevenson, 1844.)

Boyce, Edward Jacob. *A Memorial of the Cambridge Camden Society, Instituted May, 1839 and the Ecclesiological (late Cambridge Camden), May, 1846.* (London: G. Palmer, 1888.)

Bouyer, Louis. *Liturgical Piety.* (Notre Dame, Indiana: University of Notre Dame Press, 1955; Liturgical Studies.)

Briggs, Martin S. *Goths and Vandals: A Study of the Destruction, Neglect, and Preservation of Historical Buildings in England.* (London: Constable, 1952.)

Brilioth, Yngve. *The Anglican Revival: Studies in the Oxford Movement.* (London: Longmans, Green and Co., 1925.)

Brose, Olive J. *Church and Parliament; The Reshaping of the Church of England 1828–1860.* (Stanford: Stanford University Press, 1959.)

The Builder: an Illustrated Weekly Magazine for the Architect, Engineer, Archaeologist, Constructor, & Artist. (London: 1859, vol. XVII.)

R   243

Cambridge Chronicle and Journal and Huntingdonshire Gazette. (Cambridge: 1845.)

Carpenter, S. C. *Church and People, 1789–1889: A History of the Church of England from William Wilberforce to 'Lux Mundi'.* (London: S.P.C.K., 1933.)

'Church Architecture', *Christian Remembrancer: A Monthly Magazine and Review,* III (1842), 353–60.

Church, R. W. *The Oxford Movement: Twelve Years 1833–1845.* (London: Macmillan and Co. Ltd., 1897.)

Clark, Sir Kenneth. *The Gothic Revival: an Essay in the History of Taste.* (Revised and Enlarged Edition; London: Constable, 1950.)

Clarke, Basil F. L. *Anglican Cathedrals Outside the British Isles.* (London: S.P.C.K., 1958.)

Clarke, Basil F. L. *Church Builders of the Nineteenth Century: A Study of the Gothic Revival in England.* (London: S.P.C.K., 1938.)

Clarke, C. P. S. *The Oxford Movement and After.* (London: A. R. Mowbray & Co., 1932.)

Clarke, W. K. Lowther and Charles Harris, editors. *Liturgy and Worship: A Companion to the Prayer Books of the Anglican Communion.* (London: S.P.C.K., 1940.)

'Clericus Connorensis', *Ecclesiologism Exposed: Being the Letters of 'Clericus Connorensis' as Originally Published in the Belfast Commercial Chronicle.* (Belfast: George Phillips, 1843.)

Close, Francis. *Church Architecture Scripturally Considered, from the Earliest Ages to the Present Time.* (London: Hatchard and Son, 1844.)

Close, Francis. *A Reply to the 'Remarks' of the Rev. T. K. Arnold, M.A., upon Close's 'Church Architecture'.* (London: Hatchard and Son, 1844.)

Close, Francis. *The Restoration of Churches Is the Restoration of Popery: Proved and Illustrated from the Authenticated Publications of the 'Cambridge Camden Society': A Sermon Preached in the Parish Church, Cheltenham, on Tuesday, November 5th, 1844.* (London: Hatchard & Son, 1844.)

Collison, F. W. *Remarks on A Sermon by Professor Scholefield, Entitled The Christian Altar: Being a Vindication of the Catholic Doctrines Therein Impugned.* (Cambridge: University Press, 1842.)

Collison, F. W. *Some Further Remarks on the Christian Altar and Eucharistic Sacrifice: With Strictures on Vedilius and Williams.* (Cambridge: University Press, 1843.)

Bibliography

Cook, G. H. *The English Mediaeval Parish Church*. (London: Phoenix House Ltd., 1954.)

Douglas, Winfred. *Church Music in History and Practice: Studies in the Praise of God*. (New York: Charles Scribner's Sons, 1937.)

Durandus, William. *The Symbolism of Churches and Church Ornaments: A Translation of the First Book of the Rationale Divinorum Officiorum, Written by William Durandus, Sometime Bishop of Mende*. Introductory Essay, Notes, and Illustrations by the Rev. John Mason Neale, B.A., and the Rev. Benjamin Webb, B.A. of Trinity College Cambridge. (Leeds: T. W. Green, 1843.)

Eastlake, Charles L. *A History of the Gothic Revival: An Attempt to Show How the Taste for Mediaeval Architecture Which Lingered in England During the Last Two Centuries Has Since Been Encouraged and Developed*. (London: Longmans, Green and Co., 1872.)

'Ecclesialogy', *British Critic and Quarterly Theological Review*, XXI (1837), 218–48.

Elliott-Binns, L. E. *Religion in the Victorian Era*. (London: Lutterworth Press, 1946.)

'An Enquirer'. *A Re-Print of a Letter Addressed to a Revd. Member of the Cambridge Camden Society by M. de Compte de Montalembert Accompanied with a Few Remarks & Queries*. (Cheltenham: Richard Edwards, 1845.)

Every, George. *Christian Discrimination*. (London: Sheldon Press, 1940.)

Fairchild, Hoxie Neale. *Religious Trends in English Poetry. Vol. IV: 1830–1880 Christianity and Romanticism in the Victorian Era*. (New York: Columbia University Press, 1957.)

Faulkner, R. R. Circular: *An Appeal to the Protestant Public Respecting the Popish Abominations of a Stone Altar and Credence Table, in St. Sepulchre's Church, Cambridge*. (n.p. 1844.)

Ferrey, Benjamin. *Recollections of A. N. Welby Pugin, and His Father, Augustus Pugin: With Notices of their Works*. (London: Edward Stanford, 1861.)

Circular: *The Following Statement Is Submitted to the Members of the Cambridge Camden Society*. (Cambridge: 17 May 1845.)

Circular: *The Following Statement Was Submitted to the Members of the Cambridge Camden Society*. (Cambridge: 13 June 1845.)

Freeman, Edward A. *Principles of Church Restoration*. (London: Joseph Masters, 1846.)

F[reeman], P[hilip]. *Thoughts on the Proposed Dissolution of the Cam-*

bridge Camden Society Suggested for the Consideration of the Members. (London: Francis and John Rivington, 1845.)

Frere, W. H. 'Introduction', *Hymns Ancient and Modern for Use in the Services of the Church with Accompanying Tunes; Historical Edition with Notes on the Origin of Both Hymns and Tunes and a General Historical Introduction. Illustrated by Facsimile and Portraits.* (London: for the Proprietors, 1909.)

Gladstone, W. E. *Gleanings of Past Years; 1843–78.* (London: John Murray, 1879.) Vol. VI.

Godwin, George and John Britton. *The Churches of London: A History and Description of the Ecclesiastical Edifices of the Metropolis. With Biographical Anecdotes of Eminent Persons, Notices of Remarkable Monuments, etc.* (London: C. Tilt, 1839; 2 vols.)

Goodchild, Thomas. 'Gothic and Classic', *The Builder: an Illustrated Weekly Magazine for the Architect, Engineer, Archaeologist, Constructor, & Artist,* xv (1857), 25.

Goode, William. *Altars Prohibited by the Church of England.* (London: J. Hatchard and Son, 1844.)

Goodhart-Rendel, H. S. *English Architecture Since the Regency: an Interpretation.* (London: Constable, 1953.)

Graham, John. *A Sermon Preached at the Re-opening of the Church of the Holy Sepulchre in Cambridge; on Sunday, August 10, 1845.* (Cambridge: University Press, 1845.)

Gwynn, Denis. *Lord Shrewsbury, Pugin and the Catholic Revival.* (Westminster, Maryland; Newman Book Shop, 1946.)

Gwynne, Walker. *The Beginnings of Church Architecture in America.* Reprinted from *American Church Monthly,* American Ecclesiological Society Bulletin No. 1, n.p. [1917].

Hitchcock, Henry-Russell. *Early Victorian Architecture in Britain.* (New Haven: Yale University Press, 1954; 2 vols.)

Hitchcock, Henry-Russell. 'G. E. Street in the 1850's'. *Journal of the Society of Architectural Historians,* XIX (1960), 145–71.

Hope, A. J. B. Beresford. *The English Cathedral of the Nineteenth Century.* (London: John Murray, 1861.)

'D. C. L.' [A. J. B. Hope]. *Letters on Church Matters. Reprinted from the 'Morning Chronicle'.* (London: James Ridgway, 1851–2; 3 vols.)

Illustrated London News. Vol. xx (1852). (London: William Little, 1852.)

Jebb, John. *The Choral Service of the United Church of England and Ireland: Being an Enquiry Into the Liturgical System of the Cathedral and Collegiate Foundations of the Anglican Communion.* (London: John H. Parker, 1843.)

Jebb, John. *Three Lectures on the Cathedral Service of the Church of England.* Second Edition with Additions. (Leeds: T. W. Green, 1845.)

Johnston, John Octavius. *Life and Letters of Henry Parry Liddon. D.D., D. C. L., LL. D., Canon of St. Paul's Cathedral, and Sometime Ireland Professor of Exegesis in the University of Oxford.* (London: Longmans, Green and Co., 1904.)

Langley, B[atty] and T[homas]. *Gothic Architecture Improved by Rules and Proportions. In many Grand Designs of Columns, Doors, Windows, Chimney-Pieces, Arcades, Colonnades, Porticos, Umbrellos, Temples, and Pavillons &c. with Plans, Elevations and Profiles Geometrically Explained.* (London: John Millan, 1747.)

Law, Henry William and Irene. *The Book of the Beresford Hopes.* (London: Heath Cranton Limited, 1925.)

[Lee, Samuel]. *A Letter to the Venerable Archdeacon Thorp, President of the Camden Society, on Its Late Re-organization and Apparent Objects.* (London: Cahn & Co. [1845].)

[Lee, Samuel]. *A Second Letter to the Venerable Archdeacon Thorp, President of the Cambridge Camden Society on Symbolism.* (London: Seeley, Burnside and Seeley, 1845.)

Lesser, George. *Gothic Cathedrals and Sacred Geometry.* (London: Alec Tirenti, 1957; 2 vols.)

Liddon, Henry Parry. *Life of Edward Bouverie Pusey.* (London: Longmans, Green & Co., 1893-7; 4 vols.)

'The Literature of the Gothic Revival', *Eclectic Review*, New Series, vol. xxv (1849), 33-50.

Lowe, Thomas Hill. *A Few Thoughts on the Interior Arrangement of Churches: Being the Substance of a Paper Read at a General Meeting of the Members of the Exeter Diocesan Architectural Society, March 24, 1842.* (Exeter: P. A. Hannaford, n.d.)

Maurice, Peter. *The Popery of Oxford Confronted, Disavowed, & Repudiated.* (London: Francis Baisler, 1837.)

'Member of Trinity College'. *The Claims of the Camden Society Considered in Connection with the Church of England.* (Cambridge: W. P. Grant, 1842.)

Montalembert, Le Comte de. *A Letter Addressed to a Rev. Member of The Camden Society, on the Subject of Catholic Literary Societies, on the Architectural, Artistical, and Archaeological Movements of the Puseyites.* (Liverpool: Booker and Co., 1844.)

Bibliography

Molyneux, John W. H. *Preaching the Gospel to the Working Classes Impossible under the Pew System.* (London: General Committee on the Pew System, 1858.)

Mozley, T[homas]. *Reminiscences Chiefly of Oriel College and The Oxford Movement.* (Boston: Houghton Mifflin and Co., 1884; 2 vols.)

Neale, John Mason. [Church Schemes.] Five volumes in the Library of the Royal Institute of British Architects, London, filled out by Neale, and others, 1839–41.

Neale, John Mason. *A Few Words of Hope on the Present Crisis of the English Church.* (London: Joseph Masters, 1850.)

Neale, John Mason. *Hierologus: or, The Church Tourists.* (London: James Burns, 1843.)

Neale, John Mason. *Hymns, Chiefly Mediaeval, on the Joys and Glories of Paradise.* (London: J. T. Hayes, 1865.)

Neale, John Mason. *Hymns of the Eastern Church: Translated, with Notes and an Introduction.* (Third Edition; London: J. T. Hayes, [1866].)

Neale, John Mason. *Letters of John Mason Neale, D.D., Selected and Edited by His Daughter.* (London: Longmans, Green and Co., 1910.)

Neale, John Mason. *Notes, Ecclesiological and Picturesque, on Dalmatia, Croatia, Istria, Styria, with a Visit to Montenegro.* (London: J. T. Hayes, 1861.)

Neale, John Mason. *The Place Where Prayer was wont to be made. The Re-introduction of the System of Private Devotion in Churches Considered in a Letter to the Venerable The President of the Cambridge Camden Society.* (Rugeley: John Thomas Walters, 1844.)

Neale, John Mason. *A Statement of the Late Proceedings of the Lord Bishop of Chichester Against the Warden of Sackville College, East Grinstead.* (n.p., 1849.)

Neale, John Mason. *The Symbolism of Churches and Church Ornaments: A Translation of the First Book of the Rationale Divinorum Officiorum, Written by William Durandus, Sometime Bishop of Mende.* Introductory Essay, Notes, and Illustrations, by the Rev. John Mason Neale, B.A., and the Rev. Benjamin Webb, B.A. of Trinity College, Cambridge. (Leeds: T. W. Green, 1843.)

Neale, John Mason. *The Unseen World: Communication with It Real or Imaginary, Including Apparitions, Warnings, Haunted Places, Prophecies, Aerial Visions, Astrology, etc.* (London: James Burns, 1847.)

248

Bibliography

Neale, John Mason. *The Unseen World.* Second Edition with additions. (London: Joseph Masters, 1853.)

Newman, John Henry Cardinal. *Apologia Pro Vita Sua Being A History of His Religious Opinions.* Edited by Charles Frederick Harrold. (New York: Longmans, Green and Co., 1947.)

Newman, John Henry Cardinal. *Correspondence of John Henry Newman with John Keble and Others, 1839–1845.* Edited at the Birmingham Oratory. (London: Longmans, Green and Co., 1917.)

Newman, John Henry Cardinal. *The Idea of a University Defined and Illustrated.* (London: Longmans, Green and Co., 1898.)

Newman, John Henry Cardinal. *Loss and Gain: The Story of a Convert.* (London: Longmans, Green and Co., 1900.)

New-York Ecclesiological Society. *Annual Report of the New-York Ecclesiological Society, 3rd: 1851.* (New York: Stamford and Swords, [1851].)

New York Ecclesiologist. Vols. I–II. (New York: New-York Ecclesiological Society, 1848–50.)

New-York Ecclesiological Society. *Transactions of the New York Ecclesiological Society, 1855.* (New York: D. Dana, 1857.)

Ollard, S. L., Gordon Crosse, and Maurice F. Bond, editors. *A Dictionary of English Church History.* (Third Edition. Revised; London: A. R. Mowbray & Co. Limited, 1948.)

Ollard, S. L. *A Short History of the Oxford Movement.* (London: A. R. Mowbray & Co., 1915.)

'On the Present Condition and Prospects of Architecture in England' *Weale's Quarterly Papers on Architecture,* II (1844), 1–16.

Oxford Architectural Society. *Rules and Proceedings of the Oxford Society for Promoting the Study of Gothic Architecture.* (Oxford: 1840 et seq.)

Pace, G. G. 'Pusey and Leeds', *Architectural Review,* 98 (1945), 178–80.

Paget, Francis E. *Milford Malvoisin: or, Pews and Pewholders.* (London: James Burns, 1842.)

Petit, J. L. *Remarks on Church Architecture. With Illustrations.* (London: James Burns, 1841; 2 vols.)

'Pews', *British Critic and Quarterly Theological Review,* XXXII (1842), 436–505.

Pugin, A. Welby. *An Apology for the Revival of Christian Architecture in England.* (Edinburgh: John Grant, 1895.)

Pugin, A. Welby. *Contrasts: or, a Parallel Between the Noble Edifices of*

Bibliography

the Fourteenth and Fifteenth Centuries, and Similar Buildings of the Present Day: Showing the Present Decay of Taste: Accompanied by appropriate Text. (London: Printed for the Author, and published by Him, at St. Marie's Grange, near Salisbury, Wilts., 1836.)

Pugin, A. Welby. *Contrasts.* (Second Edition, reprinted. Edinburgh: John Grant, 1898.)

Pugin, A. Welby. *An Earnest Appeal for the Revival of the Ancient Plain Song.* (London: Charles Dolman, 1850.)

Pugin, A. Welby. *The Present State of Ecclesiastical Architecture in England.* (Republished from the Dublin Review; London: Charles Dolman, 1843.)

Pugin, A. Welby. *The True Principles of Pointed or Christian Architecture: Set Forth in Two Lectures Delivered at St. Marie's Oscott.* (London: John Weale, 1841.)

Purchas, John. *Directorium Anglicanum; Being a Manual of Directions for the Right Celebration of the Holy Communion, for the Saying of Matins and Evensong, And for the Performance of Other Rites and Ceremonies of the Church According to Ancient Uses of the Church of England.* (London: Joseph Masters, 1858.)

Quarterly Papers on Architecture. Vols. I–IV. Edited and published by John Weale. (London: John Weale, 1844–5.)

Ratcliff, E. C., 'The Choir Offices', in *Liturgy and Worship*, edited by W. K. Lowther Clarke and Charles Harris. (London: S.P.C.K., 1940, 257–95.)

'Review. Publications of the Oxford Architectural Society', *Quarterly Papers on Architecture*, IV (1845), 1–6.

Rickman, Thomas. *An Attempt to Discriminate the Styles of Architecture in England, from the Conquest to the Reformation: with a Sketch of the Grecian and Roman Orders; Notices of Numerous British Edifices; and Some Remarks on the Architecture of a Part of France.* (Fifth Edition. London: John Henry Parker, 1848.)

Robertson, J. E. P., editor. *The Judgment of the Rt. Hon. Sir Herbert Jenner Fust, Kt. Dean of the Arches, &c. &c. &c. in the Case of Faulkner v. Litchfield and Stearn, on the 31st January, 1845.* (London: William Benning & Co., 1845.)

Rothenstein, John. 'Newman and Littlemore', *Architectural Review*, 98 (1945), 176–7.

Ruskin, John. *Modern Painters.* (London: George Allen, 1904; vol. III.)

Ruskin, John. *The Seven Lamps of Architecture.* (London: J. M. Dent & Sons Ltd., 1956.)

Bibliography

Ruskin, John. *The Stones of Venice*. (New York: John B. Alden, 1885; 3 vols.)

Scholefield, James. *The Christian Altar; A Sermon Preached before the University of Cambridge, on Sunday Morning, Oct. 23, 1842*. (Cambridge University Press, 1842.)

Scott, Geoffrey. *The Architecture of Humanism: A Study in the History of Taste*. (Garden City, N.Y.: Doubleday Anchor Books, 1956.)

Scott, Sir George Gilbert. *Personal and Professional Recollections*. Edited by G. Gilbert Scott. (London: Sampson Low, Marston, Searle & Rivington, 1879.)

Scott, Sir George Gilbert. *A Plea for the Faithful Restoration of Our Ancient Churches. A Paper Read before the Architectural and Archaeological Society for the County of Bucks, at Their First Annual Meeting in 1848, and Repeated at a Joint Meeting of the Architectural Societies for the Archdeaconry of Northampton and the County of Bedford in 1849*. (London: John Henry Parker, 1850.)

Sedgwick, Tom E., J. T. Micklethwaite, R. Norman Shaw et al. *Description and History of the Church of St. Mary Magdalene, Munster Square, London, N.W.* (London: Henry J. Glaisher, 1902.)

Simpson, W. J. Sparrow. *The History of the Anglo-Catholic Revival from 1845*. (London: George Allen & Unwin, Ltd., 1932.)

Simson, Otto von. *The Gothic Cathedral: Origins of Gothic Architecture and the Medieval Concept of Order. With an Appendix on the Proportions of the South Tower of Chartres Cathedral*. (New York: Pantheon, 1956.) (Bollingen Series.)

[Smith, J. J.]. *A Few Words on The Last Publication of the Cambridge Camden Society*. (Cambridge: University Press, 1843.)

Staley, Vernon. *Hierurgia Anglicana, Documents and Extracts Illustrative of the Ceremonial of the Anglican Church after the Reformation*. (New Edition, Revised and Considerably Enlarged by Vernon Staley; London: Alexander Moring, 1902–4; 3 vols.)

Stephens, W. R. W. *The Life and Letters of Walter Farquhar Hook, D.D., F.R.S.* (Seventh Edition; London: Richard Bentley & Son, 1885.)

[Stokes, S. N.]. *A Christian Kalendar For the Use of Members of The Established Church Arranged for the Year of Our Lord MDCCCXLV*. 'By a Lay Member of The Cambridge Camden Society.' (Cambridge: Norris Deck, [1845].)

Storr, Vernon F. *The Development of English Theology in the Nineteenth*

Bibliography

Century, 1800–1860. (London: Longmans, Green and Co., 1913; vol. I.)

Stuart, Edward. *The Pew System the Chief Hindrance to the Church's Work in Towns: A Sermon*. (Third Edition; London: Joseph Masters, n.d.)

'Styles of Church Architecture', *Christian Remembrancer; A Monthly Magazine and Review*, IV (1842), 257–70.

Summerson, John. *Heavenly Mansions and Other Essays on Architecture*. (London: Cresset, 1949.)

S[wainson], C. A. *A Letter to a Non-Resident Member of the Cambridge Camden Society, on the Present Position of That Body*. (Cambridge: Privately Printed, 1845.)

Thorp, Thomas. *A Charge Delivered at the Visitation of the Archdeaconry of Bristol in July, 1842*. (Bristol: W. Strong, 1842.)

Thorp, Thomas. *A Charge Delivered at the Visitation of the Archdeaconry of Bristol in July, 1843*. (Bristol: W. Strong, 1843.)

Towle, Eleanor A. *John Mason Neale. D.D.: A Memoir*. (London: Longmans, Green & Co., 1906.)

Tracts for the Times. (By Members of the University of Oxford.) (London: J. G. F. & J. Rivington, 1839–41; 6 vols.)

Transactions of the St. Paul's Ecclesiological Society. (London: Printed for the Society by Alabaster, Passmore, and Sons, 1879–1920; vols. I–VIII.)

Venn, J. A. *Alumni Cantabrigienses: A Biographical List of All Known Students, Graduates, and Holders of Office at the University of Cambridge from the Earliest Times to 1900; Part II: From 1752 to 1900*. (Cambridge: University Press, 1940–54; vols. I–VI.)

[Wade, John]. *The Extraordinary Black Book: Being an Exposition of the United Church of England and Ireland; Civil List and Crown Revenues; Income, Privileges, and Power, of the Aristocracy, Privy Council, Diplomatic, and Consular Establishments, Law and Judicial Administration; Representation; and Prospects of Reform Under the New Ministry; Profits, Influence, and Monopoly of the Bank of England and East-India Company, with Strictures on the Renewal of Their Charters; Debt and Funding System; Salaries, Fees, Emoluments in Courts of Justice, Public Offices, and Colonies; Lists of Pluralists, Placemen, Pensioners, and Sinecurists: The Whole Corrected from the Latest Official Returns, and Presenting a Complete View of the Expenditure, Patronage, Influence, and Abuses of the Government in Church, State, Law, and Representation*. (London: Effingham Wilson, 1831.)

Bibliography

Warren, Charles. *The Lord's Table the Christian Altar, in Some Remarks upon Professor Scholefield's Late Sermon.* (Cambridge: J. and J. J. Deighton, 1843.)

Webb, Benjamin. *Sketches of Continental Ecclesiology or Church Notes in Belgium, Germany, and Italy.* (London: Joseph Masters, 1848.)

Webb, Benjamin and John Mason Neale. *The Symbolism of Churches and Church Ornaments: A Translation of the First Book of the Rationale Divinorum Officiorum, Written by William Durandus, Sometime Bishop of Mende.* Introductory Essay, Notes, and Illustrations, by the Rev. John Mason Neale, B.A., and the Rev. Benjamin Webb, B.A. of Trinity College Cambridge. (Leeds: T. W. Green, 1843.)

Sermons Preached in the Church of St. Andrew's, Wells Street on St. Andrew's Day and on Sundays in Advent 1885 after the Death and Funeral of the Rev. Benjamin Webb, M.A., Vicar and Prebendary of Portpool in St. Paul's Cathedral. Together with Other Published Notices of His Life and His Work. (Printed for Private Circulation, 1886.)

Webb, Clement C. J. 'Benjamin Webb', *Church Quarterly Review*, LXXV (1913), 329–48.

Webb, William. [Letter requesting withdrawal of members of the Cambridge Camden Society]. [Cambridge, 1845.]

Whichcord, John. 'Observations on the Polychromatic Decorations of the Middle Ages', *Quarterly Papers on Architecture*, IV (1845), 1–15.

The Widow's Lament, Literally Rendered, into Verse and Respectfully Addressed to the Parishioners of the Parson Deserted Parish, Called the Holy Sepulchre. (Cambridge: J. W. Doughty, 1845.)

Wightwick, George. 'Ancient English Gothic Architecture', *Quarterly Papers on Architecture*, II (1844), 1–9.

Wightwick, George. 'Modern English Gothic Architecture', *Quarterly Papers on Architecure*, III and IV (1845), 1–18 and 1–7.

Wren, Christopher. *Parentalia: or, Memoirs of the Family of the Wrens; Viz. of Matthew Bishop of Ely, Christopher Dean of Windsor, etc. but chiefly of Sir Christopher Wren, late Surveyor-General of the Royal Buildings, President of the Royal Society, etc. etc. Compiled by his Son Christopher. Now published by his Grandson, Stephen Wren, Esq.* (London: 1750.)

PLATES

EXPLANATION OF PLATES

PLATE I

A TYPICAL ANGLICAN CHURCH INTERIOR IN THE 1830's—St Olave's, Hart Street, London, a medieval town Church as arranged for Anglican worship in the nineteenth century. The high private pews, the pews beside the altar, the galleries, the three-decker pulpit in the centre alley, the classical funeral monuments on the walls and hatchments in the south clerestory, the altar rails of twisted balusters, and the classical reredos with the Command-ments, Creed, and Lord's Prayer are characteristic of the period. The font stood in the east end of the north aisle. This Church was subsequently refurnished, and then burnt during the bombings of 1941. (Plate from Godwin and Britton, *The Churches of London*, 1839, Vol. I.)

PLATE II

THE LITURGICAL ARRANGEMENT ADVOCATED BY THE CAMBRIDGE CAMDEN SOCIETY—based on a plate which appears in the sixpence edition of *A Few Words to Church Builders*, Cambridge, 1841. On the preceding page (page 32) appears the following description:

PLATE I is intended to illustrate the Catholick arrangement of a church. The ground plan is that of a village church in Sussex; the arrangement, however, adopted in the original is sadly at variance with the principles inculcated in this Tract.

S. The Chancel. TT. The Transepts. N. The Nave. OO. The Aisles. P. The Porch. A. The stone altar. a. The sedilia. B. The three flights of three steps. CC. Misereres. A double row on each side. D. Roodscreen. Z. Priest's door. [This might equally well have been on the other side.] T. The founder's tomb. E. The steps to the Chancel. Two are perhaps better than three. ffff. Lantern piers. These support a light Decorated spire. F. Font. KK. Piers. H. Pulpit. I. Eagle desk. Facing west. G. Faldstool. Facing east. A better position—at least on

Explanation of Plates

Litany days—would be on the east side of the Roodscreen. W. Transept door. Q. S. western door. VV. Wooden seats. The whole of OO. TT. are, if necessary to be filled with chairs.

PLATE III

GABLE CROSSES SUGGESTED FOR IMITATION—*Instrumenta Ecclesiastica* became the source of numerous details and furnishings of Victorian Churches. These stone crosses were advocated as coming 'from old examples' (Plate XLV, 1847 series).

PLATE IV

RECOMMENDED FURNISHINGS FOR CHURCHES—The iron kneeling rail (*above*) was to be portable and could be used before the altar at Communion or at the west end of the church for the Churching of Women. The idea of the altar desk (*below*) came from medieval illuminations. Both designs were made by William Butterfield. (*Instrumenta Ecclesiastica*, 1847 series, Plate LXXII.)

PLATE V

'A REAL CHURCH'—St Paul's Church, Brighton, built by R. C. Carpenter, 1846–48, deserved 'very high commendation' according to the *Ecclesiologist*. The style was the favoured Middle Pointed, the chancel was 'just suited for the Anglican ritual to be solemnly and statelily celebrated', the only major defect being 'a prayer-desk looking west in the nave' (*E.* x, 207). (Plate from *Ecclesiologist*, v, 156.)

PLATE VI

A TYPICAL ECCLESIOLOGICAL CHURCH IN THE 1850's —St Mary Magdalene's, Munster Square, London, built in 1852 by R. C. Carpenter, one of the Cambridge Camden Society's favourite architects. Though lacking a full roodscreen or altar rails, the June 1852 issue of the *Ecclesiologist* called it 'the most artistically correct new church yet consecrated in London'. The building is in the approved Decorated style, and included benches in the nave, a pulpit, a lectern, chancel seats, sedilia, an altar, two candlesticks, and a dossel 'of a rich diaper of gilding, upon which is emblazoned a floriated cross in still richer gilding'. (Plate from *Illustrated London News*, xx (19 June, 1852), 480.)

Explanation of Plates

PLATE VII

THE SOCIETY'S MODEL CHURCH—All Saints', Margaret Street, London, was a building closely supervised by members of the Ecclesiological Society during its construction, 1849–59. Butterfield's use of colour in the interior and exterior are conspicuous features of a building showing great originality. In the words of the *Ecclesiologist*, 'we have never had occasion to notice a more suitable and dignified adaptation to the Anglican ritual than this magnificent church presents' (xx, 188). (Plate from *The Builder*, XVII (4 June 1859), 377.)

PLATE VIII

'A TRULY EXCELLENT DESIGN'—St Helen's, Little Cawthorpe, Lincolnshire, was to be rebuilt by R. J. Withers. The *Ecclesiologist* liked the scheme for rebuilding this small country church partly because 'the arrangements are thoroughly correct'. But it also indicates that by 1859 the Society had accepted the use of red and black brick and a certain amount of originality in details. (*Ecclesiologist*, xx, 288.)

Plate I

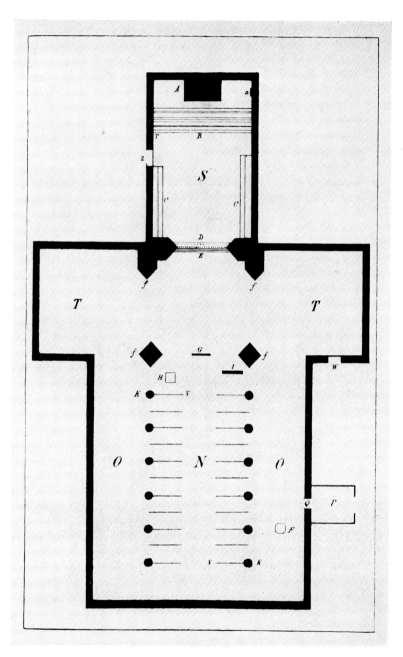

Plate II

SCALE OF FEET

Plate III

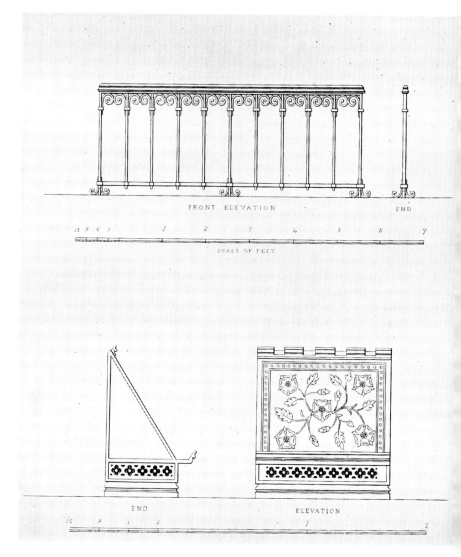

FRONT ELEVATION

END

SCALE OF FEET

END

ELEVATION

Plate IV

Plate V

Plate VI

Plate VII

Plate VIII

INDEX OF PERSONS

Index of Persons

Wade, John, 16
Walpole, Horace, 8
Walton, Isaak, 60
Ward, W. G., 19, 144–5, 146
Warren, Charles, 136
Weale, John, 20, 43, 128, 187
Webb, Benjamin, 17, 20, 22, 27, 36, 37, 40, 45, 46, 56n., 58, 61, 62, 66, 68, 79, 81, 89, 125, 148, 149, 169, 183, 193, 196, 199, 200, 201n., 209–10, 213, 218, 220n., 222
Webb, William, 153

Wightwick, George, 130–1, 132
Wilberforce, Samuel, 18
Wild, James William, 123
Williams, Isaac, 24
Willis, Robert, 119
Withers, R. J., 256
Woodyer, Henry, 112
Wordsworth, William, 28, 32, 153
Wren, Christopher, 2–3, 122, 173–4
Wren, Matthew, 68
Wykeham, William, 71

Young, James G., 45

INDEX OF PLACES

263

Index of Places

INDEX OF SUBJECTS

Index of Subjects

Few Hints on the Practical Study of Ecclesiastical Antiquities, 57
Few Words series, 113–16, 134
first pointed, see Early English Gothic
flowers, 188, 207
font, 5, 102, 160, 254
foreign art, 13, 31–2, 216
  and architecture, 189–190
  continental ecclesiology, 61–2
Foreign Office Building, 212
French Academy, 8
French churches, 177
frescoes, 171, see also painted walls
functionalism, 12–13, 71
funeral monuments, 109
funerals, 215

galleries, 8, 67, 77, 112, 159, 162, 193, 254; condemned, 97–8, 115
gardens, 32
General Committee on the Pew System, 108
Geometrical Gothic, 165
Georgian architecture, 91, 109, 172, see also classical styles
Gorham Case, 146n., 211
Gothic architecture, 24, 38–9, 43, 129, 176, 185, 212, 221
  and tropical climates, 106
  early revival of, 8, 9
  knowledge about, 52–3
  Newman and, 23–4
  only Christian architecture, 12, 86–7
  Pugin's advocacy of, 10–14
Gothic styles
  nomenclature, 9, 88
  preference for Decorated, 87
  see also 'debased', Decorated, Early English, Perpendicular
Great Exhibition of 1851, 211
Great International Exhibition of 1862, 212, 222

hagioscope, 142

Hakluyt Society, 65
Hand-Book of English Ecclesiology, 58
Hierologus, 29n., 60
Hierugia Anglicana, 67, 205–7
History
  architectural, 85–91
  ecclesiastical, 85–6
History of Pews, 67, 106
Holy Communion, 3, 5, 17, 21, 97, 206, 211, 255
Holy Orders, 101
Hymnal Noted, 218–20
hymns, 17, 218–19
Hymns Ancient and Modern, 220

ideal church, 92
Illustrations of Monumental Brasses, 61
imitation of medieval buildings, 81, 93, see also drawings for imitation; models for imitation
Incorporated Society for Promoting the Enlargement, Building and Repairing of Churches and Chapels, 82–3, 178
Instrumenta Ecclesiastica, 111–12, 215, Plates III and IV
iron church, 112
Irish Ecclesiological Society, 44n.
Irvingism, 182, 196
Italian architecture
  See classical styles, Georgian architecture, pagan architecture, Renaissance

Knightsbridge Church's Defence Fund, 208

Ladies' Ecclesiastical Embroidery Society, 212
laity, 100–1, 103, 105
lancet windows, see western triplets of lancets
Laws, architectural, 80 ff., 147
lectern, 102, 112, 132, 254, 255
  see also desk
libraries, 65

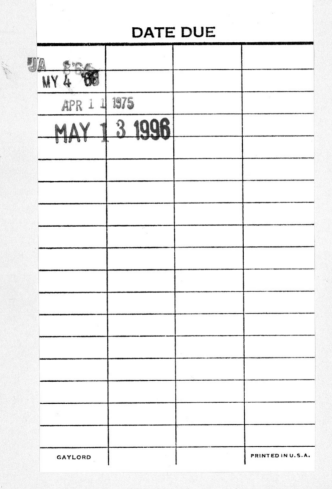

DATE DUE